Design in Texas
A Retrospective Exhibition
AIGA-Texas
1986

American Institute of Graphic Arts-
Texas Chapter

Graphic Design Press

Acknowledgements

Design in Texas
© 1986
Graphic Design Press and
American Institute of Graphic Arts-
Texas Chapter

The works reproduced in this book are under prior copyright, by the creators or by contractual arrangements with their clients. They are published here under one-time publishing rights permission granted by the individual design firms. Nothing shown in this book may be reproduced in any form without obtaining the permission of the creators and other persons who may have copyright ownership.

Graphic Design Press has taken every precaution to insure that proper credit has been given.

Published by
Graphic Design Press
1216 Hawthorne
Houston, Texas 77006
(713) 526-1250

Distributed by
Texas Monthly Press
P.O. Box 1569
Austin, Texas 78767
(512) 476-7085

•

Printed in Japan

Library of Congress
Catalog Card Number:
86-82243

ISBN 0-917001-05-2

Design in Texas
Jerry Herring and Philip Waugh
Book Design

Ellis Vener
Exhibition Photography

Jolynn Rogers
Interviews

Professional Typographers, Houston
Book Typography

San Jacinto Graphics
Reproduction Materials

Steve Freeman
Editorial Assistance

Tom McNeff, Diane Mitten, Angie Alvarez
Production Assistance

Neill Whitlock
Photographs of Show Judges

Jack Summerford, Mike Hicks, Bill Hill,
University of Texas
Research Assistance

Sandy Herring
Public Relations, Marketing

Bill McClung
Distribution

•

Design in Texas, The Exhibition
Special Recognition

Don Sibley and Rex Peteet
Show Chairmen

Don Crum, Olivette Hubler, Jim Jacobs,
Cap Pannell, Carol St. George
Show Committee

Jim Jacobs, Cap Pannell, Carol St. George,
Shel Hershorn, Dick Jones
Call for Entry

Contents

Acknowledgements
4

AIGA-Texas Board
6

AIGA-Texas
7

Design in Texas,
A Look Back
9

Design in Texas,
An Interview with
Stan Richards and Bill Hill
10

Design in Texas,
An Interview with
Fred Korge, Lowell Williams and Ron Scott
16

Design in Texas,
An Interview with
Mike Hicks and Leonard Ruben
20

Design in Texas,
The Exhibition Jury
25

Design in Texas,
The Exhibition
26

Index
268

Members of AIGA-Texas
272

AIGA-Texas Boards

Founding Board

Mike Hicks
President
Austin

Steve Freeman
Austin

Sue Heatly
Austin

Jerry Herring
Houston

Chris Hill
Houston

Jim Jacobs
Dallas

Janis Koy
San Antonio

Eric Morrell
Austin

Woody Pirtle
Dallas

Ron Sullivan
Dallas

Jack Summerford
Dallas

1985–86 Board

Steve Freeman
President
Austin

Jerry Herring
Past-President
Houston

Bill Carson
Houston

Roger Christian
San Antonio

Don Crum
Dallas

Rick Gavos
Dallas

Mark Geer
Houston

Scott Goodwin
El Paso

Mike Hicks
Austin

Olivette Hubler
Dallas

Jim Jacobs
Dallas

Alison Klassen
Austin

Janis Koy
San Antonio

Ed Lindlof
Austin

Jay Loucks
Houston

Cap Pannell
Dallas

Rex Peteet
Dallas

Paula Savage
Houston

Barbara Shimkus
San Antonio

Don Sibley
Dallas

Pat Sloan
Ft. Worth

Lowell Williams
Houston

The American Institute of Graphic Arts (AIGA) is the national, non-profit organization of graphic design and graphic arts professionals. Founded in New York City in 1914, the AIGA conducts an interrelated program of competitions, exhibitions, publications, educational activities, and projects in the public interest to promote excellence in, and the advancement of, the graphic design profession.

Members of the Institute are involved in the design and production of books, magazines and periodicals as well as corporate, environmental and promotional graphics. Their contribution of specialized skills and expertise provide the foundation for the Institute's program. Through the Institute, members form an effective, informal network that is a resource to the profession and the public.

In 1984 a Texas chapter of the AIGA was formed, and has provided an active forum for the exchange of ideas and information among Texas members. Meeting around the state, AIGA-Texas has become a vital proponent for design awareness and excellence in Texas.

Design in Texas
A Look Back

Over the past several years, the perception of design in Texas has undergone some striking changes. From a secondary market of little consequence and less impact, Texas graphic design has ascended to a position of international prominence.

Admittedly, the decades of the seventies and eighties have been extremely productive ones for Texas designers, but the hand of the designer has been around far longer, even as far back as the early days of the Republic of Texas when printers and mapmakers were our foremost visual communicators. To gain a true perspective of how the Texas market has evolved, however, we need go back only as far as the early fifties, a time of great importance not only to the infant Texas design community but to the communications industry as a whole, a time when advances in communications technology were reshaping and changing forever the way we view ourselves and the world.

Although we can explain the factors that hastened the development of design in Texas, one very important question remains unanswered: "What makes Texas design so special?" Is it the healthy economic climate in which we've been privileged to operate? Or is it Texas itself—bold, brash, iconoclastic, bigger than life?

For answers, we talked to leading design professionals in Dallas, Houston and Austin who have been witness to, and a part of, the emergence of Texas as a state of design.

Design in Texas

An Interview With Stan Richards and Bill Hill

Stan Richards has been called the "Father of Texas Design." His influence on Texas has come not only from his considerable personal achievements, but also from the many designers that he has hired, taught and mentored over the years. Stan came to Texas from New York in 1953, and after a year of freelancing, worked with Bloom Advertising. He formed his design firm, Stan Richards & Associates in 1955. Today he is the president of that same firm, now known as Richards, Brock, Miller, Mitchell & Associates and of the advertising agency, The Richards Group.

Bill Hill was hired by Stan at Bloom Advertising and rose to become the agency's President and Director of Creative Services. A graduate of the Kansas City Art Institute, Bill worked in Philadelphia and New York before moving to Dallas. Bill has been honored as the Dallas Art Director of the Year, as well as being selected one of the top 100 Creative Men in the U.S. Today he is the Chairman of Levenson, Levenson & Hill, a Dallas advertising agency.

Stan and Bill were interviewed in Dallas.

Q: We're here to talk about 25 years of Texas design. So let's go back to where we started—what did you find when you moved to Dallas in the fifties?

STAN: I got here in '53, about three years before Bill. Dallas was like a lot of other little markets around the country. It had an inconsequential advertising and design community. There was almost no good work being done. It was unthinkable that a piece done in this part of the country would make it into the New York Art Directors Show. Today it's the most commonplace thing in the world for Texas designers to be very well represented in all the international shows. But the market was a long time maturing.

BILL: I had been advised by an instructor not to go to New York or Los Angeles, or Chicago, but to pick a market that was about to break loose. He thought that either Dallas or Atlanta would be a real graphic arts center in the future. When I came to Dallas I interviewed with every agency and every studio in town. But there was really only one that was doing work that was outstanding, at least as far as my eye had been trained at that point, and that was Bloom. The work that was coming out of there was very, very different. Stan was art director and was totally responsible for it. I don't think everything they did was great, but they were really trying to break some molds. It was a small agency, a small department, but it was exciting. Stan had grown up at Pratt, and he had had a great amount of exposure to the things that were happening in New York and Los Angeles. I profited from that and—I don't think this is ego—I honestly think there was nobody else at any other shop in Dallas really trying to achieve a responsible, legitimate design effort. In the rest of the United States, a revolution was taking place. Advertising and design coincided. Some West Coast designers were breaking loose with Saul Bass...

STAN: Yes, that was when Saul Bass moved from New York to Los Angeles and was doing some very exciting stuff.

BILL: And Paul Rand had been laying the groundwork. But I personally think that what happened in one agency in particular—Doyle Dane Bernbach—really revolutionized advertising. A designer went there as art director, and his design eye influenced the look of advertising for the next 25 years.

STAN: The fifties were a remarkable period in advertising when extraordinary work was being done. Production budgets were, for the times, beginning to be adequate to do terrific pieces. The influence of Doyle Dane was staggering, influencing a half dozen agencies in New York and spreading to other agencies and designers throughout the country. When you look back at the early and middle fifties you realize that here was a time when virtually everything was letterpress. There was little offset equipment. Obviously, you can't do much with letterpress printing. Offset printing began to come into widespread use in this part of the country, and we had to push the printers awfully hard to get them to deliver a product that was fully competitive with what was being done in a couple of shops in the East and West. The suppliers were very unsophisticated. There was no real expectation of a high level of quality, you just put an image down on a piece of paper and that was good enough. The same thing was true for engravers. They didn't have the capability, and needed to be pushed to get the equipment and the expertise. That was also before Foster & Kleiser came into this part of the country, so you couldn't even get an outdoor board painted properly. Here we sat in Dallas designing bulletins to turn over to some hamhanded painter who would absolutely destroy any integrity that was in the piece. They couldn't even match a type face. We looked at boards on the West Coast that Foster & Kleiser was painting and they were superb. But we couldn't get it. So that gives you a pretty good picture of how different it was. It was a really tough time here. It was tough to do good work.

BILL: There were old habit patterns here that just weren't going to be broken until a new generation of craftsmen came in. The electronic media at that time was rushing into the invention of the wheel. Most of the television, well, there were just not many broadcasting accounts here, and it was just as common to have them produced at Channel 8 and Channel 4.

STAN: Remember, it was the middle fifties, before tape was even available to us. So most television, that is the show content, was done live. We had some small production companies but they were basically in the business of doing industrial films. They would also do television production that was just awful.

When I came to Dallas I was really headed for Los Angeles. I knew I didn't want to stay in New York. Saul Bass had intrigued me by moving his operation from New York to California. He was doing terrific work, and I thought that was where I would like to be. I came through Dallas and was encouraged to stay. All I was interested in was finding a job, or finding a way to generate some income. My needs were small, and the art director in what was then the largest agency counseled me to stay. But I couldn't get a job. I interviewed at a lot of places, but no one would hire me because I had a Pratt book and it was very different from anything that was being done in this part of the country. It was the kind of book that was very heavy in design. What most agencies were looking for in an art director was somebody who could draw a picture of a housewife holding a can of something, and that wasn't what I was particularly good at. I could draw, and draw well, but I wasn't interested in doing it. I was a designer. I was interested in working with content and concept and form and typography, and all the things that were of little consequence to the agencies in Dallas. No one hired me, so I started a freelance practice.

BILL: The book that Stan brought to Dallas, and to some extent, the one that I brought, was a completely different book. To the advertisers and agency people, it was probably as astounding to look at Stan's book as the first Impressionist exhibit was to traditional eyes in France. It was a totally different way of looking at communications. The people in the agencies and studios were living in a different era, a different time, as were the clients. Their clients weren't sitting there waiting for a revolution in graphics, so it was tough to sell the stuff. A lot of times the account executives would walk out quaking at some of the things we gave them to sell. In retrospect, I'm surprised that as much of it sold as it did.

STAN: We were a really bad department. We would get even with our account supervisors when they didn't sell something by being late on the next assignment. Really it was a tremendous disservice to the agency that was paying us, but at the same time it allowed us to make some progress. Of course, if anybody here did that I'd kill them. I think to some extent we were a bit full of ourselves.

BILL: But we were thinking differently than most of the industry in Dallas at the time. There weren't a lot of companies in Dallas that were absolutely advertising and marketing dependent for their existence. It was a commodity, sort of a necessary evil that they appropriated budgets for, but people who were looking for exciting communications that carried a message as well as an image of their company along with it were practically nonexistent.

Q: Did either of you ever regret coming to Dallas in the early years?

STAN: We both did. I went to New York and interviewed with Doyle Dane Bernbach because I was tired of fighting all the wars. But on the cab ride from LaGuardia to midtown my wife, Betty, who had never been in New York before, said, "I don't want to live here." I looked at it long and hard through her eyes and said, "I don't either. I made that decision once; let's just make it again." I went through with the interview, had a tentative job offer, and decided not to leave Dallas after all. So I went back and toughed it out. Bill actually left.

BILL: I went to Philadelphia—which I found out was even more in the Dark Ages in a lot of ways— and New York, which was disappointing because the logistics of living were a real pain. But what I really found that convinced me that Dallas was the place to be was that the amount of good work coming out of New York was equal proportionate to what was coming out of Dallas. The work that was getting the visibility and influencing trends was being done in a minority of the organizations up there. Plus, I found that what I loved about Dallas was a certain amount of spontaneity, a lack of sacred cows. There was a "go for it" attitude that I hadn't recognized; I just thought that's the way the world is. In New York I found all kinds of mores, in both the organizations and the clients, that didn't exist here.

Q: Do you think Texas has a climate conducive to innovation?

BILL: I went to the film festival's tribute to Shirley MacLaine last year. In her acceptance speech she said she loved being in Texas because there was some sort of rough-hewn combination of sophistication and bawdiness that she never felt anyplace else.

STAN: There's a different social structure in this part of the country that engenders an adventurous spirit. Texas will probably change over time, because homogenization is exactly what's happening. How often do you sit with a business leader with a pronounced Texas accent anymore? And it's not because he isn't from Texas but because he spends part of his time watching national television newscasts and he lessens his accent.

BILL: Where my office is in Las Colinas, 100 major corporations have moved in from the East Coast in the last ten years. They bring in a certain sophistication, a different way of working, new corporate policies. They affect Dallas, and Dallas affects them.

And I think that communications and design in this part of the world are being judged now by the same standards as New York or London or Los Angeles. We have reached the point where we have to understand that we are in competition with the rest of the world because advertisers here can afford to go anyplace they want. And New York agencies are just as happy to come here because DFW is an easy trip.

Q: How is the designer influenced by what is going on around him?

BILL: While Stan and I were working together a speaker that we admired, Jerome Gould, came to Dallas. We spent two evenings with him just talking and having dinner, and Stan asked him, "Don't you think that a good, responsible designer should be equally good in his judgement of music, painting, architecture, or any of the other arts and crafts?" His answer was, "Yes, because a good designer has a trained eye and ear, and that taste level should apply across the board because every one of those things in one form or another will touch in the area of communication." And I think that is true. Incidentally, I've hired a lot of art directors who grew up in electronics and never did quite get that grounding in print which is a 100 percent the design function. They never could make it. On the other hand, people who might not have been innately as talented but who grew up in print had a discipline that allowed them to make the transition to television much easier. It was two different disciplines, and it showed up on everything including the supers at the end of a spot.

Q: What about other influences—politics, music, society in general?

BILL: To give you an idea of the sort of environment that existed in Dallas in the fifties: There was a traveling exhibit at the Dallas museum featuring primarily contemporary artists called *Sport in Art*. In it was a piece by Picasso, a communist, and one by Ben Shawn who was a socialist. The curator of the museum and the committee raised so much hell about it that they threw the thing out because it was a "communist" exhibit.

STAN: The biggest influences have always come

Dallas Civic Opera Poster
1961

Stan Richards,
Designer, Illustrator

Early evidence that Stan Richards had brought his Pratt style to Texas.

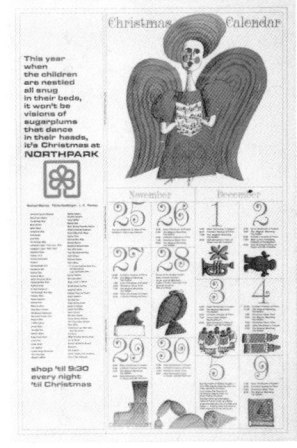

Northpark Ad
1960

Bill Hill
Art Director, Designer Illustrator

From a series of illustrated ads for the opening of Northpark.

11

Lomas & Nettleton
Annual Report
1971
Jack Summerford
Art Director, Designer
One of the first
Lomas & Nettleton annuals
featuring a progressive
front to back theme.
Photographed by Greg Booth,
the report shows
L&N's relationship to
the different stages of
a man's life.

from outside. It may sound awfully simplistic to say it but the primary influence on every designer is what he is seeing in the *CA* show, the Clio's, the One Show. He aspires to be in those competitions.

Q: How about client influences?

STAN: The client's role is to provide an environment in which the designer will flourish. When the designer presents something that is provocative and exciting and well-done, the client recognizes it and appreciates it. And although a lot of terrific ideas come from clients—and when they do we're more than happy to accommodate them and build off those ideas—it's not really the client's primary role.

BILL: It's a partnership. There's mutual respect there. Respect on the part of the designer or the agency for that client, that company, that product or service. The company, or the decision maker, also has to respect the designer. It's the responsibility of the designer himself to prove that he has a genuine understanding of the problem to be solved, and that his solution is going to accomplish the client's needs. Once that's established you're over the major hurdle of selling something that may break the mold because they trust you. They believe you have their best interests at heart. Whether they 100 percent understand it or not, that's not their job. They spend twenty-four hours a day doing other things and they are experts in their areas. We're experts in another area and those two disciplines should complement each other and provide the very best combination.

Let me tell you another thing that happened during the fifties that was a big influence nationally on corporations as well as the design or communications community. The chairman of Container Corporation of America initiated through the NW Ayer agency a series called *Great Ideas of Western Man*. It was probably, in my mind, the best corporate series ever. It helped establish an image or a state of mind around Container Corporation, a company that was very innovative in three-dimensional as well as two-dimensional design. Their main source of revenue was boxes, big boxes; they wanted to sell paper, and they did it through design. The campaign was what it said it was, great ideas of western man. Each one featured a phrase from great thinkers in history interpreted by a different designer who was told, "this is your interpretation, it will run exactly the way you do it." There was no sell in it at all. But you don't find clients like that very often. The chairman happened to be a very unusual man.

STAN: We've been doing annual reports for Lomas & Nettleton for the past 17 years. It started out as one book for Lomas & Nettleton Financial, and they added another company and another company, and now I guess we're doing five books a year, just for Lomas & Nettleton. It's been a 17-year partnership in which the working environment could not have been better. We sit down with the CEO at the outset of each book, talk for 45 minutes or so about how he sees the company, how he puts the past year in perspective, what he is looking for in the immediate future. Then we go off and come up with a concept. Amazingly, the meetings at which we present concept are never more than 15 minutes because the client is a brilliant guy who thoroughly understands what we are trying to accomplish. We'll present a concept, sometimes two or three, and he'll say, "that's terrific for this year, why don't we save that concept for next year and then look at it again to see if it's appropriate for what has happened to the company."

That one client has probably done more for the graphic arts industry in this part of the country than anyone else. They allowed us to push printers into areas they had never gone before.

BILL: Another one of Stan's clients that has the same sort of relationship is MBank. From the time Stan did just design for them until he took over their entire advertising effort, MBank has maintained a specific image. It has been consistently above average in quality, and it has consistently separated itself from any other financial institution.

STAN: The client can provide an environment in which extraordinary things can happen. Let me give you a very recent example. We just did an incredible campaign for Tom Thumb Page Supermarkets. It's a series of commercials produced live in front of a studio audience with Harry Anderson, a brilliant comedian, as spokesman. Imagine, I walk into a meeting with the parent company of Tom Thumb Page and sit down with four of their key decision makers including the president, and I have no way to demonstrate what we're going to do because it's never been done before. We talked through the concept and when we finished they said, "that sounds good, go ahead." The risk they were willing to take at that moment was enormous. First of all, there were a lot of dollars involved. Secondly, we were going to have an audience of 600 people who were officers and senior employees of the Cullum Companies, and about 100 members of the press. If we had a disaster it was going to be the most visible of all time. For a client to be willing to assume that risk is an extraordinary thing. The risks that we take as creative people are inconsequential compared to the risks that clients take as entrepreneurs and heads of major corporations. I have enormous respect for that. The guys who allowed us to produce those commercials made us friends for life.

BILL: It's a cliche in our business, but for the client to be willing to take a risk...that's absolute trust.

Q: How hard was it to get that kind of response in the early years?

STAN: Really tough. But part of the reason was that we were kids. When I was at Bloom I was 22, and how much faith can you put in the judgement of a 22-year-old? The fact that both of us have been successful through the years has helped. We've obviously made a lot of right decisions, and we have enough gray hair now that people recognize that our judgement is probably pretty good.

BILL: But to a great extent, you never really get

there. It's a day-to-day thing. As Stan said, if you work for a company for 17 years that you don't have a contract with that means that every time you go in it becomes a "what have you done for me lately" situation. He doesn't just have to do as well as he did last time, they're really expecting something better. There's a continuing responsibility on both sides that has to be fulfilled constantly.

STAN: It all comes down to the competitive spirit of the individual. The fifty or so people in Creative that I supervise are intensely competitive among themselves and with everyone else in the creative community. They want their stuff in *CA* every year, they want Clios, they want One Show awards. They don't talk about it, and they know never to mention it in front of a client because that's not what a client needs or is interested in. But they care a lot about the individual recognition they will get from the national and international award shows.

BILL: I really hate sports analogies, but there is a lot of correlation between our profession and professional football. Everyday when you get up and go out on the field, it really doesn't matter what happened last week, you're back to how well you can do this week. It's really a matter of individual desire and competitiveness, but the best people in any field are those who are their own worst critics. When you're in an environment where quality and excellence are expected, you absorb something from it.

STAN: Back to this concept of risk... We talked about how clients are willing to take risks too. What they really have to do is be willing to put their jobs on the line in order to make the breakthroughs that are going to advance their careers, and advance the design community. When a client says it sounds good, he's also saying that if it doesn't work you have a problem. So there's an enormous risk on the part of the agency or the designer, when he goes in with a concept that is revolutionary because if it does fail, he has to pay for it, and it's only proper that he pay for it.

BILL: Our business as it exists today is a combination of art and science. Maintaining the balance between the two is difficult in an agency or design firm. Too often, organizations hide behind science, and if it doesn't work—because ultimately, this is not an exact science—they're able to say, "You can't blame me, the numbers said it would work; you can't hold me responsible." But that is the most blatant irresponsibility because they aren't willing to put their tail on the line and say, "I believe" or "I think" rather than "this number proves it." Once an organization wants it proved in black & white, the spontaneity and the risk taking and the desire are dead.

STAN: A lot of good Texas designers learned to take risks at our places. I don't mean to take credit for it because the people who have been with our organization through the years have learned much more from each other than they have from me. But the fact is, that's where they began to understand that they have to take risks if they are going to do great work.

Q: But how do you maintain that? When you're 22-years-old, taking risks is easy because you have nothing to lose. But when you become successful...

STAN: People have to understand that it is only a job. A designer who takes a risk and gets fired has only lost one thing, a job. There are other jobs.

BILL: It all starts at the top. In an organization like this there is pressure. There is pressure to be right and to be good, but there's got to be that pressure without threat. You've got to know that you have the right to make a mistake. That can only come from the person who creates the tone and the environment and the atmosphere. If the message says to protect your turf, don't allow anything to go wrong, what happens is you spend your time trying not to be wrong rather than trying to be right. And those are two very different things.

I've been caught up in that before with certain clients. There are many levels of people, but all of them are protecting their P & L. In many cases they can say no, but not many of them can say yes, so they try to justify their existence by making little changes. When the meetings are over there's a great sense of relief, we finally won. But when you sit down and look at the results, it has no resemblance to what you originally took in there. It's been committed to the point that every bit of the blood has been drained out and it's just another ordinary piece of communication.

STAN: Let me put another perspective on the risk taking aspect of what we do. Sometimes you simply cannot do a great commercial within a given environment, and therefore, it's not in your best interests to continue in that environment. We just signed a new multi-million dollar office lease, and if we lose all of our clients because circumstances are such that we are not able to do the kind of work that we want to do, I still have to pay it, it's not going to go away. It puts risk taking in a slightly different light, but it's important to do it anyway.

Q: How much of the development of Texas design had to do with our earlier status as a secondary market?

BILL: There may have been some underdog attitudes over the last 25 years, especially in the fifties. You could look at a piece and say that's better, that's different from what I'm doing. But that exposure did not put us in competition with New York, we learned from it.

STAN: One of the things that is probably comforting to the designers in Texas who have done good work and been recognized for it is that it would have been easier in New York. The designer who is functioning particularly well in Texas—he's good, he's gained recognition, he's busy all the time, he's operating profitably—could have done it in half the time in New York, with half the effort.

BILL: And if absolute growth was your objective, you'd grow twice as fast just because of what's available to you there.

STAN: But I don't think any designer thinks in the

Bart Forbes
1975

Jim Jacobs
1977

Jack Unruh
1985

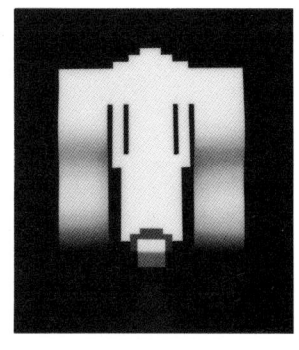

Woody Pirtle
1986

Design in Dallas has been dominated by illustration.

13

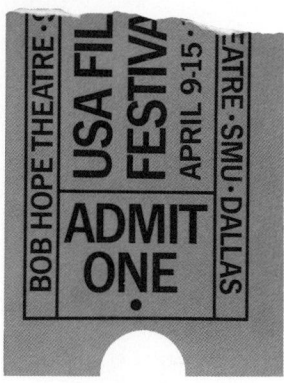

USA Film Festival Program
1973
Larry Sons
Designer

The first Texas piece to win a gold medal in the New York Art Directors Show.

context of making Texas the most exciting design community in America. What he's really after is being *the* designer of all time.

Q: So what's the reason for working in Texas?
STAN: Because you like to live in Texas, that's all.
BILL: Remember, we may mentally spend 24 hours-a-day with our profession, but our bodies are other places, and we do have other responsibilities. And all those elements in an individual's life contribute to the product he produces, no matter what his chosen field. I guess I've hired hundreds of people from New York, some of them confirmed New Yorkers, and now you couldn't get them out of Dallas. They swear that there's no difference between New York and Dallas as far as the demands, the pressures and the quality standards. But outside the office there's a big difference, and they feel that they can cope and grow a lot better here with fewer pressures in their day-to-day lives.

Q: You've hired some very bright, very talented people. What do you look for?
STAN: I look for at least one brilliant piece in a portfolio. I'll hire a person on that basis. For the most part, I don't even care to look at a television reel and the reason is simple: television has too many participants. I can visualize a scenario where I'm looking at a whole series of books and the same terrific commercial is in the book of the writer, the art director, the broadcast producer, the editor, the cinematographer. Who did it? Where did it come from, and how did it get to be terrific? With print, that is not the case. It is relatively easy to identify who was the responsible party when you look at a piece of print. The other considerations are, does this person have the personality and demeanor that will allow him or her to function well within my organization? And, no matter how strong the book may be, I never hire arrogance. I don't want arrogant people in my organization, and I don't want to expose my clients to arrogant people.

Bill embodied all the characteristics that I look for: a very talented designer and a very gentle kind of person who would work well within an organization, and also be terrific with clients. Bill was a perfect example of the kind of people I've tried to hire over the years.

Woody Pirtle's another super example of a guy who in the right environment absolutely flourished. He had a bad book when he came here, and he knew it. Woody was indefatigable. He could outwork any three people, and I always felt that was part of the reason for his success. He has a great eye, he has a great sense of taste, and he will flat outwork anybody who tries to compete with him.

Larry Sons was another example. He had a lot to learn because his background was primarily in illustration. But he became a first-rate writer and a first-rate designer. The best portfolio I ever hired was Ed Brock, who is still a principal of our design group. He had an extraordinary body of work, a magical portfolio that had stuff in it like I'd never seen before.

Q: We always hear about the Texas mystique, is there something about Texas that fires the creative spirit?
STAN: Back in the East where I came from there was a limit to how high I could climb. My dad was a bartender. I knew that at some point I would be interfacing with people who had gone to Princeton and Harvard and I knew I was not going to be comfortable in that social set. I always felt there was that kind of limitation. Here that absolutely does not exist. I can tell you that a dozen times a year I'll come out of a meeting at which I've been counseling with a business or political leader who has me in there because he values my judgement, and as I walk out of the office I think to myself: "Pretty good for the bartender's kid."

Q: Is there a Texas style?
STAN: I don't think there is a Texas style. There are many different approaches to problem solving in the advertising and design communities. I would hope that you could sit down with our work and the work of a half dozen terrific agencies or design groups, and no one would be able to pick it out and say: "That one came from Richards, that one came from so-and-so."
BILL: If I look at a whole bunch of different work I can tell the difference between a definite West Coast style and a definite New York style. I can even see some differences between Los Angeles and San Francisco. To me, what has happened in Texas is that it's the best of both worlds. Maybe it's because of the influx of people from both coasts. I can see a lot of sophistication here, but there's still a kind of Texas-style risk taking. It's a much better balance.
STAN: I think it has a lot to do with the strength of the influential designers in Texas. I seldom see a book come out of New York that is done in seven colors and two varnishes. But because designers here tend to work with a limited group of printers, they are able to push things. They may be at the end of the budget, but if the printer recognizes that one run of dull varnish is going to make a difference to the piece, he will go ahead and run the dull varnish.

A lot of the things that tend to be seen as trends are a result of some technological breakthrough. For example: fifteen years ago I was having problems getting a black & white look that I wanted and that I knew could be achieved through gravure. So I began to work with one of the printers here to develop a way of using a four-color press to print black & white. That only occurred to me because we would have a four-color press just sitting there while we did a black & white book on a two-color press. The cost of the press time is not that significant. So I thought, "Why can't we move this book over to this four-color press and print some combination of greys and blacks to give us this gutsy gravure look?" I worked with Heritage Press to get to the point where we were printing something that we eventually called quadratones. Mixing two blacks, a grey and a dull varnish gave us a really powerful, solid look. Suddenly the images we were putting down on the printed page looked exactly as they looked when the prints came from the photographer. Because we were successful with it we did several books in this quadratone black & white process. And because our books looked so good, other designers did exactly the same thing. It became part of the vernacular in this part of the country. So there was probably a period of time when if you were judging the *CA* show you would see four books by four different designers in Texas and they'd all be done in black & white quadratones. That's a trend! But it really isn't a trend, it's just something that was made possible by the way the equipment was used. You see the same things happening with the capability of retouching. All of a sudden we've got computers that can take this little chunk of background and move it from up here to down there, and if we're willing to build $5000 into a job for retouching, we can do anything. We can create any image we want.

BILL: One real influence on the design community in Texas was Stanley Marcus of Neiman-Marcus. The influence of Neiman's came from the kind of merchandise that was brought in and the way it was marketed. Stanley Marcus created a certain style that became associated with Dallas. The pieces that came out of Neiman-Marcus—the advertising, the catalogs, the His & Her Gifts, the Fortnights—were international. And I think, to some extent, it created a little bit of halo under which other things could develop.

STAN: I totally agree. As a matter of fact, when I came here the only thing I knew about Dallas was Neiman-Marcus. I knew there was at least one entity that was doing good work. They were a major influence. I can well remember when we were building into a substantial design organization how our goal at the annual Society of Visual Communicators show was to win more awards than Neiman's.

BILL: It was all done in-house except for the outside people who were used for catalog covers and posters. And it happened because there was one person there who could control it and let it happen, Stanley Marcus.

STAN: Bill made the point very early that much of what we do was strongly influenced by Doyle Dane Bernbach. Prior to that the traditional way of doing things was the assignment went to the writer who wrote a headline and a piece of body and sent it by messenger to the art director's desk, and the art director would try to figure out some way of laying it out. All of a sudden, here was this new force doing brilliant work, and they didn't do it that way. They had a writer/art director working on it alone, or they had a writer and an art director working together as a team until the answer was achieved. So now we're dealing in a verbal/visual concept on a unified basis.

Q: What design trends do you see developing?

BILL: The biggest changes I see coming are from outside influences. Corporations have become information organizations. Our tools are changing. The ways people hear and see and read are changing—they have less time for it now. Stress is a fact of modern society. As communicators, we're going to have to be much more aware of people's state of mind and how it's influenced by what is going on in the world. Society is also becoming more fragmented. It's going to be more difficult to get someone's message across and make it important.

STAN: Isaac Azimov said something that I thought was really significant. We've always worried about the computer being a depersonalizing device, but it turns out that the computer is precisely the opposite. It is the ultimate personalizing device. In the past you have had to divide people into groups—socio-economic, ethnic, companies, schools, regions—in order to deal with them. You don't have to do that anymore. The computer sees you as an individual and can process data fast enough to identify you and every characteristic you have. That opens up all sorts of possibilities for the future. The fact that we as communicators can now target very, very specific audiences gives us a way to market to people that we haven't had in the past.

Publications are becoming more vertical. They're used for reaching a specific part of the population. If I determine that my customer base has certain geo-demographic characteristics, I can locate those customers who live in a certain type of neighborhood in a certain zip code and then reduce those zip codes down to census tracts and blocks. And I know that I can be much more efficient if I mail my message to this specific block than if I put it on television and send it out to everybody in the Dallas/Forth Worth area. The same thing applies to printing and production. There are probably 7000 typefaces to choose from, and they're all available at every typographer. That's a wonderful thing because it just expands the tools available to us.

BILL: It will be much more demanding. The people who are coming into our business have to be a lot smarter than they were 10 or 20 years ago. Fifteen years ago the rule of thumb for agencies was to have ten people for every million dollars in billing. Today it's two-and-a-half people per million dollars which means that they're probably being paid higher, but there are also more demands being placed on them to be smarter, more efficient, and considerably more astute in everything they do because the business is more complicated.

Q: It's interesting that although each of you has been in the business for more than 30 years, you are still as excited as someone who is just starting.

BILL: This business is demanding, it wears you down, and it kills people who aren't made for it. So you have to have a love for it and a tolerance.

STAN: The enthusiasm that you read in the two of us is characteristic of the best people in the industry. It's there among people who are doing what they want to do and doing it well.

If you were to ask me what I wanted to do for the next 15 or 20 years my answer would be: just exactly what I'm doing today.

Neiman Marcus Poster
1957
Savigar
Designer

Neiman Marcus Ad
1961
Push Pin Studios
Design Firm

Neiman Marcus of Dallas has set a consistent standard of excellence with international as well as Texas talent.

Design in Texas

An Interview With Fred Korge, Lowell Williams and Ron Scott

Fred Korge is a design pioneer in Houston. A graduate of the School of Industrial Arts in New York, Fred found his way to Texas by way of the Air Force. In 1957 Fred founded, with illustrator Norman Baxter, what is now known as Baxter+Korge, for years the dominant design studio in Houston and the starting place for practically every working designer in the city. Fred has been honored by every Houston organization associated with communications.

Lowell Williams, a native of Houston, attended the University of Houston. He worked with Fred at Baxter+Korge, and later at Saul Bass in Los Angeles, before forming his own firm in 1974. Lowell Williams Design has led the Houston design community to a new standard of professionalism.

Ron Scott is a Ft. Worth native who received a B.S. in Physics at Tulane in New Orleans, and has been a staple of the Houston communications field since forming his studio in 1972. Ron's early images for *Texas Monthly Magazine* covers have become a part of Texas lore, while some of his recent images have been generated out of his sophisticated computer graphics system.

Fred, Lowell and Ron were interviewed in Houston.

Q: How would you compare Houston design 25 years ago to the way it is now?

FRED: Houston was a very laid-back, small town in the fifties. There were maybe a dozen agencies and a lot of printers with big art departments; the design was controlled by those people. It was a freelance town, a lot of freelancers. I don't think we were doing design work, we were just doing layouts and pasteups of what the agencies were creating. Designers had not come into being then. There was a band of people here, but we really weren't called upon to think creatively, conceptually. I don't think we even said "designs," we called them "layouts." When I came to Houston there was one studio in town. It was a bona fide studio where someone was paying you a salary as opposed to Bill Shield's place where there were four or five guys sharing space.

Ever do a four-color job on a single color press? That's what we were doing. And once in a while someone would get in a two-color press and we'd say, "wow, we can do two at a time." Now I just heard that we are getting an eight-color press.

RON: When I started in photography everybody else around the country had just discovered 35mm film and were shooting with small cameras and shooting lots of film, bracketing, then editing down to one or two shots. But, when I came here in 1970 the printers didn't have the scanners and the techniques. They wanted large transparencies, so everybody was shooting 4x5's, even 4x5 aerials, and that was pretty strange because it was obvious that wasn't the way to do advertising or collateral photography. As the scanners came in, it flip flopped. Things really started breaking loose in the seventies because that's when the oil business really boomed and the economy boomed and Houston really grew.

FRED: I think the seventies was a boom period and not just because of what was happening with the entrepreneurs. The influx of major companies moving in from the northeast and Chicago brought different mentalities, different thought processes, and technology followed.

LOWELL: Also it came from companies here that were small market or middle market, or even some of the major oil companies who saw other things happening. That was when the Landors and Basses were beginning to do corporate identity programs. People here would fly up to New York and see somebody's symbol on a building and come back to Houston and say, "gee, I'd like to have one of those," or, "we're getting too big and we need to reorganize the way all of this stuff looks." So the need was created. I don't think it was a case where all of a sudden there were a bunch of guys here ready to work. I think the industry evolved with the need.

FRED: Before, clients were printers and advertising agencies. We didn't call on Humble or Prudential or Bank of the Southwest directly. Editors from these companies were letting printers not "design" a piece, but "do" a magazine. And they would do it based on their equipment.

RON: That gets back to what I was saying about the way the photographers shot pictures. It wasn't based on the best way to make a picture, it was determined by the separation house and how it worked. And that only makes sense. You have to form a critical mass. There was no critical mass of design people in Houston so there was no design. When that critical mass formed, it took over.

I came from a small town, Fort Worth, and up in Fort Worth where I started in photography I did a lot of work for advertising agencies. I had never heard of an art director. There was an artist, but he was the guy who sat at a board somewhere and drew stuff and did type and you only saw him if you happened to go to an agency to deliver something. I worked with what would now be considered account executives. When I came to Houston that was the first time I met an art director and actually had somebody go on a shoot who wasn't in a suit and tie. That's what Houston was like.

LOWELL: As staggering as that sounds, it's only been in the last couple of years that an agency has ever called a designer in and said, "we have a special problem and we'd like you to work with our client." In other words, it's become more of a joint venture between agency and designer.

FRED: When Tom Ballinger hit Houston back in the early sixties he was an unbelievable thing here. He had long hair before people did that, but he was a fantastic talent. We couldn't afford him and didn't want to let him go so Earl Littman and I made a deal and split his salary just to keep him in town. Because the work is not going to get better unless you get better people. The better the people, the more challenging it is. I can remember someone telling me once, "Damn, Korge, what are you hiring these people for, they're so damn good." Well how are we going to get better if somebody isn't pushing us to get better?

Q: Texas designers are getting a lot of recognition. What are the elements of the Texas style?

RON: People talk about Texas design like it's something that was invented and all we had to do was to go out and fill in the blanks. People are always looking for a way to hang a handle on something. Whatever Texas design is grew out of our needs here.

Houston offered a terrific opportunity for photographers because there was such a tremendous need for pictures, pictures of ugly things. A photographer could go out and shoot a mass of pipes and do some kind of weird thing with it and make a real interesting photo. If you're doing fashion and you've got a beautiful girl, you've got a beautiful girl. But if you have something challenging, it forces you to do something. I think there needs to be a little bit of angst in everything you do in order for it to be good. I know that the times I think the photo is going to be the worst, many times it comes out the best because you really have to dig down deep in your bag of tricks to come up with something.

FRED: I think it's kind of difficult to pin a handle

on Texas design. When you think of the talented designers, art directors, illustrators, and photographers that we have here, look at where they've come from. It's what they learned outside that brings them into the area of opportunity. I don't know how you'd categorize so-called Texas design.

LOWELL: One way to look at it might be to consider that before the seventies you didn't have a lot of interaction between Texas and New York and Los Angeles. The gaps were tremendous from city to city. Plus, people here were not doing projects in other parts of the country, there was no need. So what happened was that as people began to be more cosmopolitan, or international even, and more publications like *CA* offered Texas designers a forum to show what they could do, Texas became more prominent. Now, if you look at the New York annuals or the *CA* annuals, you'll probably find more work by Texas designers than any other state. That may just be because the economy was so great here in recent years. Houston may not have had a good economy for the past three years but if you go back and look at the annuals I think you'll find that Texas as a whole was doing well. Of course, when you have a Woody Pirtle that gets 15 or 20 pieces in *CA*, the rest of us don't have to be that good. He's carrying the ball. As long as he's not in Louisiana, you get credit for Texas design.

Q: So the development of Texas design has come about because of the economic boom?

RON: There's no doubt that what has attracted many companies here are certain economic factors. The fact that Texas is a non-union, right-to-work state certainly can't be overlooked. It's a low tax state, there's no state income tax. And the weather is a major factor.

FRED: You have 11 months of workable time in Texas as opposed to New York where you have maybe seven months of workable time. That's attracted people here.

RON: From my perspective as a photographer, when these companies moved here there was a growth in the collateral area and the need to do corporate brochures and annual reports. These are very picture hungry devices. That certainly drew a lot of photographers here. One thing I like about Houston is that it is a very open town. The people have always been that way. You never meet anybody who wants to be somewhere else. They came here to be successful and make money. It's sort of a no-nonsense approach. Even now with the economy the way it is, people hustle. Everybody wants to work; they want to make a buck.

FRED: I think one of the greatest things that happened to Houston was when these non-Texas people came here to live and build and grow. It broke the mold of the good-old-boy type of business and advertising. They allowed us to use our minds, not just our hands. They would actually call us in for a concept meeting where writers and photographers and designers worked together instead of executing in a vacuum. Before, you'd get the copy from somebody, you'd get a thumbnail layout from an art director, and you'd lay it out. You didn't know what the hell you were doing. A client would ask for a 12-page brochure, but nobody would ask them "why," "what are you going to use it for", "who is the audience", or, maybe "what you really need is a direct mail piece." It probably sounds stupid today, but 25 years ago those questions were never asked. You had no opportunity even of discussing the copy with the client.

RON: There's no doubt we've become a lot more sophisticated. But I keep thinking about the question that somebody picking up this book would want answered and that is: if all these Texas people are winning all these awards, what is it that makes Texas so great? And I think you have to get back to the fact that Texas has been a very productive environment. It's an open place, a "can do" place, and the money was here. If you had a client from the oil patch with a lot of money and you show him something that's good, and if you're clever enough to get him to give up a little of his money, he'll spend it. Like my dad always taught me, anything worth doing is worth doing well. And I think that's probably as true a Texas ethic as anything. If a guy in Texas tells you he's going to do something, he's going to do it or die trying.

FRED: I find it very difficult to see any mystery in the growth or development of our business or the quality of work we do. There are a lot of okay people. But there are those who really want to do quality work and they're going to work extra hard to do it. There's nothing mysterious about it. They've worked harder; they've worked longer; they've worked smarter; they've allowed themselves to be exposed to worldly things. Another thing that helped the design community here is when we became a bigger community, we joined national organizations. We associated with other people; we didn't get inbred.

RON: I've always felt that once I get a job from somebody, I'm no longer as concerned about that job as much as the next one. By that I mean that I want the job to go well, but it's not enough just to solve that client's problems. I want to do more than that. I want to solve their problem and make them ecstatic, but I also want to have other people look at it and say, "wow, look what he did for them." It's much better if your work precedes you. And to do that you have to make each job more than just enough to satisfy that particular client.

I know for a fact that's what it was like when I first came here. Many of the clients were willing to accept less because they didn't know any better. They were happy if everything was in focus. No one shot at "magic hour," dusk, because the security guards didn't stay that late. People would shoot at banker's hours when everything is flat. I'd be out there at 8:30, 9:00 at night still taking pictures and I'd actually get into trouble over that because I was

Extra! Will Big John move from the third estate to the fourth?

Texas Monthly Editorial
1983
Tom Ballenger
Illustrator

Galveston-Houston
Annual Report
1979
Joe Baraban
Photographer
Design for
Houston's industrial base
has been dominated
by photography.

making waves. So I'd have to explain that at that time of the day you get more color in the light, the light's softer, there are more variations. In 30 minutes you get the equivalent of a full day's change in light, and that's what a photographer looks for.

One thing that is true of Texas: it has great light. It has the best light of any state I've ever been in. It may just be the fact that there aren't any mountains or trees to clutter up the view. The sun goes down, and then there's that magic moment where the whole sky lights up and glows. In West Texas you'll have light for an hour after legal sunset. If you look at our work, you'll see that it's influenced us.

LOWELL: Fred made the point about hiring guys from the outside. When I was just starting to do real work at Fred's he hired a guy named Gary Cook who had been at Stan Richards. It was the first time I can recall of somebody coming into town and immediately winning a bunch of awards. The way he worked, the way he solved problems was different. The fact that he had learned to do quick thumbnails as opposed to laying out every page in a booklet was a totally new thing. The fact that he used little bitty type instead of great big type or medium-sized type was a whole new thing. So from my standpoint the Stan Richards influence brought to us by Gary Cook really opened a lot of doors.

RON: When I did my *CA* interview there was an underlying tone in the questions like, "okay, now that you've gotten this good, when are you going to leave this turkey patch and go someplace where good photographers work—New York, L.A., Chicago." My answer to that was, that's not a measure of success. Where you are is not important. However, being here is probably an advantage over being in a crowd scene in New York where there are clearly established patterns and you would have a much more difficult time establishing yourself. In Texas there wasn't anything established. I think that a very important thing about Texas is it's simply a fertile ground for people to grow.

Q: Many of Houston's top designers got their start at Baxter+Korge. What sort of people do you look for when you hire?

FRED: Because of the pressures we're under, I basically look for good people who care about themselves and their fellow man and are nice people to be with. If the talent's there, fine. But if the talented people are selfish and difficult to work with, I don't want them around. Everybody that has come through has helped make B+K what it is. This is a very transient community. If somebody stayed three years, that's a long time. Because of the kind of business we had 25 years ago—agricultural, petroleum, financial—you could get bored doing ads for drill rigs. So you'd move over to Tracy-Locke and do Maryland Club for a while.

LOWELL: The portfolio can only hurt you. You can't afford to look at the work and hire somebody based on that. You can tell by how a person dresses, how they talk, what they know about you, whether they like the kind of work you've done. Of the people who have left here in the past 13 years, only one has not left to go into business for themselves.

FRED: You mention dress... Back in the sixties and seventies when we began to be business communicators and were dealing directly with clients, our whole attitude toward dress changed. I probably wore suits more than most because I wanted to meet the chairman of the board, I wanted to meet the guy who was making the decisions because by the time I went through the advertising manager, the vice-president of marketing, and the senior vice-president of marketing, the idea was watered down four times.

Q: You seem to be demystifying the whole idea of "Texas design." Are you saying that there is a universality to good work? That what makes people good is the same in New York or Europe or Texas?

RON: If there's anything unique about Texas it's openness. People talk to each other. Like the photographers here, we all know each other and we're all good friends. We wouldn't hesitate to walk into each other's studios at any time and we wouldn't cover anything up.

FRED: I think there's a trust and a faith and a belief in each other's honesty and integrity. I would never hesitate to call Lowell about any problem, either business or personal, and get an opinion from him. And I know he would do the same.

Q: How much influence did the clients have on what has happened with Texas design?

LOWELL: I'll tell you the influence the clients have had...in 12 or 13 years of business I've only had one client not pay.

FRED: I don't think that's what she's asking about.

LOWELL: No, but that's the way I'm answering it.

FRED: I can probably see a bigger change in clients than they can because they came on board when clients were inspiring people, when clients wanted to do great things, when clients had bigger dreams. I don't want to keep harping back to that, but only in the past 12 to 15 years when we got to see clients directly and they had ideas that weren't homespun...

RON: So the client wasn't really important then.

FRED: My clients were of the opinion that we were a damn good art studio, but they told me what to do all the time.

RON: So when do you think clients first started being an influence, if they are?

FRED: Maybe 15 years ago. And it was definitely a positive influence. It gave you an opportunity to see the problem firsthand. It gave you the opportunity to meet with people of a different frame of mind, from different parts of the country, different parts of the world.

LOWELL: The seventies were really when the outsiders started moving in. When people were coming from New York and Detroit and other places. The clients themselves were growing and becoming more aware and also more competitive. I think that happened in Dallas a little earlier.

FRED: Their location as the hub of a whole region is far greater than ours.

LOWELL: Also, they were more retail, more cosmopolitan, if you will. The Dallas thing has been nothing more than great for the people in Houston. There is very good work being done in Dallas and it's very tough being competitive with those guys on a daily basis. But don't discount the importance of the client's ability to pay and willingness to pay.

Q: You are all so pragmatic. What about philosophy?

RON: People don't want to hear that it takes hard work to be successful. What they want to hear is that there's some mystical metaphysical reason for it. I know I hated to hear it. You can have all the philosophy in the world, but if you're not going to work hard it's not going to do you any good.

Q: What do you think the future will hold for Texas design?

LOWELL: I see it being a different time here than it has been the last 15 years. There will never, ever be another boom here like there was in the seventies. It may happen again in some other part of the United States, but it certainly won't happen in Houston. A lot of the people who started businesses during that boom are now going to fall by the wayside.

FRED: There will be fewer people to do the work, it will be more competitive, and I think it will be better.

LOWELL: Also, the good people will not just be doing work in Texas. It will be more international.

RON: We're not a plumbing business. We don't have to work where the trucks will go. When I first started, it cost over a hundred dollars to get a package to New York overnight. Then Federal Express came along and completely revolutionized the business. We're getting to be much more of a global village. Just around the corner is high speed facsimile transfer that will be good enough to send layouts and portfolios and stock photography. It's already started, but once we settle on a standard it will be even more that way. Today, you can hop on a plane and go anywhere. That's another great thing about Texas, we're in the central time zone. We can be in New York shortly after noon, scout a location, and do a shot. In a lot of ways, our location serves us in good stead for doing work across the country.

Q: What about the "look" of Texas design?

RON: That's the thing. People want to find a cactus in every photo. We shot a job in Denver for an agency in Minneapolis and when we got there the art director was sort of disappointed because she expected two guys in cowboy boots and hats to get off the plane. People expect to see some kind of Texas mystique.

LOWELL: I think if there was a Texas look it was the *Texas Monthly* look a couple of years ago. *Texas Monthly* was a tremendous vehicle for that, and it has a tremendous circulation outside of Texas. It was the whole urban cowboy thing. Well, that look is gone, probably forever.

RON: The one thing the judges always comment on is the great printing and lots of paper and...

LOWELL: I hear about the dollars that are being spent. People marvel at the money. But, you see, that's a contradiction because half to three-quarters of our work is not done in Texas. So how could someone look at something we've done and say, "I'm amazed at the amount of money that you guys are getting down there to spend for production values" when it could be for a client in New York? It's not Texas money, it's not Texas design, it's not a Texas project. It's a New York project.

The thing that has helped Texas is that there is no tradition to fall back on, there is no accepted value of what's good or what's not good because all of this has happened overnight.

FRED: And what about the mixture of cultures that we've had in the last 25 years? There was a tremendous influx of all kinds of people.

LOWELL: There's been a situation here where the design industry could springboard off other people's success. A Gerald Hines who is perceived as the megabuilder, the benchmark, is one company's coattails that we've all latched onto. There are other companies—Lomas & Nettleton, for one—who have hired good designers to do good work. They've been a tremendous vehicle for designers to jump on.

RON: The technology of doing business is changing, too. I think people in Texas are just as adaptable as anyplace else, if not more so.

LOWELL: The fact that we are very service-oriented, and this is a service industry, means that we get wagged by a lot of dogs. The success that the dogs are having directly relates to the success that our general industry has. As the different dogs have their peaks, that will inevitably influence what we do.

RON: One of the problems we have is that people tend to look at Texas as one stereotype when they should see that Texas is very diverse. We don't all try to design like Woody Pirtle. There was a time when only New York or maybe Chicago or L.A. had the technology. Today we have all the same technology. There are excellent printers here, excellent separators, we probably have the country's greatest retoucher—Raphaele—and there's no reason for her to be anyplace else. That in and of itself pretty well explains why Texas design has grown.

LOWELL: Of all the things said, that is probably the keynote: there is no reason for someone like Raphaele to be anyplace else.

RON: Why reinvent the wheel and go someplace else just to fly out of another airport?

LOWELL: You know I really don't think there's a Texas style at all. It's just happened that Houston and Dallas have had the opportunity to do a tremendous amount of work and have had a tremendous amount of money to work with. If there were three states between Houston and Dallas there wouldn't be any Texas style. It just happens that this place is so big you get lumped together.

Gerald D. Hines
Interests Brochure
1984

Ron Scott
Photographer

Developer Gerald D. Hines Interests has been a national leader in the promotion of real estate through graphic design, and a major influence on the Texas design style.

Design in Texas

An Interview With Mike Hicks and Leonard Ruben

Mike Hicks is a native Texan, educated in Texas, and has worked his entire career in Texas. After being a founding partner in the Houston illustration and design firm Flat Lizard Graphics, Mike moved to Austin in 1978 to form Hixo, Inc. The firm has been celebrated for its marketing, book and restaurant design and especially for its promotion of Texana. Mike was one of the founding board members of AIGA-Texas, and its first President.

Leonard Ruben received degrees in New York from Pratt, Columbia University and New York University. After working as an art director in several agencies, including Young & Rubicam, Leonard eventually found himself back in school at the University of Texas, where he is the F.J. Heyne Centennial Professor in Communication. Leonard's list of credits, his students, now extend throughout the country's major advertising agencies.

Mike and Leonard were interviewed in Austin.

Q: What would you say are the most significant changes you've seen in the past 25 years?

LEONARD: I go back to the distant past. I went to Pratt Institute. Back then you'd start off as a designer or an illustrator and go off from there in different directions. I started as a designer; there was no title of Art Director then.

When Push Pin Studio started in the mid-fifties the field broke into two pieces: art direction and graphic design. I took the art direction route. That was when art directors started to write. Before, we were considered illiterate, we'd just draw and make it look good; copy originated on another floor. I was at Young & Rubicam at the time. On another floor above us in a remote area the idea would originate, clear the supervisor and come down to us. It was humiliating. Doyle Dane Bernbach changed that around and it became a good field.

Q: Tell me what you found when you came from New York to Texas in 1970?

LEONARD: I want to be totally honest: I thought it was terrible. First of all, there were no ideas here. At best, there was decoration. There was a little bit of spark. Jim Franklin and a few people like that were doing unusual posters for the Armadillo World Headquarters. They were a little off-group in Austin that were really terrific designers. They didn't call themselves designers, but they were. Street people doing brilliant work. There was a kind of Texas look that was refreshing and Austin was the center of it. Dallas was doing nothing—well, Stan was doing his work and there was a little movement starting up in Houston. In fact, Houston was more vital than Dallas.

MIKE: I thought it was, too, until about 1974. It wasn't as established. Dallas was more conservative than Houston. Houston had no rules, it had no zoning. They didn't know how they were supposed to be—so they were more likely to be themselves out of ignorance. In Dallas, they were educated enough to know what the work was supposed to look like. It was even more vital here in Austin where they didn't have any idea; they didn't even know where they were. If they knew what block they were in they were doing well.

LEONARD: There was a primitive vitality here with the music scene as well. Dallas, being the sophisticated city that it was, should have done like Minneapolis, but it never took the lead. And Houston never did either; Houston got involved in a sidetrack. With me, the idea always came first. I didn't care too much if it didn't look great as long as it had a good idea. But they didn't seem to be interested in that in Dallas or in Houston, it was no concern of theirs. You'd get these vacuous beautiful-looking things, and they'd invite critics down from New York who would invariably pan the shows, and they'd say, "Get out of town you Yankees, we don't want you here." Well what they were telling them was, "Your stuff is terrific-looking, but there's no content." But that's changed.

MIKE: Yeah, now it's got content, and it doesn't look good anymore.

Q: Is there a Texas style?

MIKE: Stan Richards had a tremendous impact on establishing a style that became associated with Texas, but it wasn't necessarily generic. In recent times, a style has been emerging. It used to be that clients who were educated and cultured would go to New York. And to some extent, it's still true. It's interesting that only in the last five or six years have Texas designers been getting work from other markets. That's when you can start saying, "Okay, there's now content here which has a national parity." And when people doing business in New York start wanting to use a Texas designer, art director or agency, then I would say, "Okay, now we have a style and the style has substance." That's only happened recently. I think it's real encouraging that it's happening at last.

LEONARD: I think you've left out something important here, and that is the illustrators. Dallas had some very gifted illustrators: Bart Forbes, Jack Unruh, and people like that. They were being used nationally. They were the strongest illustrators in the country outside of Westport, Connecticut. So you had an enclave who did start a Texas style. It was an ironic style, because it had a high degree of design sophistication that you wouldn't expect to find in a Texas illustrator. They and Stan together may have started a movement of Texas breaking out of its boundaries.

MIKE: Certainly the illustrators and photographers made it easier to open up the market. For some reason there seemed to be better photographers in Houston and better illustrators in Dallas.

Q: What changes have you seen, Mike?

MIKE: When I started out in Houston in 1970, you worked for an advertising agency. There were no freelance writers, and I don't believe there were more than ten freelance designers, and they were really illustrators who could work in design occasionally. So if you were a designer or a writer or an art director, the only place you could work was an advertising agency. And the advertising agencies were exactly as Leonard described them. They were from another era. They had pretty cut-and-dried ideas about what you were supposed to do and how things worked.

So as a consequence, a lot of people abandoned advertising agencies. When I started we couldn't get any real clients. I had been in music for a long time, so the only contacts I had were in the music field. For the first two years we did rock & roll posters and album covers. It wasn't because it paid well or because we wanted to do it, but simply because they were the only people who would talk to us. As a consequence, the only idea work was done for low budgets—the hair salon or the deli where you traded, or for music accounts who had no preconceived notions. Necessity affected the style. I still think in black & white because for years and years none of my clients could afford color. If we had used a rubber stamp and a second ink color, that was considered a color job. It was discouraging.

Texans are real independent, and as a consequence, they've made some mistakes that have become embodied into a form. A lot of illustration that came out of Texas was flat and two-dimensional. I don't know why that is except that Texas is real flat and two-dimensional. I feel like a lot of guys for years did real quick work because of the low budgets. If you could draw in an hour you could make money at it. If it takes you two hours you're dead. I began as a designer and became an illustrator because I couldn't find an illustrator. I worked and worked and worked to try and develop the ten-hour illustration because I figured if you couldn't do it in ten hours you'd never make money as an illustrator. I got it down to 12 hours, which was the quickest I could physically get it done, and then I lost interest in the game. But for a long time, the style I was doing—which embodied copy machines and cameras and pasting stuff together—was a style that evolved solely out of necessity. There was no way in the world I could sell an illustration for what I was able to get, produce it in more than 10 or 12 hours, and be able to do enough of them to pay for my car.

We were doing work for Howard Stein out of New York who was using us because word got out in the music field that we were so cheap. I didn't hear that until years later. I thought at the time it was because we were so good. I remember we did a job for the opening of the Who coming to the U.S. We were asked to do it, and Milton Glaser was asked to do it. I was probably 26 at the time, and I thought, "We'll show them." A year later a producer told me they just couldn't believe we were so cheap. They were all ready to use Milton, but they wanted to see what we'd do. We cost so little that they would just as soon try us, and if they didn't like us, they could still use him and get away with it. Meanwhile, the people I knew in the art directors club were doing $90,000 TV commercials where they're helicoptering cars up to the top of Pike's Peak for Shell Oil and here we were: working for a hundred dollars...and sometimes they wouldn't pay us. That era was crazy.

Q: What were some of your early influences?
MIKE: I will always credit *CA* Magazine for being a huge influence on Texas. Ads for the same products were different in the South than they were in the rest of the country. Those first 7-Up ads in the early seventies that were wonderfully animated, I never saw them. Everybody in the country was talking about them but they didn't show them in Texas. *CA* was something you could hold and look at, and it was real and you knew it. And then, as Leonard pointed out, many people from New York and other places began to come to Texas, and their presence contributed a lot of sophistication to the market.
LEONARD: Now Texas is in New York. You can go into any agency in New York—big, little, tiny—and they're staffed with Texans. You can look in awards annuals and you wouldn't know who's Texan

and who's not, but you can find a large percentage. I counted about 45 out of my classes alone in the last New York art directors annual. At J. Walter Thompson, the third largest agency in the country, we have one whole group, the Burger King group, that's almost entirely our people. The thing is, you can go to New York and you'll find a hell of a lot of Texans up there. They're starting to get in the position right now where their influence is being felt. And it's a good influence.

Q: Why suddenly all these Texans on the national advertising scene?
MIKE: I could say it's the raw vitality of our pioneer heritage, the bold courageous spirit of our forefathers. Except that most of our forefathers weren't from Texas. When I was young, jet planes always flew over, but they never stopped. When they started stopping, Texans started going places. Maybe it is as simple as that: cheap air fares.
LEONARD: I still wonder how the sophistication developed. Everybody says Stan Richards developed it because he's the father of graphic design here.
MIKE: I don't quite credit him with that. I don't think he created it, I think he made the rest of the country aware that you could operate in Texas and do sophisticated work that had content.
Q: Mike, you're from Texas. How has that influenced your work?
MIKE: I grew up in Lubbock. I went to Texas Tech back when it was still a small college, before it became a university. Larry McIntyre was in class with me, and Sybill Broyles, who later became the art director of *Texas Monthly*. Speaking of Lubbock, the reason so many people there were in music or art was because there was such dire isolation, and a repressive society. There were proportionately more churches there than there were in Houston. It was the world's largest dry city. It was 400 miles to anywhere. When I was a kid we used to drive up to the Cap Rock, this large flat rock 200 miles long and 300 miles wide. We would drive up to the edge of it where the whole world fell off, and wonder what was out there. We were 13, and none of us had ever been off the Cap Rock. It was a big flat physical barrier that was more than two tanks of gas away from anyplace. You either were so overpowered by the system that you became part of it and worked on your dad's ranch—if you were fortunate enough to have a ranch—or you worked at somebody else's dad's ranch, or you worked at the cotton gin, or you sold cars, or you left. The only thing to do if you played a guitar was to play a guitar, because there was nothing else to do.
LEONARD: It was sort of like *The Last Picture Show*.
MIKE: Frighteningly so. The Beatles hit when I was in high school. It was a raising of consciousness; people who felt the need for a creative outlet could channel whatever resources they had, assuming they weren't totally uncoordinated, into music; whereas it was hard to get into art. At the same time, a guy named Mouse, Big Daddy Roth and a few others in

Armadillo World
Headquarters Poster
1970

Jim Franklin
Designer, Illustrator

Texas Monthly
Magazine Poster
1979

Mike Hicks
Designer, Illustrator

Austin based
Texas Monthly Magazine
became a major market
for Texas illustrators
and photographers.

21

Texas Monthly
Magazine Cover
1973

Ron Scott
Photographer

Texas Monthly
Magazine Cover
1978

Ron Scott
Photographer

Early issues of
Texas Monthly Magazine
celebrated Texana.

California were painting cars and T-shirts at raceways. Car culture, dragsters and all that, was big at the time. They'd set up an airbrush in the pits and draw on the back of sweatshirts for drivers or whoever. It was drag racing art. And that's what the kids I knew were doing; they were drawing on the backs of shirts and playing guitar because it was easy and you could buy an electric guitar at Sears for fifty-nine bucks.

LEONARD: We had an illustrator out of Texas when I was at Y&R, and he was the first Texan I ever saw. He even looked like one: six-six, blond hair, cowboy hat, boots, and he was terrific.

Q: What were some of the early influences on Texas design?

LEONARD: I think the real influence on Texas was the Push Pin style.

MIKE: Push Pin was a real influential studio, with many gifted people and two or three incredibly gifted people. Glaser was probably the foremost. Good illustrators, good writers, good designers— they published their own books, did their own products, they were years ahead of everyone else. They were very, very strong during the sixties and seventies when Texas was just kind of pecking its way out of the egg in terms of developing a style. Push Pin was the style at that point, so naturally, when they poked their heads out of the egg in Texas and looked around what they saw was Push Pin. They developed a style that was real design intensive, which appealed to Texans because most couldn't draw. There were no good art schools here. You want to be an artist? That was like saying you wanted to go off and join the ballet. In Texas it had the same connotation.

LEONARD: I wanted to go to Pratt Institute. My parents wouldn't hear of such a thing, but it was semi-respectable because it was commercial art and you could make a little money.

MIKE: Now, "designer" means money to a lot of parents. Designer jeans, designer furniture, designer cars, they think designers are rich guys. Of course, now the market is glutted with designers.

I'll tell you another thing that makes Texas neat is that designers in Texas write. And I think that's because the state is not as rigorously specialized as larger markets have been.

LEONARD: All of our students write. They're trained in two aspects: to write and to design. And actually, what is writing? It's conceiving an idea.

MIKE: That's another thing I think people should be beholden to Stan for: he wasn't so narrow in his definition of what a design firm was. It was what he said it was.

LEONARD: You may not have thought of this, but he was a school unto himself. He is as much of a school as any school.

Let me put in a plug for the University of Texas. We have people all over the country—Fallon McElligott Rice, Chiat/Day, all the top agencies— and they wouldn't hire them if they weren't good. This is a Texas product that's known throughout the country. I remember the first Texan I sent up there. She went up to New York and they said, "Texas! You can't be serious, you got this book out of Texas! We thought all they knew was football." They were surprised to see someone with a really sophisticated product coming out of Texas.

MIKE: In a way this new-found success may be because a lot of people from Texas, when they were growing up, said, "We want to show those bastards in New York and Los Angeles that we can get by without them looking down their noses at us." I think that's part of the reason they work so hard, and the reason they go to New York and get their first job. They want to prove, by God, that they're better than anybody and can do twelve times what anybody in their position can. It's a nice thing to have, really; otherwise, you'd probably start going to plays and enjoying the city and get too comfortable. Comfort is a horrible thing for keeping yourself motivated.

LEONARD: Let me be a critic here for a minute. Why isn't Austin better known than it is? Austin should be a center of design, it's perfect for it.

MIKE: I think what happened to Austin is what happened earlier to Texas. Austin will come around, but it's like every other rural community. Houston and Dallas are pretty much relating to the nation now. Austin is still in the shadow of Houston and Dallas and has an inferiority complex.

Q: But surely Austin is in a transition period now. There's a lot of activity going on.

MIKE: It will change. There's already signs of it happening. There are certainly instances where extremely nice work is being done. There's work from Austin in the New York shows, even in the Dallas show.

Q: What trends do you see developing in Texas design?

MIKE: I don't think Texas design will be as distinct. Look at the New Wave style which I associate with Los Angeles. When it becomes that renowned and that much of a commodity, I think there's a tendency for it to become part of the American style, the greater overall trend.

LEONARD: I think there are some major trends developing that are very significant. Stan Richards, the father of Texas design, has gone into a full-fledged agency business that was picked as one of the agencies of the year by *Adweek*. Now that's significant. He's made a whole 180-degree turn. And what does that mean? That means that Texas has now abandoned its artsy-craftsy roots and gone after the big leagues in a big way. He's got big accounts; he's now billing over $70 million, and that's no small time thing. Why is it that Dallas has two first-line agencies—The Richards Group and Tracy-Locke— and all this happened in the past five years? Because it's ready for it now. I'm glad to see Texas get away from its aping of other little craft industries into a big, mammoth, and tasteful operation that doesn't have to take second place to anybody. It hasn't, I'm afraid, happened in Houston. Houston is suffering from an economic crisis, and it's really kind of tragic in a way because they showed signs of wanting to do something. It's too bad this oil crunch happened when it did because it's going to stop movement. You've got to have the impetus of money.

MIKE: I would say Houston's impact is in the design community, not advertising.

LEONARD: But Dallas is getting in the big leagues in advertising. And Stan is the leader, or at least he's on the cutting edge of it. And that for me is interesting.

Q: Getting back to the Texas style, what exactly is it?

MIKE: It's a kind of offshoot of the Push Pin style. Stan developed it further, and then Stan's offshoots developed it further. Flat, decorative, muted colors, look at the Push Pin stuff of the fifties and you'll see the genesis of the Texas style. They won't admit this, and maybe it's not complimentary, I don't know. Usually they used repetitive designs over and over again. Maybe to a fault. Because there wasn't a budget for illustration so you used the same one over and over again.

LEONARD: But that, I think, describes it. And usually, inserted somewhere, was an idea. I'll give them credit, most designers in Texas are looking for an idea. One of the cleverest things I've ever seen was a dog looking at a television set and it said, "See Spot Run." It was for some television spots that were going to run out of Dallas. I thought it was a hell of an idea. It wasn't over embellished. If I have any criticism of Texas design it's over embellishment.

MIKE: It's very complex.

LEONARD: Simplicity would be a nice, refreshing note. If someone would come in and say, "Hey, let's make it simple," I think something would be advanced in Texas design.

MIKE: I do hope never again, certainly in my professional life or even my unprofessional life, to do another picture of a cactus. That's a whole separate substyle. Usually, if you're from Texas, or the job you're doing is about Texas and you can't think of anything else, put a cactus or a boot in it, and somehow that makes it okay. That's not funny, it's hack. It's been hacked over and brought up from the dead about three or four times. It's time to bury it.

You mentioned trends. Probably everyone in the state, myself included, is not without a cactus or two in their history. But hopefully, everyone is moving away from that because Texas as a state finally has an image. It's not J.R., that's a trite image laughed at in Texas. It's now younger, more urban, glitzy; it doesn't depend so much on the heritage of the state—the saddlebags, longhorns, the wide open spaces and all that stuff that no one sees anymore anyway.

When I was in Houston, my group, Jay Loucks' group, Jerry Herring's group, Jerry Jeanmard's group—you could have put all of our offices together and you wouldn't have ever been aware that you were going from one studio to the next. They were all exactly alike. They all had Coca-Cola signs, they all had little type trays, they all had soft sculptures of cactus and cow skulls somewhere, and they all had wooden library furniture from the thirties. They were as similar to one another as suburban tract houses. Now, people's offices are a lot different. They're slicker, more modern, high rise. I think a style and identity is emerging for the state, and it's not historical. And designers themselves are changing. They're not as similar to one another and as they grow older they grow more self-confident.

There used to be a way all designers looked. Now there is a greater variety of looks, the clothes they wear, the cars they drive. For a long time, when Texas was suffering its identity crisis, there was sort of a security in everybody being alike because they were the only people you felt you had anything in common with.

LEONARD: It's a great state. You have to get away from it to see it. I just went up to Syracuse a year ago to teach, and there's a whole different feeling up there. I came from that part of the country, but I haven't been there for so long I forgot what it was like. I wanted to come back here. And that's when I knew I was a Texan.

Design in Texas
The Exhibition

In 1983 when a group of designers first met in Dallas to talk about forming a Texas chapter of the American Institute of Graphic Arts, it symbolized the coming of age of the Texas design community.

That small group was responding to the growth of Texas design, a growth in quantity as well as a growth in quality.

Being visually oriented people, it seemed inevitable that there would come a time when AIGA-Texas would want to document this change, this entering of a new age. So early on, the seeds were planted for the exhibit, *Design in Texas*.

There were precedents for shows like the one AIGA-Texas was considering. The AIGA California Graphic Design Exhibition is one example. And like other graphic design exhibits, this show would be juried—a competition—rather than curated. While a curated show would have certain distinct advantages, such as a more comprehensive look at older work, a juried show has a competitive flavor and the credibility of having been chosen by ones peers.

Judging the nearly two-thousand entries in *Design in Texas* were Seymour Chwast, James Cross, Richard Hess, Kit Hinrichs and McRay Magelby.

After the judging, the question "Is there a Texas Style?" begged to be answered. The answer? For that, the collective work speaks for itself.

Seymour Cwhast
Push Pin Studios
New York, New York

McRay Magleby
Brigham Young University
Salt Lake City, Utah

Richard Hess
Hess & Hess
Roxbury, Connecticut

Kit Hinrichs
Jonson Pedersen Hinrichs & Shakery
San Francisco, California

James Cross
Cross Associates
Los Angeles, California

Turtle Creek Center For The Arts
1983

Danny Kamerath
Art Director, Designer

Kent Kirkley
Photographer

Grant Richards
Copywriter

Richards, Sullivan,
Brock & Associates
Design Firm

The Richards Group
Agency

Turtle Creek Center
For The Arts
Client

Mercantile Texas Corp.
Annual Report
1976

Jack Summerford
Art Director, Designer

Greg Booth
Photographer

John Stone
Copywriter

The Richards Group
Design Firm, Agency

Mercantile Texas Corp.
Client

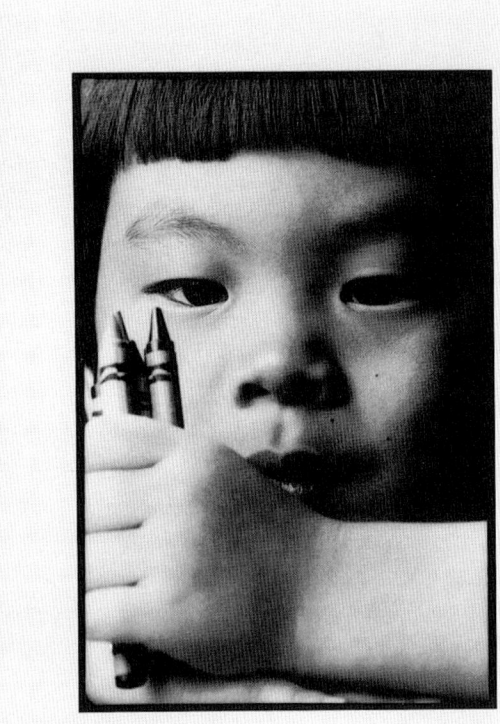
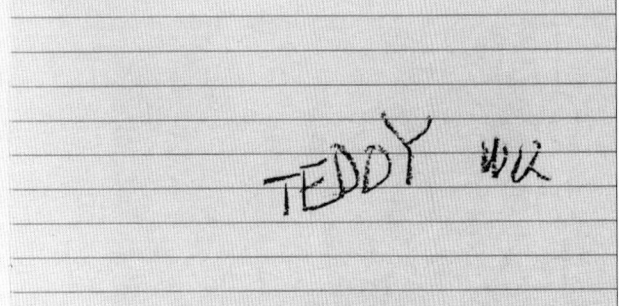

The School

From the beginning, our intent in creating this private school was to provide a select group of children with an extraordinary environment for learning. Grace School is a school dedicated not only to helping children develop their academic abilities. It is a school committed to helping children strengthen the whole of their being—their confidence, their fortitude, and especially their faith.

Today, Grace School offers pre-school, elementary, and middle school programs to children from three to 14 years of age. Though governed by Grace Presbyterian Church, the school is open to children of all religious affiliations, races, and creeds. Its facilities are excellent. The church campus was recently remodeled to encompass more than 100,000 square feet including a gym, library, and kitchen.

Class sizes are kept exceptionally small—no more than 20 students. Every child is assured of receiving an uncommon measure of individualized instruction. Here, in this very personalized setting, teachers are afforded the time it takes to stay keenly aware of each child's progress. They have the time to work quietly with each child and closely with parents, helping to assure that the child has what he needs to reach his potential.

Teddy
Kindergarten

Grace School
1985
Richard Kilmer, Mark Geer
Art Directors, Designers
Jim Sims
Photographer
Linda Bradford
Copywriter
Kilmer Geer Design
Design Firm
Grace School
Client

Zoo Quarterlies
1984–1986
Lowell Williams
Art Director
Lana Rigsby, Andy Dearwater
Designers, Illustrators
Rona Schwartz
Copywriter
Lowell Williams Design, Inc.
Design Firm, Agency
Houston Zoological Society
Client

Three's The Charm
1983
Sharon Tooley
Art Director, Designer
Frank White
Photographer
Paule Sheya Hewlett
Copywriter
Sharon Tooley Design
Design Firm, Client

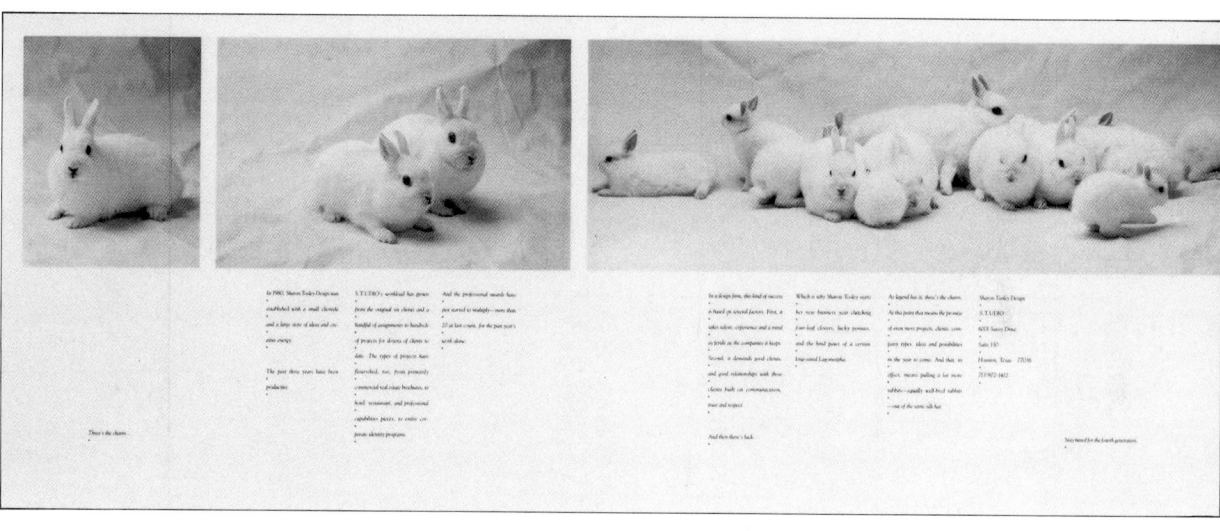

Superior Land & Cattle Brochure
1980
Blake Miller, Wayne Ford
Art Directors, Designers
Joe Baraban
Photographer
Mark Judson
Copywriter
Miller, Judson & Ford, Inc.
Design Firm
Superior Land & Cattle Company
Client

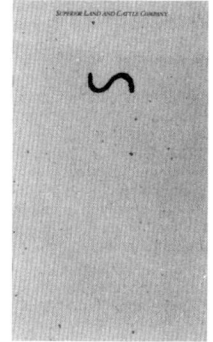

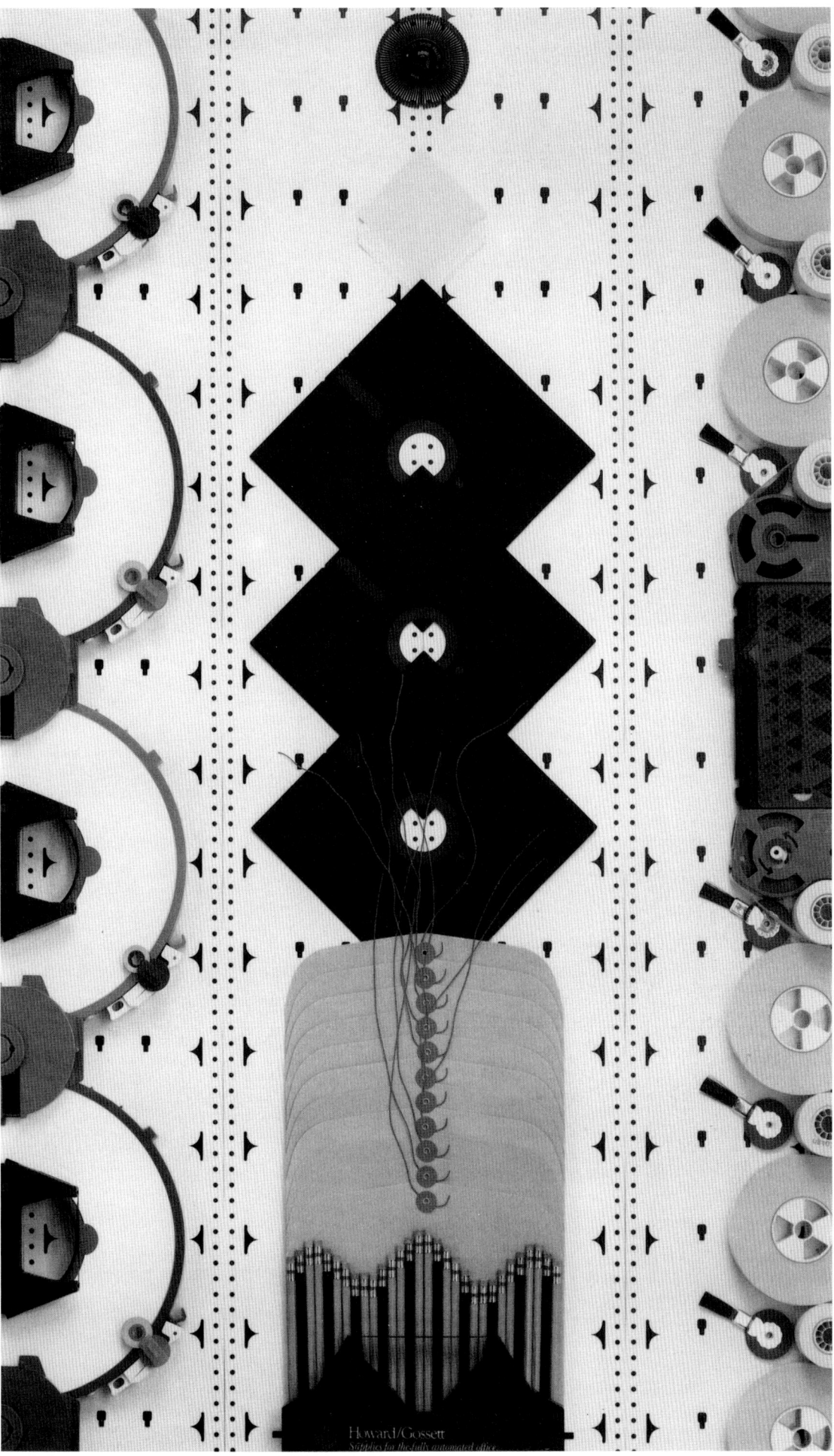

Howard Gossett Poster
1985
Richard Kilmar, Mark Geer
Art Directors, Designers
Jim Sims
Photographer
Kilmer Geer Design
Design Firm
Howard Gossett Co. /
Office Supplies
Client

Apple Poster
1985
Chris Celusniak
Art Director, Designer, Illustrator
Artworks
Design Firm
Asheland Design, Inc.
Client

Shooting Stars
1983
Michael McGrath
Art Director, Designer
Michael McGrath Design
Design Firm
Webb & Sons
Client

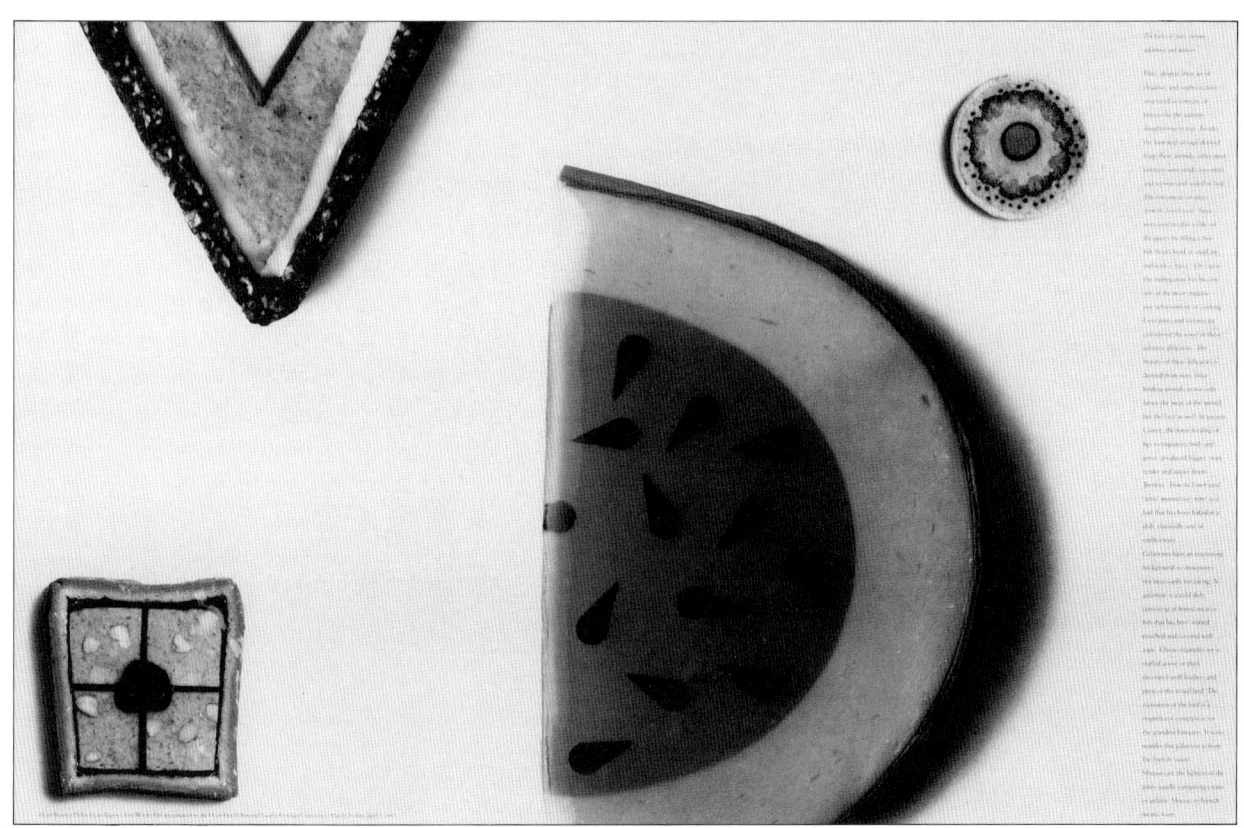

Patè
1985
Chuck Hart
Art Director, Designer
Judy Kerm
Photographer
Hyatt Regency Dallas
Copywriter
Krause & Young
Design Firm, Agency
Hyatt Regency Dallas
Client

Birth Announcement
1984
Don Grimes
Art Director, Designer
Bieber Tidwell
Copywriter
Don Grimes Design, Inc.
Design Firm
Jon & Toni Gray
Client

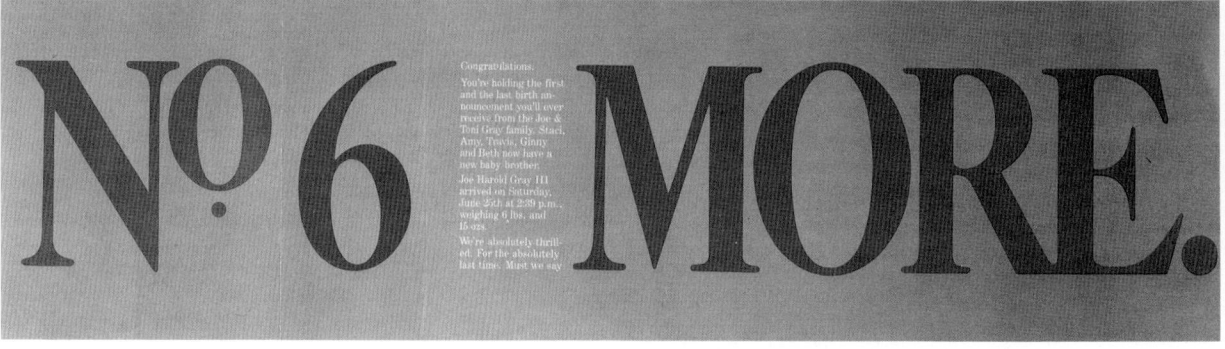

West Lovers Lane
1985
Dorothy Marschall
Art Director, Designer
Dean St. Clair
Illustrator/Photographer

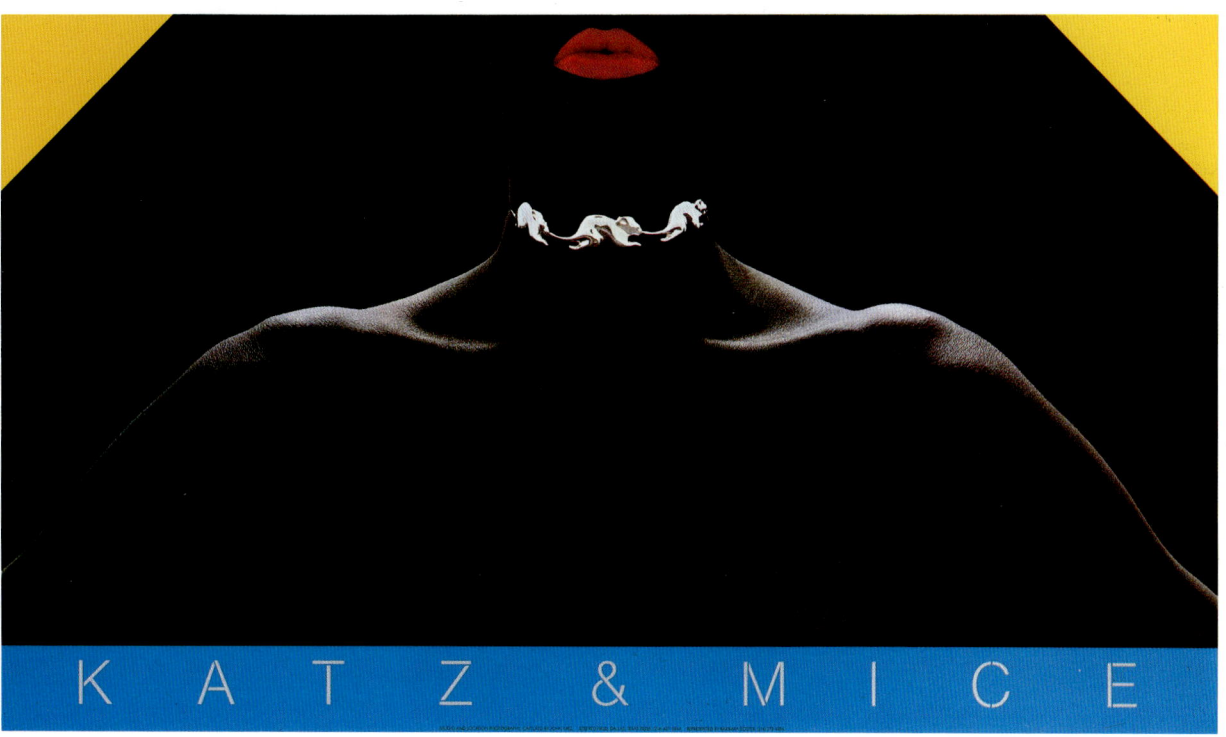

Katz & Mice
1983
John Katz
Art Director, Photographer
Woody Pirtle
Designer, Copywriter
Pirtle Design
Design Firm
John Katz Photography
Client

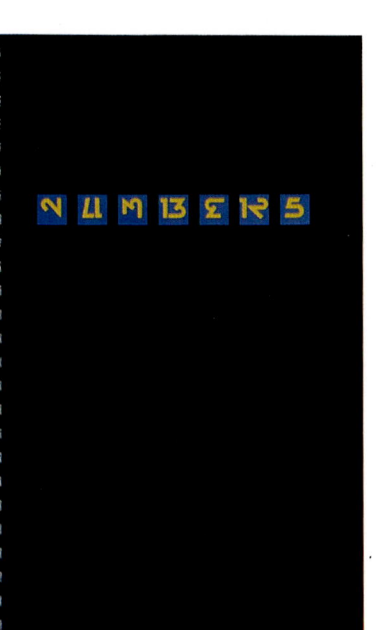 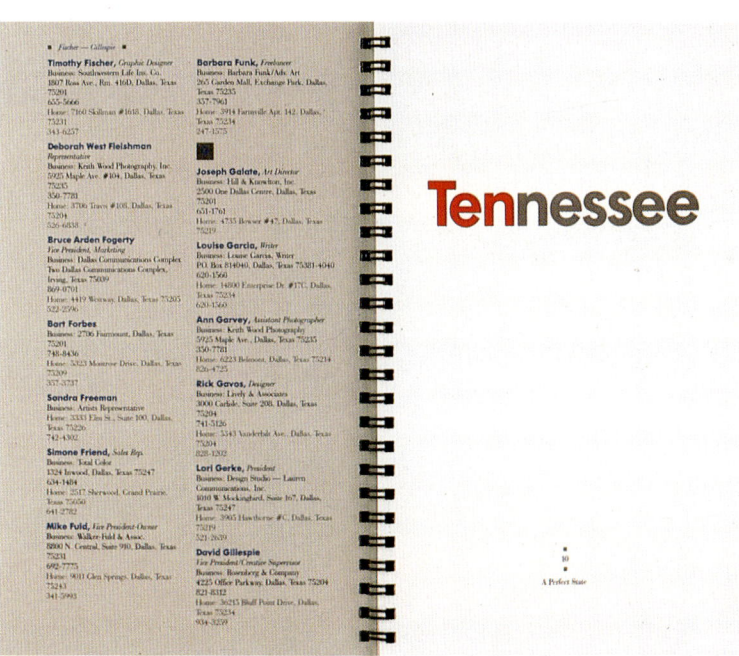

Numbers
1984
Jack Summerford
Art Director, Designer, Illustrator
Summerford Design, Inc.
Design Firm
Dallas Society of Visual Communications
Client

Night Blossom Invitation
1977
Rex Peteet
Art Director, Designer
Jack Unruh
Illustrator
Jim Hradecky
Copywriter
The Richards Group
Design Firm
Autohaus
Client

Texas Homes Poster
1980
Cap Pannell
Art Director, Designer
Cap Pannell, Cerita Smith
Illustrators
Texas Homes Magazine
Copywriter
Pannell Creative
Design Firm
Texas Homes Magazine
Client

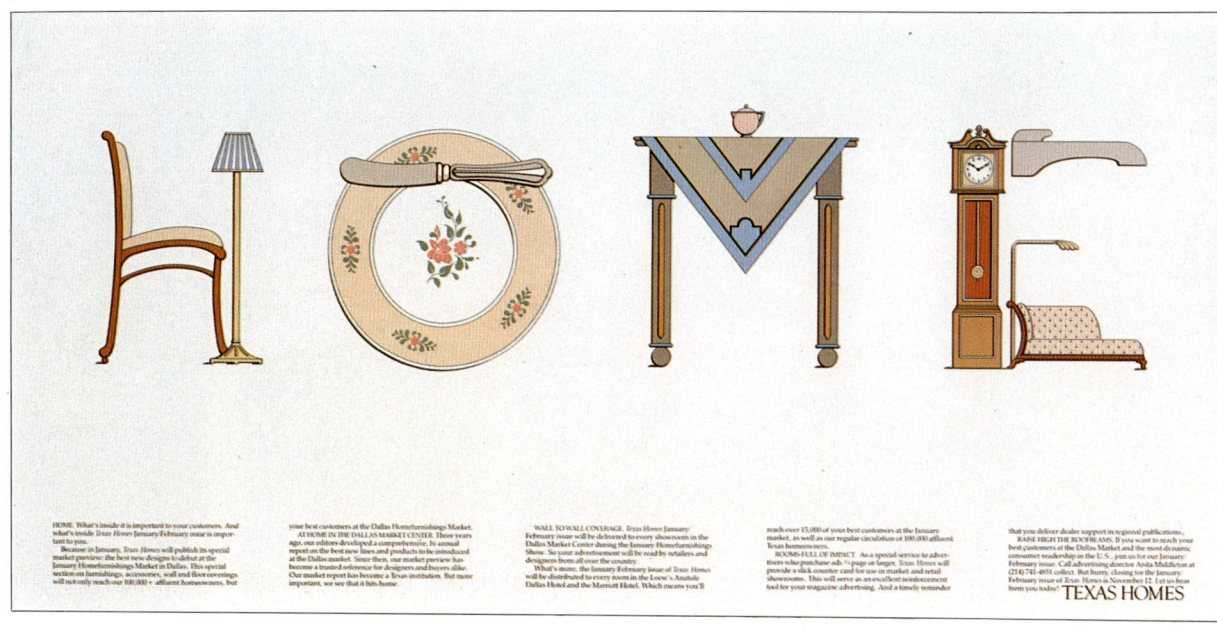

Melissa Lane Sheers
1980
Steve Connatser
Art Director, Designer, Copywriter
Kent Kirkley
Photographer
Connatser & Co.
Design Firm
Melissa Jane
Client

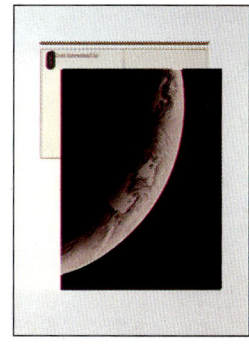

Oiltools Brochure
1980

Lowell Williams
Art Director

Lowell Williams, Bill Carson
Designers

Ron Scott, Joe Baraban, Jim Sims
Photographers

Lee Herrick
Copywriter

Lowell Williams Design, Inc.
Design Firm, Agency

Oiltools International, Ltd.
Client

Scali Invite
1979

Glyn Powell
Art Director, Designer

Arthur Eisenberg
Copywriter

Eisenberg, Inc.
Design Firm

Dallas Society of
Visual Communications
Client

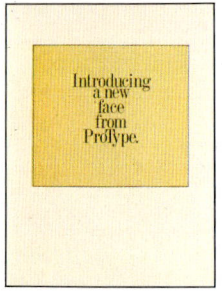

Pro-Type Baby Book
1984
Janis Koy Beveridge
Art Director
Janis Koy Beveridge,
Brad DiBaggio, Trisha Ravseh
Designers
Brad DiBaggio
Illustrator
Doug Rucker
Copywriter
Koy Design, Inc.
Design Firm
Pro-Type
Client

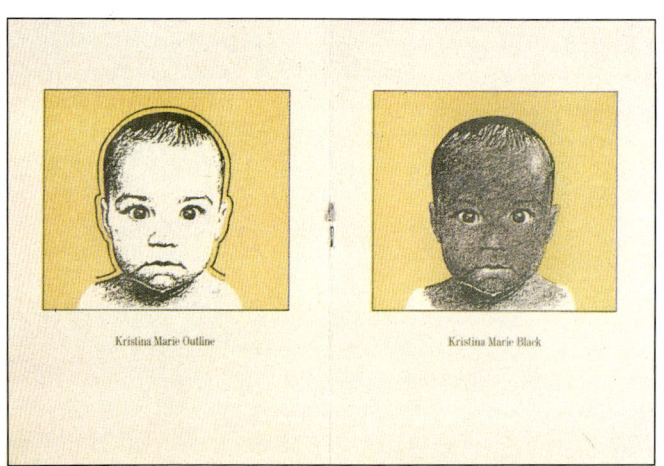

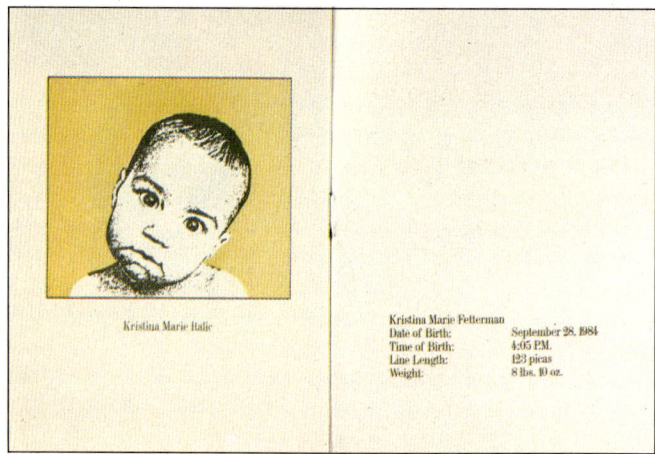

Trademark Books
1976–1983

Stand Richards & Associates,
The Richards Group,
Richards Sullivan,
Brock & Associates,
Richards, Brock, Miller,
Mitchell & Associates
Design Firm, Agency, Client

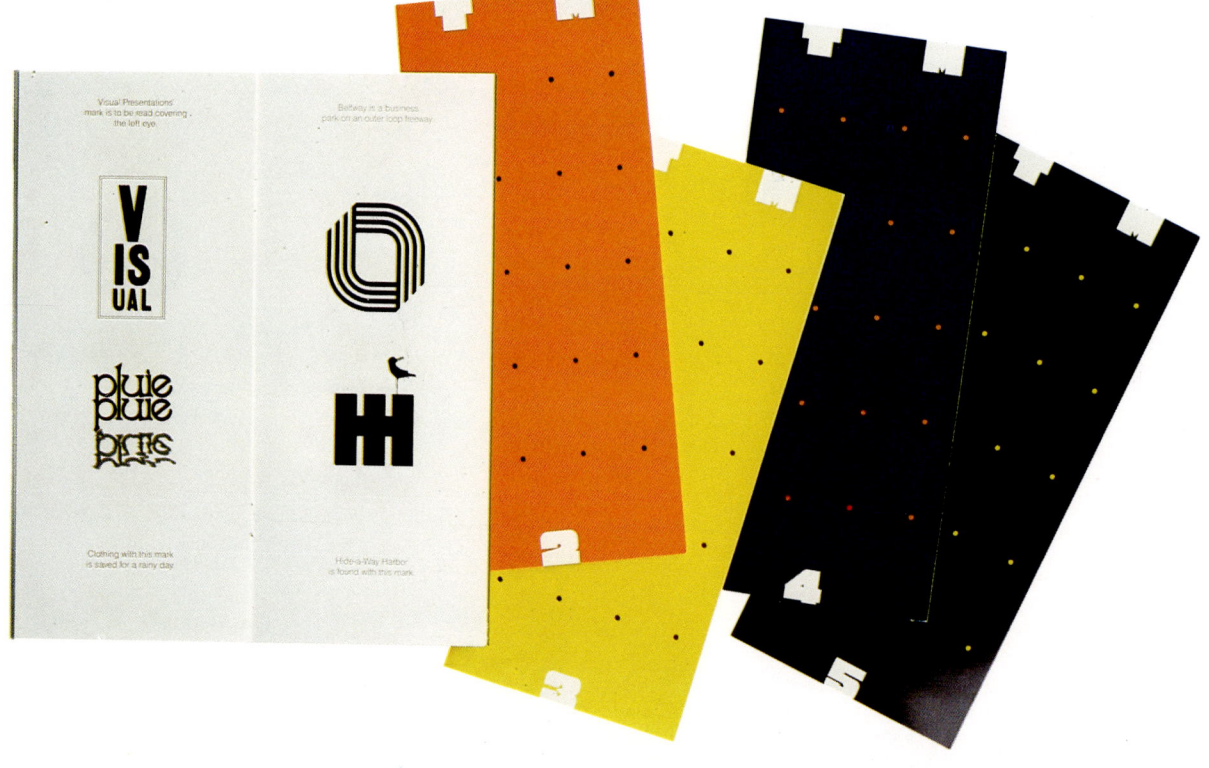

Christmas Peppers
1982
Chris Hill
Art Director

Chris Hill, Joe Rattan
Designers

Jim Sims
Photographer

HILL/A Marketing Design Group
Design Firm, Client

Miss Williams Logo
1978
Mike Schroeder
Art Director, Designer, Illustrator

Schroeder, Acevedo
Design Firm

Miss Williams, Make-up Artist
Client

Smithsonian Invitation
1985
Rex Peteet
Art Director, Designer
Rex Peteet, Paul Black
Illustrators
Rex Peteet, Marguerite Steed
Copywriters
Sibley/Peteet Design, Inc.
Design Firm
Trammel Crow Company
Client

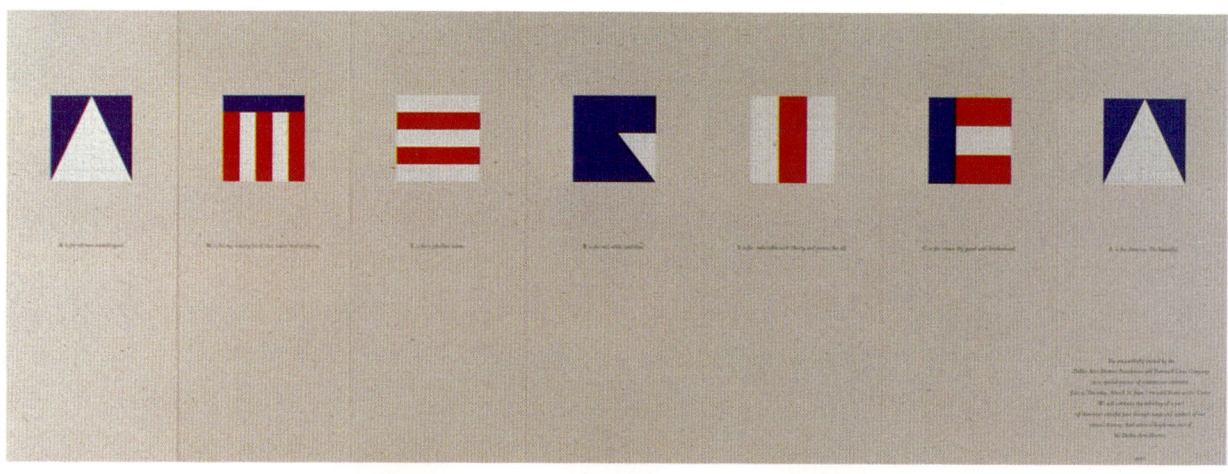

The Four Chairs
1985
Michael Muhlherr
Art Director, Designer
Robert Ziebell
Photographer
Jim Sanders
Copywriter
The Glassell School of Art
Client

Texas Toffey
1985
Brenda Kilmer
Art Director, Designer, Illustrator
Kilmer Design
Design Firm
Texas Toffey, Inc.
Client

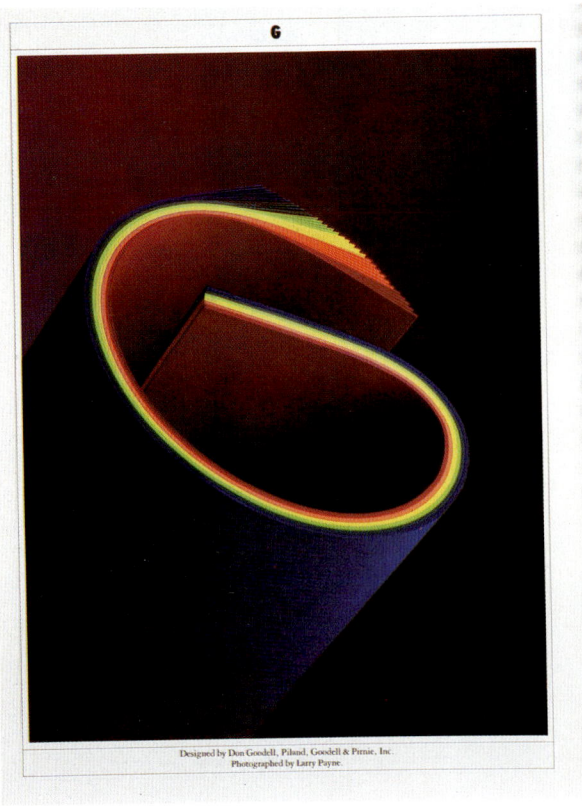
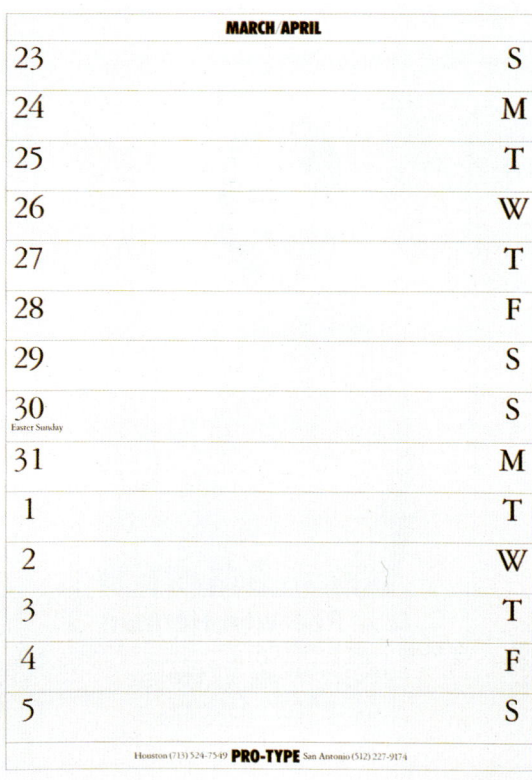

1986 ProType Calendar
1985
Jerry Herring
Art Director
John Heck
Designer
Ron Scott
Photographer
Kerry Oliver
Copywriter
Herring Design
Design Firm
Professional Typographers
Client

1984 Christmas Book
1984
Steve Gibbs
Art Director, Designer
Steve Gibbs, Don Sibley, Rex Peteet, Ken Shafer
Illustrators
Don Sibley, Rex Peteet
Copywriters
Sibley/Peteet Design, Inc.
Design Firm, Client

McDermott Songbook
1985
Ron Sullivan
Art Director

Diana McKnight, Don Roy
Designers

Sullivan Perkins
Design Firm

The Rouse Company
Client

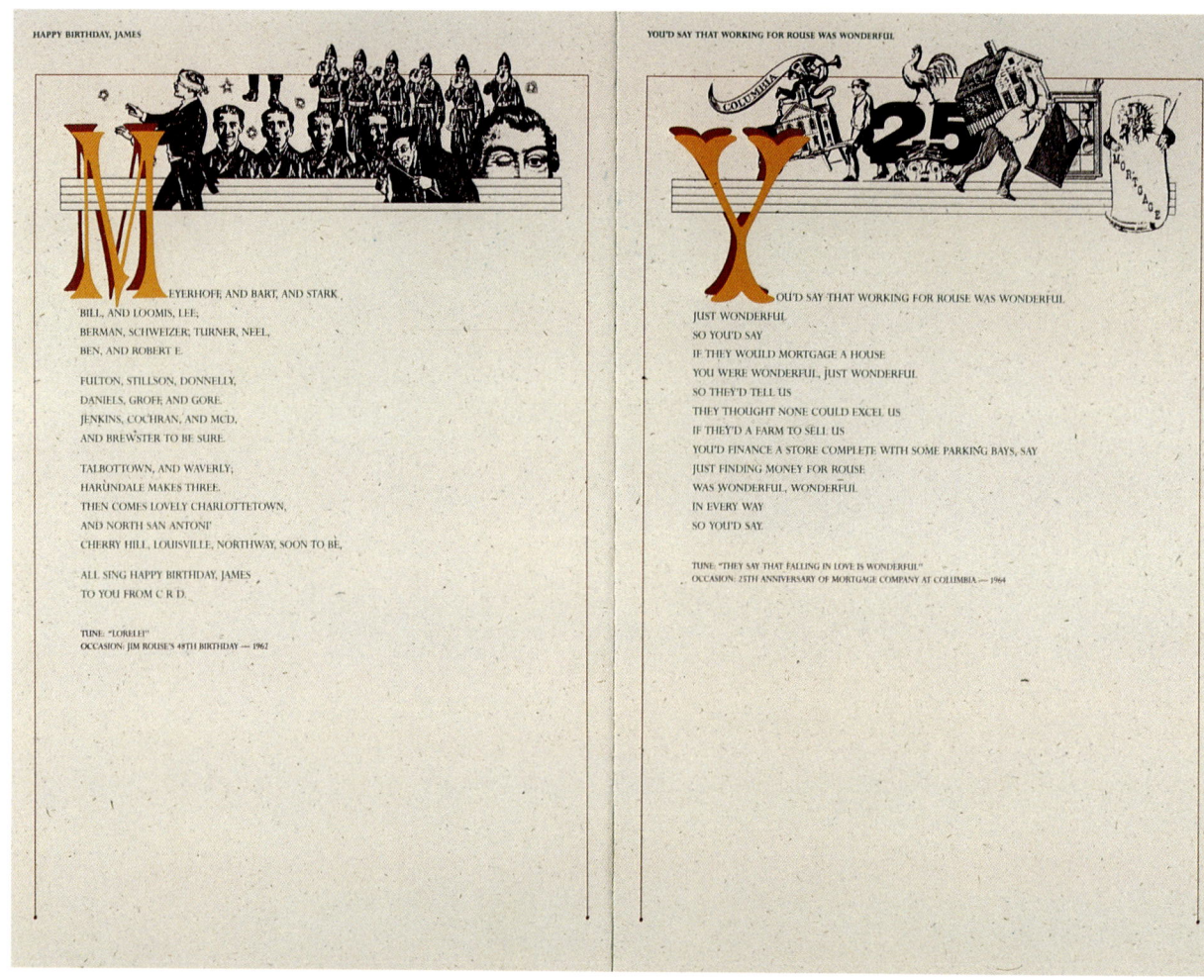

AIGA
Communication Graphics
Call for Entry
1984
Jack Summerford
Art Director, Designer, Copywriter

Jim Myers
Photographer

Summerford Design, Inc.
Design Firm

AIGA
Client

Retired in Florida
1974

John Heck
Art Director

Steve Stanley
Designer

Mike Haynes
Photographer

Jim Sanders
Copywriter

Weekley & Penny
Agency

Butyl Rubber Producers Council
Client

Lady Olive
1981

Cap Pannell
Art Director, Designer

Pannell/St. George
Design Firm

Beverly Pannell, Caterer
Client

Hot Seat Poster
1982
Woody Pirtle
Art Director, Designer, Illustrator, Copywriter

Pirtle Design
Design Firm

Knoll International
Client

MALAYSIA 1979

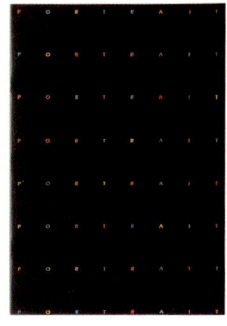

Portrait
1982
Chris Hill, Dan Daues
Art Directors
Chris Hill, Joe Rattan
Designers
Joe Baraban
Photographer
Mary Langridge
Copywriter
HILL/A Marketing Design Group
Design Firm
The Olivet Group
Client

Agriculture Dept. State Fair Bag
1982
Mike Hicks
Art Director, Designer
Melissa Grimes
Illustrator
Jim Hightower
Copywriter
Hixo, Inc.
Design Firm
State Department of Agriculture
Client

A.M. Poster
1982
Woody Pirtle
Art Director, Designer, Copywriter
Arthur Meyerson
Photographer
Pirtle Design
Design Firm
Arthur Meyerson Photography
Client

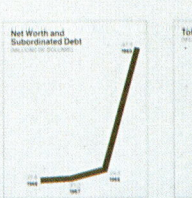

L & N Mortgage Company
Annual Report
1969

Bob Dennard
Art Director, Designer

Various Children's Schools
Illustrators

John Stone
Copywriter

The Richards Group
Design Firm

Lomas & Nettleton
Mortgage Company
Client

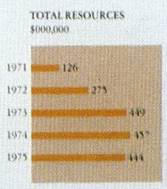
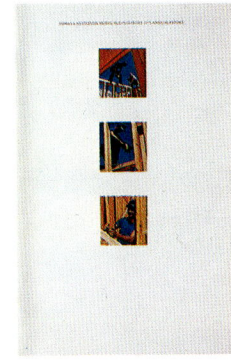

L & N Mortgage Investors
Annual Report
1975

Jack Summerford
Art Director, Designer

Greg Booth
Photographer

John Stone
Copywriter

The Richards Group
Design Firm

Lomas & Nettleton
Mortgage Investors
Client

L & N Financial Corp.
Annual Report
1985

Dick Mitchell
Art Director, Designer

Greg Booth
Photographer

Mark Perkins
Copywriter

Richards, Brock,
Miller, Mitchell & Associates
Design Firm

The Richards Group
Agency

Lomas & Nettleton
Financial Corp.
Client

DEBI BLATT *Freedom Ride Foundation volunteer*

"It's so rewarding to see children come here for the first time. Most of them can't walk, some can't even sit up, and their faces are filled with apprehension. Then they get on the horses, and it's like a light has been lit inside — the fear is gone and they become different people, with freedom and mobility they have never experienced before in their lives."

The American Red Cross recruits volunteers for Freedom Ride Foundation, a therapeutic horseback riding program that provides physical, emotional, and social therapy for the disabled. Debi Blatt first came to Freedom Ride's facilities at Zembred Ranch in Southlake, Texas because she was looking for something she could do to make a difference in the lives of the disabled. What she found was something that uplifted her own life. The program accepts riders referred from United Way, Spina Bifida Association, Scottish Rite Hospital for Crippled Children, and other organizations. At Zembred Ranch, muscles are strengthened and relaxed. Perhaps as important, riders who rarely leave their wheelchairs have a chance to see the world from on high.

L & N Mortgage Investors
Annual Report
1985

Steve Miller
Art Director, Designer

Greg Booth
Photographer

Mark Perkins, Jess Hay
Copywriters

Richards, Brock,
Miller, Mitchell & Associates
Design Firm

The Richards Group
Agency

Lomas & Nettleton
Mortgage Investors
Client

MARVA COLLINS
Westside Preparatory School–Chicago, Illinois

Marva Collins is the Chicago schoolteacher who started a private school ten years ago in her home. The successes of her students, many of them inner city kids with no history of academic accomplishment, have made her a celebrity, the subject of a television movie and hundreds of newspaper and magazine articles. There is nothing magical in the practices of Westside Preparatory School, which now has more than two hundred students and is no longer in Mrs. Collins' home. She urges educators to love what they do, to use the classics rather than watered-down textbooks, and to always promote the self-esteem of students. And she measures success by a child's continuing eagerness to learn, rather than by mere test scores. Offered the post of Secretary of Education by the Reagan Administration, Mrs. Collins declined, preferring to remain with her students.

"How many times have we taken a student's failure personally, and gone that extra mile to make certain that our students do not fail? We must settle for nothing less than excellence in all of our classrooms regardless of race, creed, color or national origin. I am the recipient of many gifts, such as rings that tarnish or candy that is sticky from being held in a sweaty palm, and when I eat that piece of candy, given me by a loving child, then I know why I teach."

46

In room after room, furnishings reveal our personal tastes and choices. There is family style in an Eames lounger that was the first piece of "serious" furniture a young couple could afford; and family history in a rocker that reminds its owners of the country auction where it was purchased. Sometimes, our favorite furniture helps us select our homes. Looking at empty houses, we measure them against what we already own. Mentally, we picture a certain chair in a particular corner or pace off a room to make sure it will accommodate an oak table. We may not literally build our homes around a piano; but, for the Burch's, whose daughter, Kristi, is a fourth-generation pianist, a Steinway that dates from the Thirties is like a member of the family and is given a room of its own.

Kristi Burch and Steinway piano at home in Landrum, South Carolina.

L & N Financial Corp.
Annual Report
1984
Dick Mitchell
Art Director, Designer
Greg Booth, John Wong
Photographers
Mark Perkins, Jess Hay
Copywriters
Richards, Brock,
Miller, Mitchell & Associates
Design Firm
The Richards Group
Agency
Lomas & Nettleton
Financial Corp.
Client

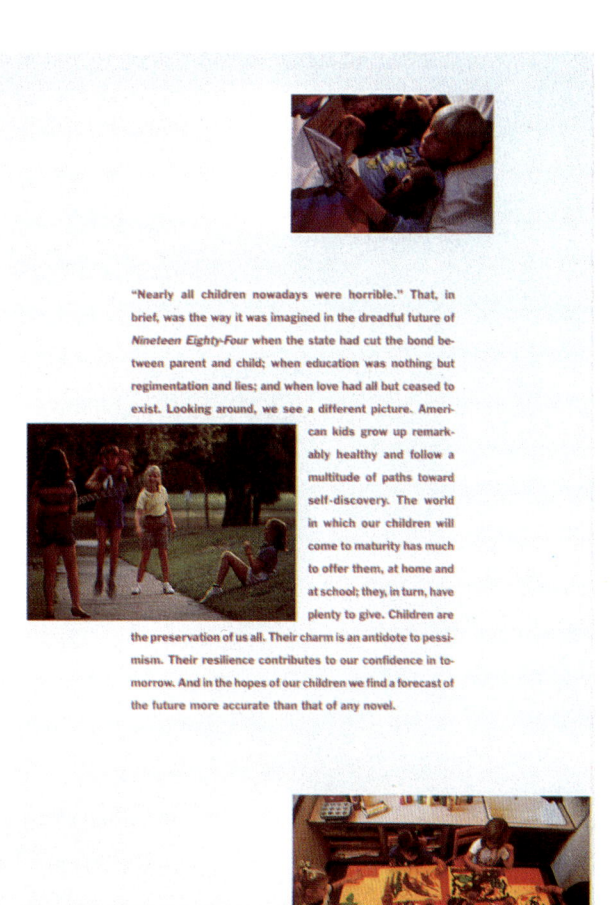

"Nearly all children nowadays were horrible." That, in brief, was the way it was imagined in the dreadful future of *Nineteen Eighty-Four* when the state had cut the bond between parent and child; when education was nothing but regimentation and lies; and when love had all but ceased to exist. Looking around, we see a different picture. American kids grow up remarkably healthy and follow a multitude of paths toward self-discovery. The world in which our children will come to maturity has much to offer them, at home and at school; they, in turn, have plenty to give. Children are the preservation of us all. Their charm is an antidote to pessimism. Their resilience contributes to our confidence in tomorrow. And in the hopes of our children we find a forecast of the future more accurate than that of any novel.

L & N Mortgage Investors
Annual Report
1984
Steve Miller
Art Director, Designer
Greg Booth
Photographer
Jack Unruh
Illustrator
Mark Perkins, Jess Hay
Copywriters
Richards, Brock,
Miller, Mitchell & Associates
Design Firm
The Richards Group
Agency
Lomas & Nettleton
Mortgage Investors
Client

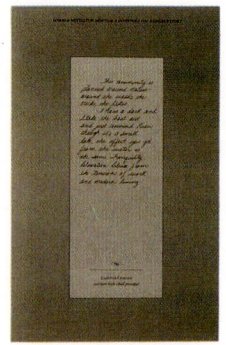

L & N Mortgage Investors Annual Report
1981

Ron Sullivan
Art Director, Designer

Greg Booth
Photographer

John Stone, Jess Hay
Copywriters

Richards, Sullivan, Brock & Associates
Design Firm

The Richards Group
Agency

Lomas & Nettleton Mortgage Investors
Client

L & N Financial Corp. Annual Report
1981

Steve Miller
Art Director, Designer

Greg Booth
Photographer

John Stone, Jess Hay
Copywriters

Richards, Sullivan, Brock & Associates
Design Firm

The Richards Group
Agency

Lomas & Nettleton Financial Corp.
Client

The neighbors are our first friends, and when neighboring children play together, they are in good company. As parents, we know the parents down the block; so we know something about our children's companions. And we can assume that the standards of behavior that apply in front of our own house will also be applied in front of our neighbor's. For children, the neighbors can be like a second family. If you don't have an older brother, you can find one on your block. If you need a respite from the seeming constrictions of your own house, try the house next door.

L & N Mortgage Investors
Annual Report
1983

Ron Sullivan
Art Director, Designer

Greg Booth, Andy Post
Photographers

Mark Perkins, Jess Hay
Copywriters

Richards, Sullivan,
Brock & Associates
Design Firm

The Richards Group
Agency

Lomas & Nettleton
Mortgage Investors
Client

L & N Financial Corp.
Annual Report
1979

Steve Miller
Art Director, Designer

Greg Booth
Photographer

John Stone, Jess Hay
Copywriters

Richards, Sullivan,
Brock & Associates
Design Firm

The Richards Group
Agency

Lomas & Nettleton
Financial Corp.
Client

L & N Mortgage Investors
Annual Report
1977

Ron Sullivan
Art Director, Designer

Jack Unruh
Illustrator

Greg Booth, Keith Wood
Photographers

John Stone, Jess Hay
Copywriters

The Richards Group
Design Firm, Agency

Lomas & Nettleton
Mortgage Investors
Client

L & N Housing Corp.
Annual Report
1982

Nancy Hoefig
Art Director, Designer

Jack Unruh
Illustrator

Mark Perkins
Copywriter

Richards, Sullivan,
Brock & Associates
Design Firm

The Richards Group
Agency

Lomas & Nettleton
Housing Corp.
Client

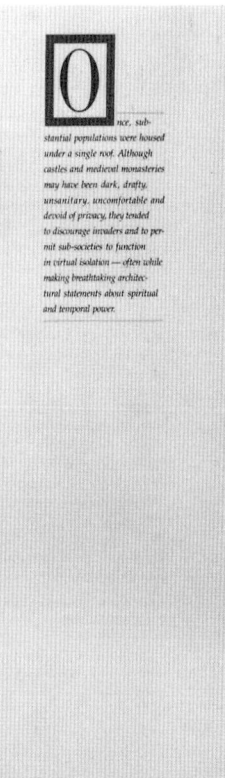

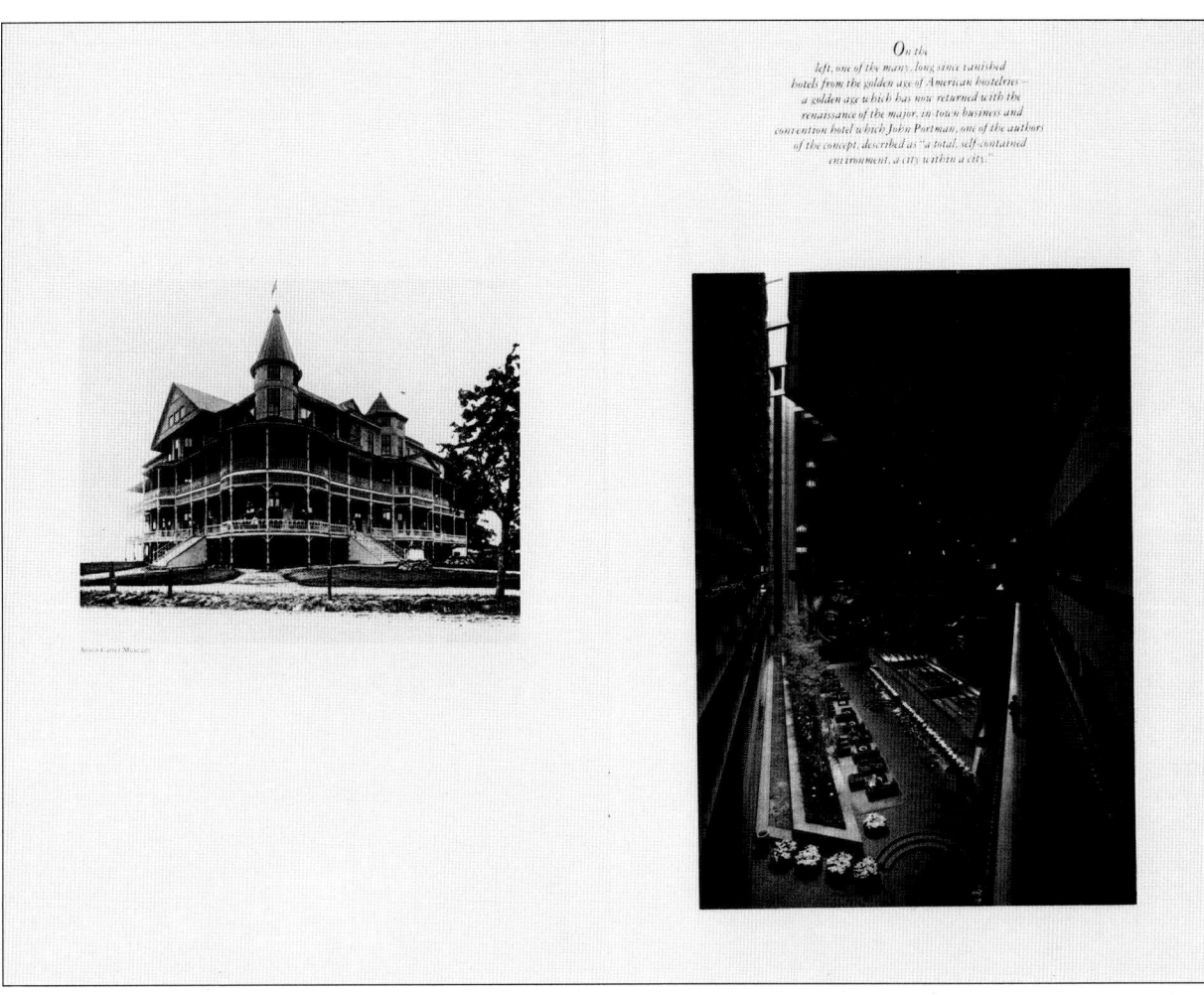

On the left, one of the many, long since vanished hotels from the golden age of American hostelries— a golden age which has now returned with the renaissance of the major, in-town business and convention hotel which John Portman, one of the authors of the concept, described as "a total, self-contained environment, a city within a city."

L & N Mortgage Investors
Annual Report
1974

Jack Summerford
Art Director, Designer

Greg Booth, UPI,
The Bettmann Archive,
Amon Carter Museum
Photographer

John Stone
Copywriter

The Richards Group
Design Firm

Lomas & Nettleton
Mortgage Investors
Client

Grandfather Ernest Schreiber was born in 1907 in what was then, and is now, a little Texas town called Windthorst, the site of this portrait. He laid the groundwork for a farming and ranching operation which is today thriving under the guidance of son Harold Schreiber. Harold's son Donnie, one of the twenty-three Schreiber grandchildren, hopes to become a rancher like his father and his father before him.

L & N Financial Corp.
Annual Report
1974

Ron Sullivan
Designer

Greg Booth
Photographer

The Richards Group
Design Firm

Lomas & Nettleton
Financial Corp.
Client

L & N Mortgage Investors
Annual Report
1978

Ron Sullivan
Art Director, Designer

Greg Booth
Photographer

John Stone, Jess Hay
Copywriters

The Richards Group
Design Firm, Agency

Lomas & Nettleton
Mortgage Investors
Client

L & N Financial Corp.
Annual Report
1976

Jack Summerford
Art Director, Designer

Daniel Schwartz
Illustrator

John Stone
Copywriter

The Richards Group
Design Firm

Lomas & Nettleton
Financial Corp.
Client

L & N Mortgage Investors
Annual Report
1982
Ron Sullivan
Art Director, Designer
Greg Booth
Photographer
McRay Magleby
Illustrator
John Stone, Jess Hay
Copywriters
Richards, Sullivan,
Brock & Associates
Design Firm
The Richards Group
Agency
Lomas & Nettleton
Mortgage Investors
Client

Whole Foods Grocery Bag
1982
Mike Hicks
Art Director, Designer
Melissa Grimes
Illustrator
Guy Bommarito
Copywriter
Hixo, Inc.
Design Firm
Whole Foods Company
Client

Christmas Party Invitation
1984

Wayne Ford
Art Director, Designer

Boswell Byers & Stone
Copywriters

Miller, Judson & Ford, Inc.
Design Firm

Boswell Byers & Stone
Agency, Client

George Hederhorst
Capabilities Brochure
1982

Lowell Williams
Art Director

Lowell Williams, Bill Carson
Designers

Lana Rigsby
Illustrator

Joe Baraban
Photographer

Lowell Williams Design, Inc.
Design Firm, Agency

George Hederhorst Co.
Client

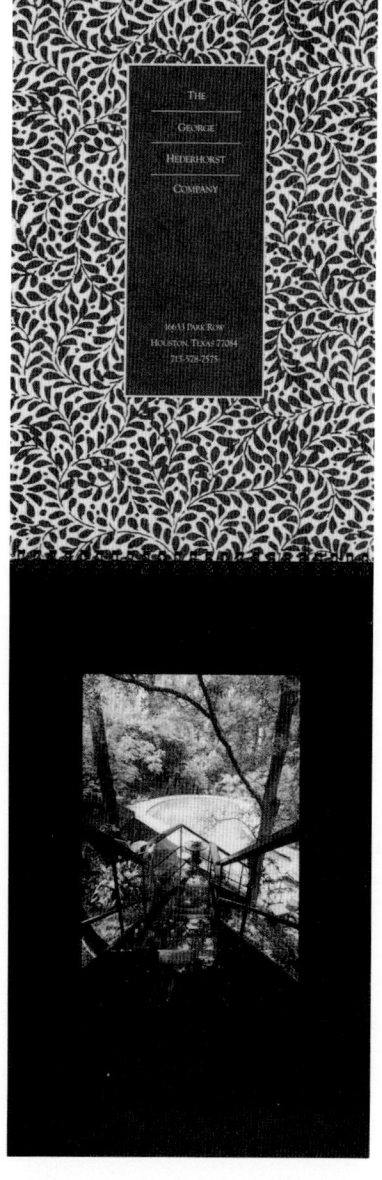

54

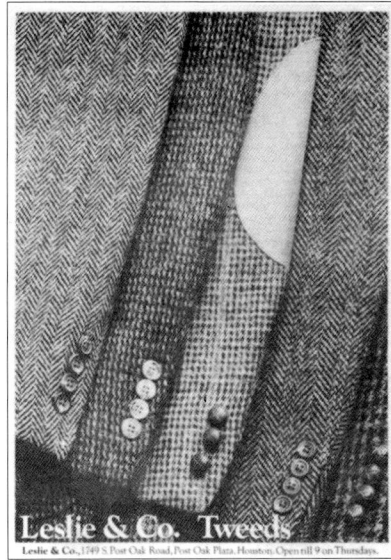

Leslie & Co. Campaign
1980
Jerry Herring
Art Director, Designer
Jim Sims
Photographer
Don Pierce
Copywriter
Herring Design
Design Firm
Leslie & Co.
Client

No Way Poster
1983
Woody Pirtle, Mike Schroeder
Art Directors
Mike Schroeder
Designer, Illustrator
Woody Pirtle
Copywriter
Pirtle Design
Design Firm
Greenville Avenue Merchants Guild
Client

55

DSVC Student Show Poster
1980

Dick Mitchell
Art Director, Designer, Illustrator

Jim Hradecky
Copywriter

Richards, Sullivan, Brock & Associates
Design Firm

The Richards Group
Agency

Dallas Society of Visual Communications
Client

Winners Circle Weekend
1982

Ron Sullivan
Art Director

Brent Croxton
Designer

Mark Perkins
Copywriter

Richards, Sullivan, Brock & Associates
Design Firm

The Richards Group
Agency

The 500 Inc.
Client

 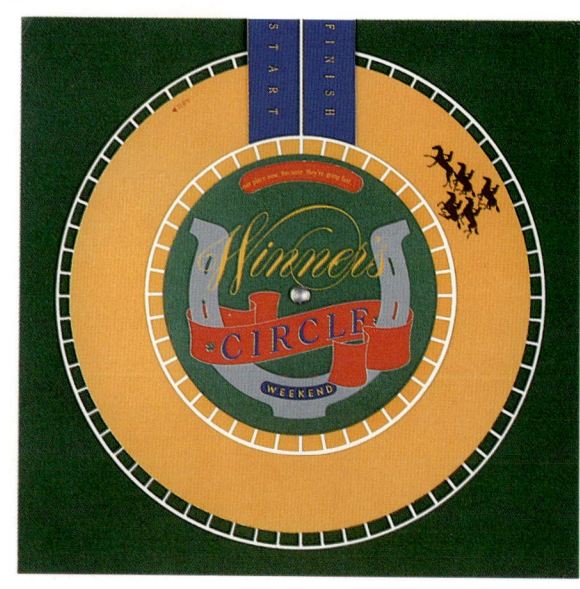

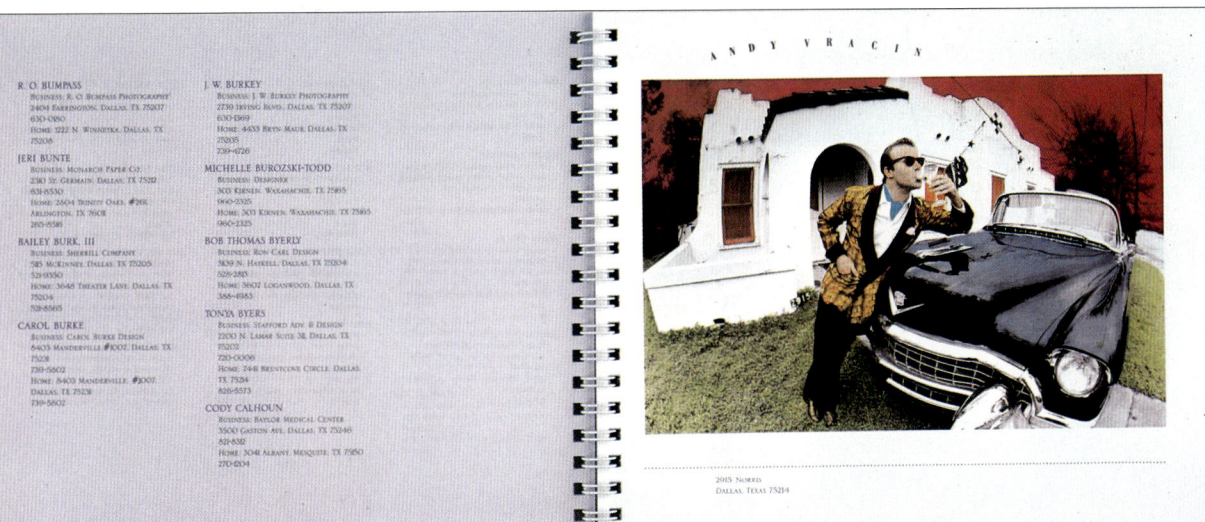

Tour of Stars Homes
1985

Don Crum
Art Director

Mo Martin
Designer

Phil Hollenbeck
Photographer

Don Crum & Co.
Design Firm

Dallas Society of
Visual Communications
Client

Flowers Invitation
1980

Bob Dennard, Cody Calhoun
Art Directors

Cody Calhoun
Designer

Bob Dennard, Don Sibley
Copywriters

Paul Broadhead & Associates
Client

Texas Junk Company
(Series)
1983
Penny Morrison
Art Director, Designer, Illustrator
Morrison Design
Design Firm, Agency
Texas Junk Company
Client

100 Years of Change
1985
Gena Rogers
Art Director, Designer
John Wong
Photographer
Gena Rogers, Mike Renfro
Copywriters
The Richards Group
Design Firm, Agency
MBank
Client

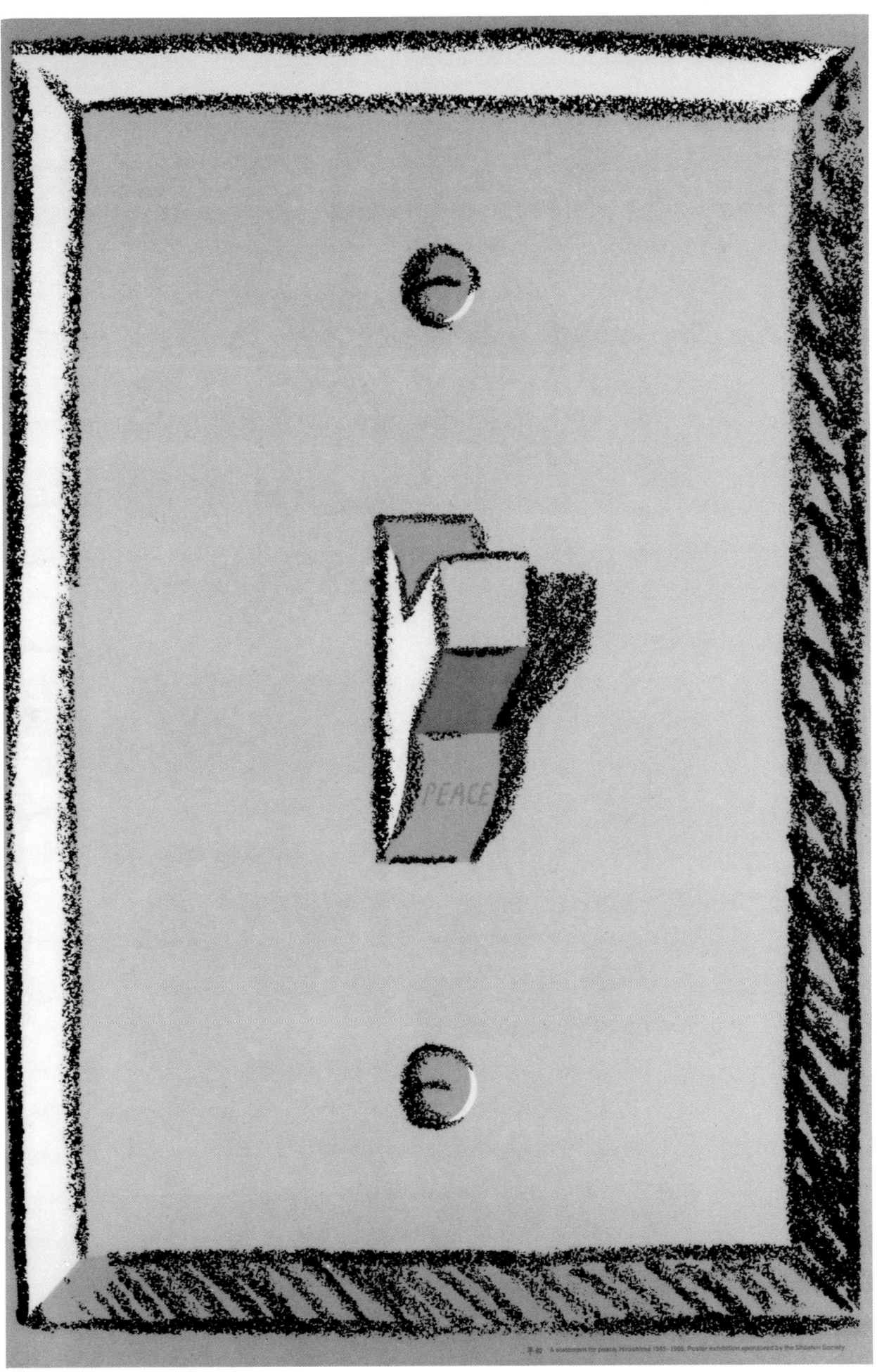

The Choice
1985
Chris Hill, Margaret Kim,
Jeffrey McKay, Regan Dunnick
Art Directors
Chris Hill, Margaret Kim
Designers
Regan Dunnick
Illustrator
HILL/A Marketing Design Group
Design Firm
The Shoshin Society
Client

Amadeus Restaurant & Bar
1985
Rex Peteet
Art Director, Designer

Rex Peteet, Walter Horton
Illustrator/Photographer

Sibley/Peteet Design, Inc.
Design Firm

Trammell Crow Company
Client

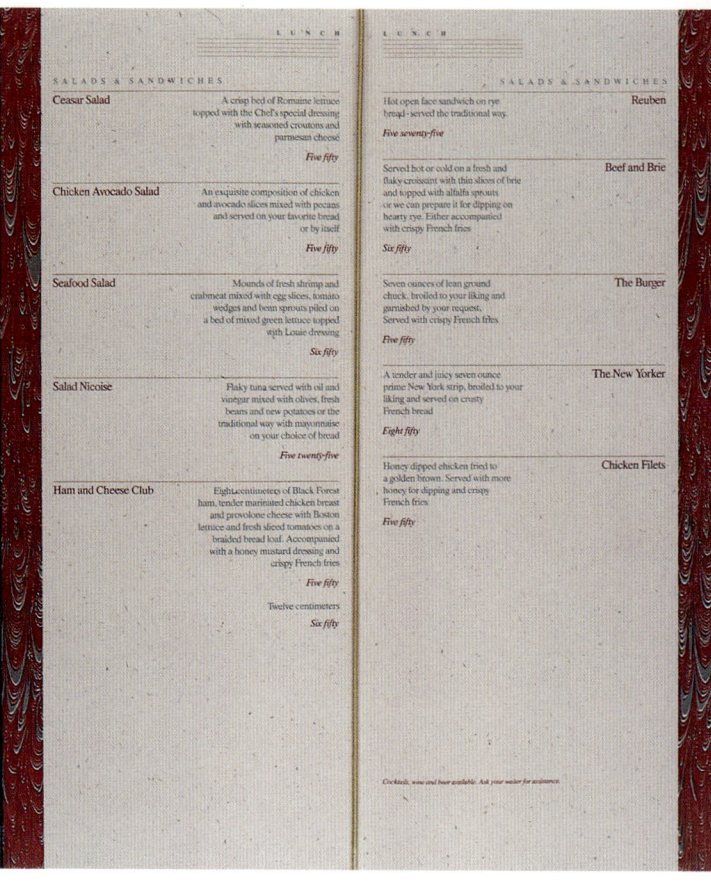

LET THE TEXAS PUBLIC RELATIONS ASSOCIATION MID-WINTER CONFERENCE GIVE YOU A NEW VIEW OF THE WORLD.   FEBRUARY 26-28, 1982 IN HOUSTON, TEXAS.

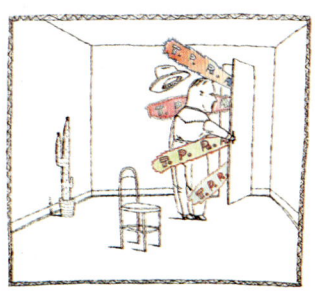

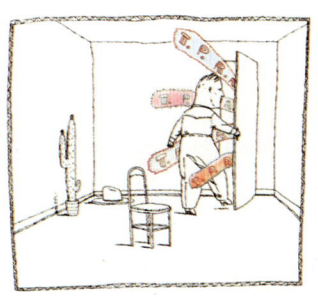
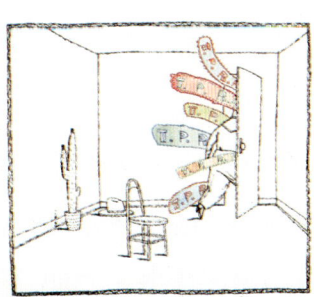
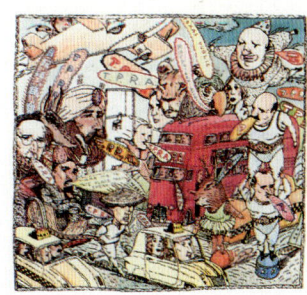

Man In Room
1982
Chris Hill, Pat Harris
Art Directors
Chris Hill, Joe Rattan
Designers
Regan Dunnick
Illustrator
HILL/A Marketing Design Group
Design Firm
Gerald D. Hines Interests
Client

Mongo Hot Chocolate
Poster
1985

Pat Sloan
Art Director, Designer

Kipp Baker
Photographer

Sharon Horton
Copywriter

Pat Sloan Design
Design Firm

Fort Worth Linotyping, Co., Inc.
Client

Woody Pirtle Letterhead
1973

Woody Pirtle
Art Director, Designer

Mike Haynes
Photographer

Pirtle Design
Design Firm

Woody Pirtle
Client

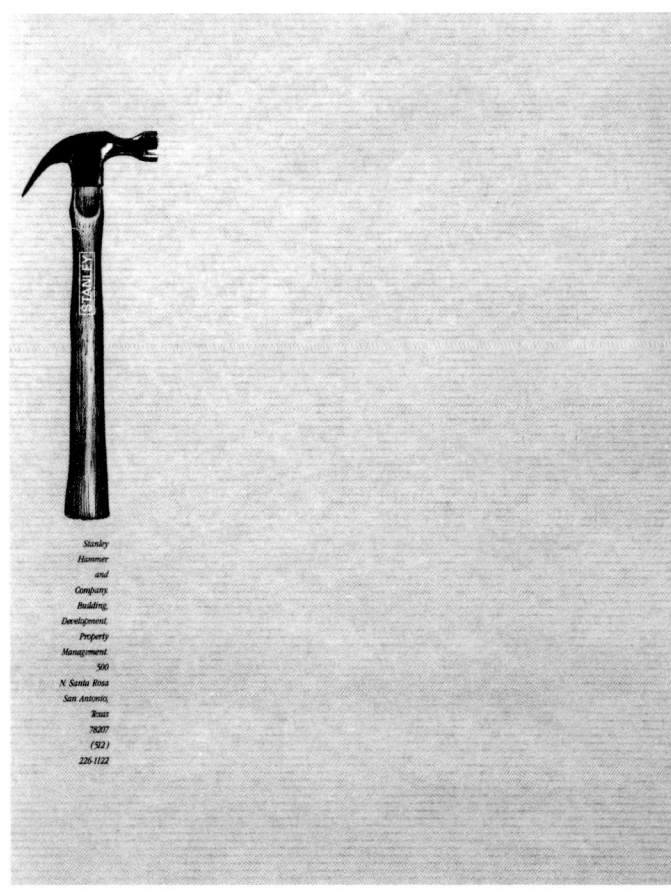

Tops Call For Entries
1983
Rex Peteet
Art Director, Designer
Madelyn Miller
Copywriter
Sibley/Peteet Design, Inc.
Design Firm
Dallas Advertising League
Client

Stanley Hammer, Builder
1978
Barbara Shimkus
Art Director, Designer
Mark Stinson
Illustrator
Shimkus Design
Design Firm, Agency
Stanley Hammer, Builder
Client

Clicks Mailer
1978
Jim Jacobs
Art Director, Designer, Copywriter

Kent Kirkley, Phil Branner
Photographers

Jim Jacobs' Studio
Design Firm

Clicks Billiards, Inc.
Client

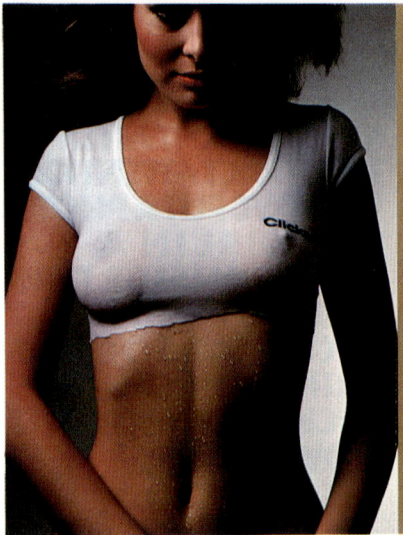

Dick Jones Business Card
1978
Jim Jacobs
Art Director, Illustrator

Jim Jacobs, Susan Crittenden
Designers

Jim Jacobs' Studio
Design Firm

Dick Jones, Retoucher
Client

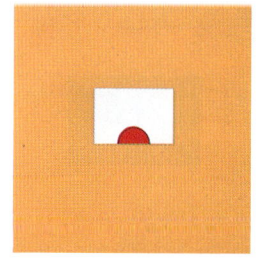

A.M. in Japan
1985
Lowell Williams
Art Director
Lowell Williams, Bill Carson,
Lana Rigsby
Designers
Arthur Meyerson
Photographer, Copywriter
Lowell Williams Design, Inc.
Design Firm, Agency
Arthur Meyerson Photography
Client

Wally Cleaver Appreciation Week
1984
Chris Hill, Regan Dunnick
Art Directors
Chris Hill, Jeffrey McKay,
Regan Dunnick
Designers
Regan Dunnick
Illustrator
HILL/A Marketing Design Group
Design Firm
Dunnick/Hill Productions
Client

Oklahoma
1982
Paul Black
Art Director, Designer, Illustrator, Copywriter
Paul Black Design
Design Firm
Eastfield College
Client

Grahnquist Birth
Announcement
1974
Woody Pirtle
*Art Director, Designer,
Illustrator, Copywriter*
The Richards Group
Agency
Mr. & Mrs. Grahnquist
Client

USA Film Festival
1971
Jack Summerford
Art Director, Designer
The Richards Group
Design Firm, Agency
USA Film Festival
Client

Luby's Cafeterias
Annual Report
1985

Janis Koy Beveridge
Art Director, Designer

Steve Brady
Photographer

Steve Barnhill
Copywriter

Koy Design, Inc.
Design Firm

Luby's Cafeterias, Inc.
Client

Bradshaw's
Prime Beef Stationery
1984

Dennis Benoit
Art Director

Laurie Foreman Adams
Designer, Illustrator

Benoit Rutter, Inc.
Design Firm

Bradshaw's Prime Beef
Client

Show Your Face
1985

Roby Odom
Art Director, Designer, Illustrator

Mark Perkins
Copywriter

The Hay Agency, Inc.
Agency

Lomas & Nettleton
Client

Newspaper Excerpts
1973

Jerry Herring
Art Director, Designer, Copywriter

Herring Design
Design Firm, Client

Dot Baker Letterhead
1979

Dick Mitchell
Art Director, Designer

Richards, Sullivan, Brock & Associates
Design Firm

The Richards Group
Agency

Dot Baker
Client

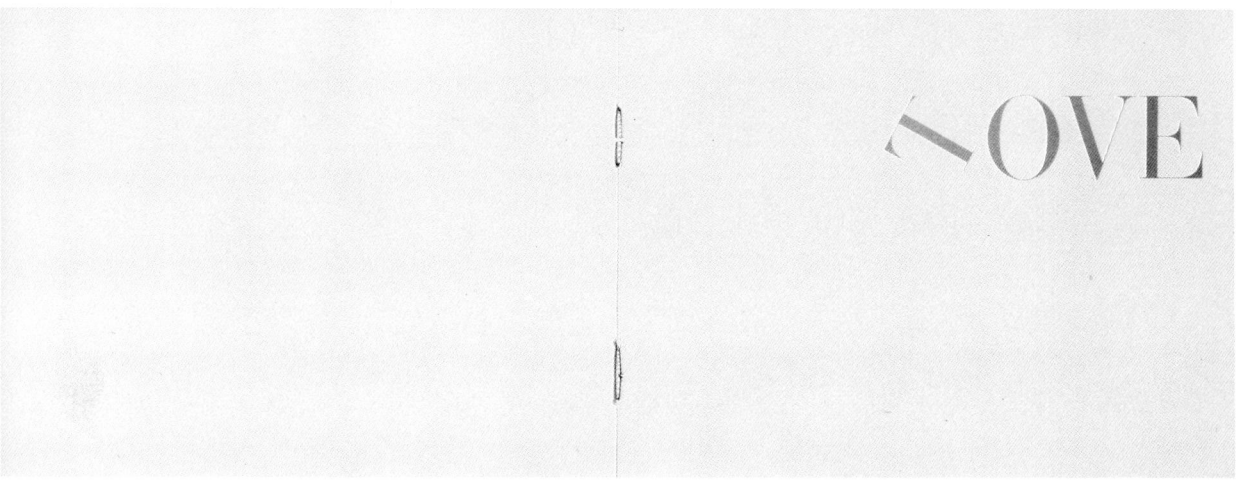

Tove Scoggin
Birth Announcement
1980

Woody Pirtle
Art Director, Designer, Illustrator, Copywriter

Pirtle Design
Design Firm

Dan Scoggin
Client

Mead Annual Report Show
Poster
1985
Woody Pirtle
Art Director

Woody Pirtle, Jeff Weithman
Designers

Pirtle Design
Design Firm

Mead Paper Company
Client

72

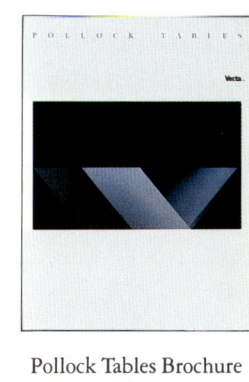

Pollock Tables Brochure
1986
Steve Miller
Art Director, Designer
Andy Post
Photographer
Owen Page, Doris Todd
Copywriters
Richards, Brock,
Miller, Mitchell & Associates
Design Firm
The Richards Group
Agency
Vecta
Client

Classic V Poster
1983
Janis Koy Beveridge
Art Director
Janis Koy Beveridge, Chris Hill
Designers
Rick Lovell
Illustrator
The Pitluk Group
Agency
Southwest Conference
Client

Valley View Shops
In Circle Ads
(Series)
1985

Rex Peteet
Art Director, Designer, Copywriter

Thom Jackson, John Parrish
Photographers

Sibley/Peteet Design, Inc.
Design Firm

LaSalle Partners/
Valley View Mall
Client

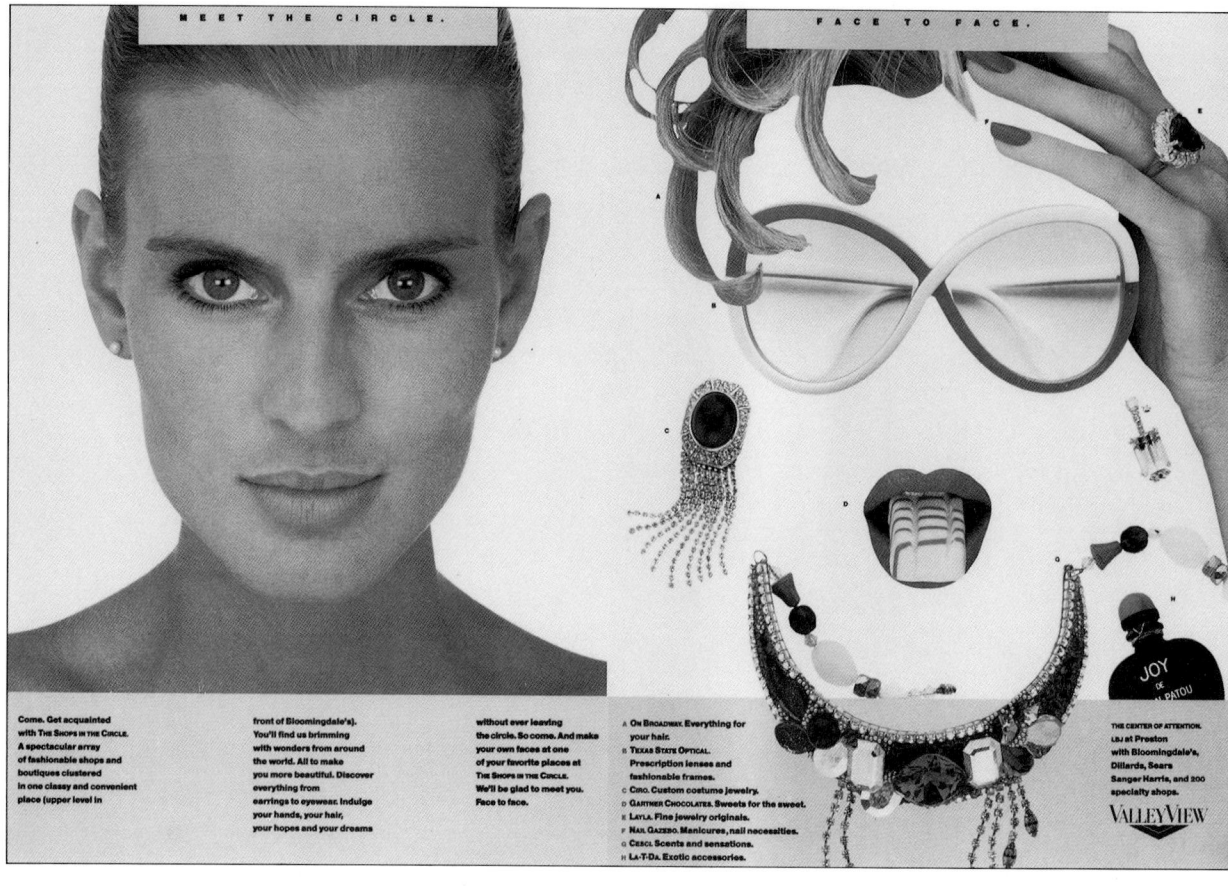

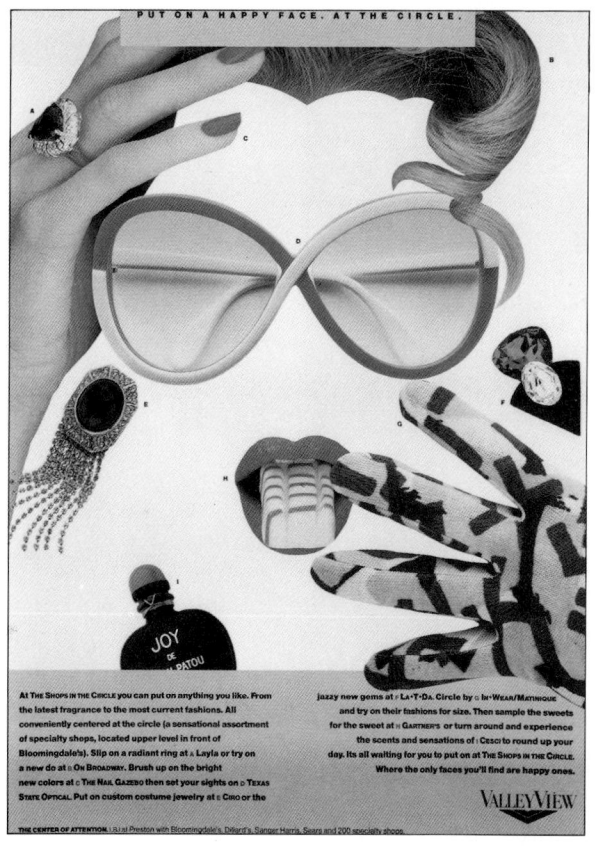

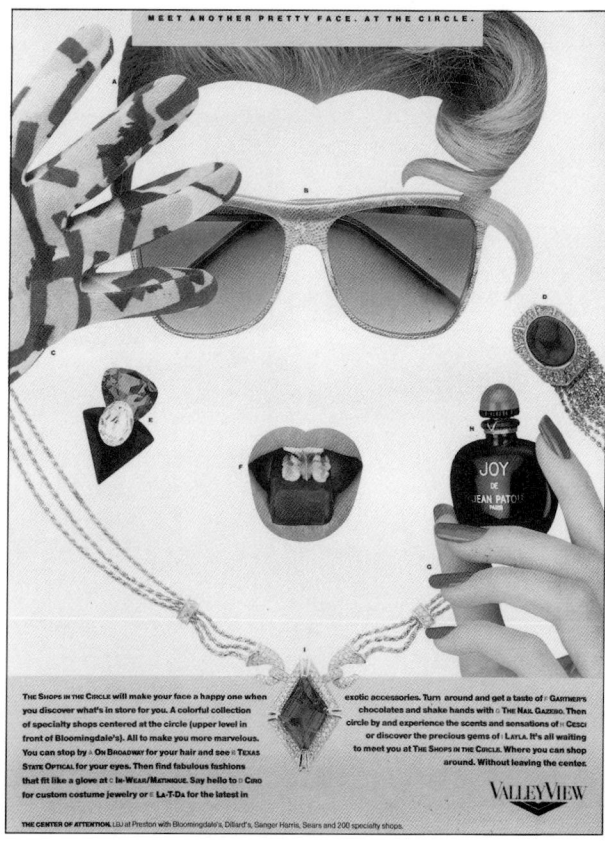

74

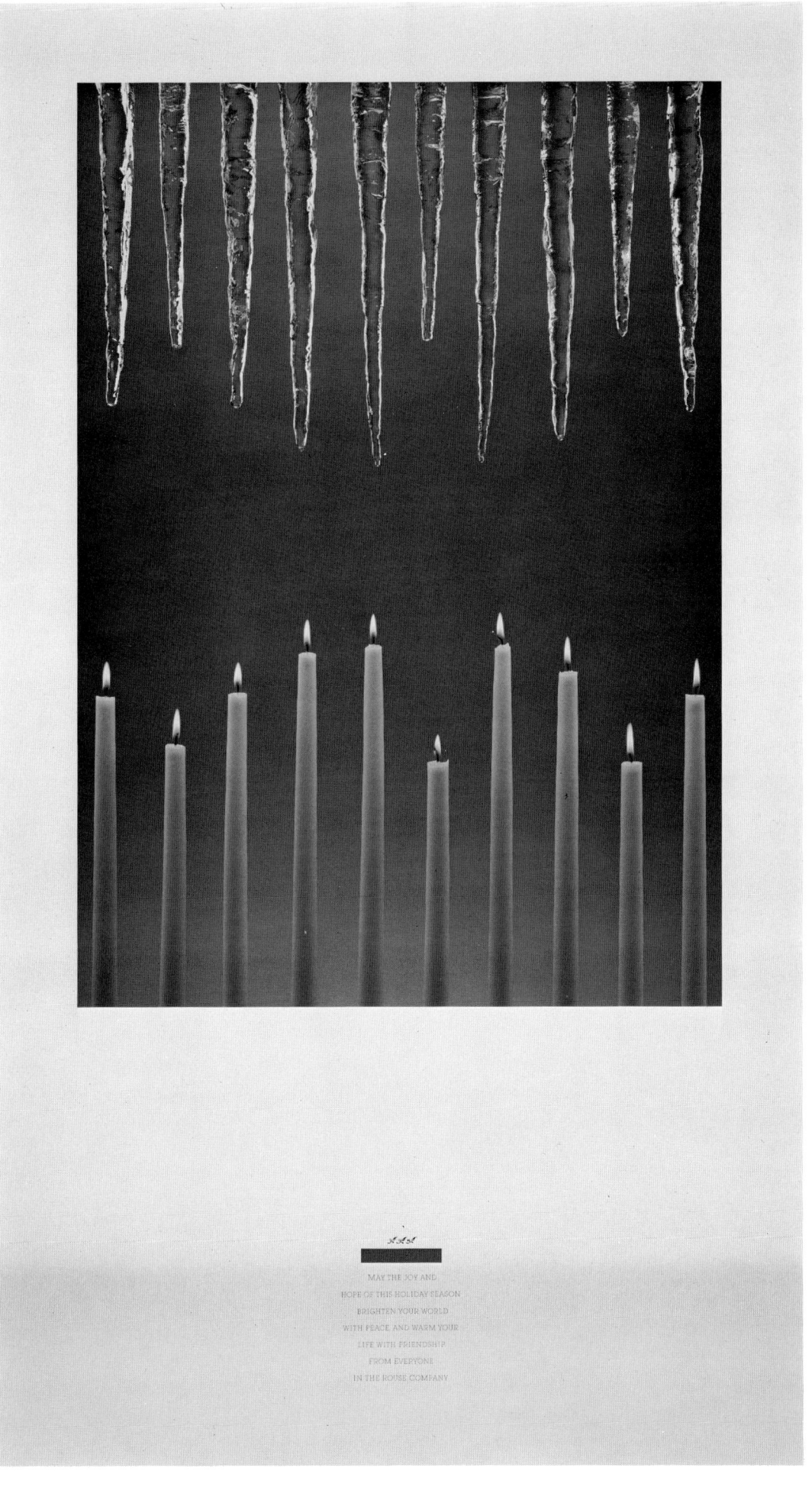

Rouse Christmas Card
1982
Scott Eggers, Ron Sullivan
Art Directors
Scott Eggers
Designer
Andy Post
Photographer
Scott Ditch
Copywriter
Richards, Sullivan, Brock & Associates
Design Firm
The Richards Group
Agency
The Rouse Company
Client

Houston Brochure
1984

Jerry Herring
Art Director, Designer

Richard Payne, Ron Scott, Steve Brady
Photographers

Lee Herrick
Copywriter

Herring Design
Design Firm

Gerald D. Hines Interests
Client

Intense scrutiny of design and material selections, coupled with mass purchasing and careful contract negotiations, has enabled Gerald D. Hines Interests to work successfully with such respected designers as Philip Johnson/John Burgee Architects; Hellmuth, Obata & Kassabaum; I.M. Pei & Partners; Kevin Roche John Dinkeloo and Associates; and Skidmore, Owings & Merrill.

This same consciousness of both quality and cost extends beyond innovative design to interior finishes that set the industry standards for attractiveness and comfort; to energy-saving features that reduce overall operating costs; and to responsible, on-site management that ensures the continued quality of all Hines Interests developments.

The result is a skillful blend of art and economy that is reflected in an entire collection of downtown office towers. Together, these buildings offer all the advantages of an office "complex": the operational efficiency, the streamlined management systems, the room for expansion. Yet separately, each maintains that distinct identity so important in a highly competitive business environment.

The exceptional value offered by these downtown projects is largely attributable to Hines Interests' unyielding commitment to excellence in every phase of project development, from architectural design and construction through operational and on-going management.

Whitmore Industrial
Lubricant Packaging
1984

Greg Chapman
Art Director, Designer, Illustrator

The Hay Agency, Inc.
Agency

Whitmore Manufacturing Company
Client

76

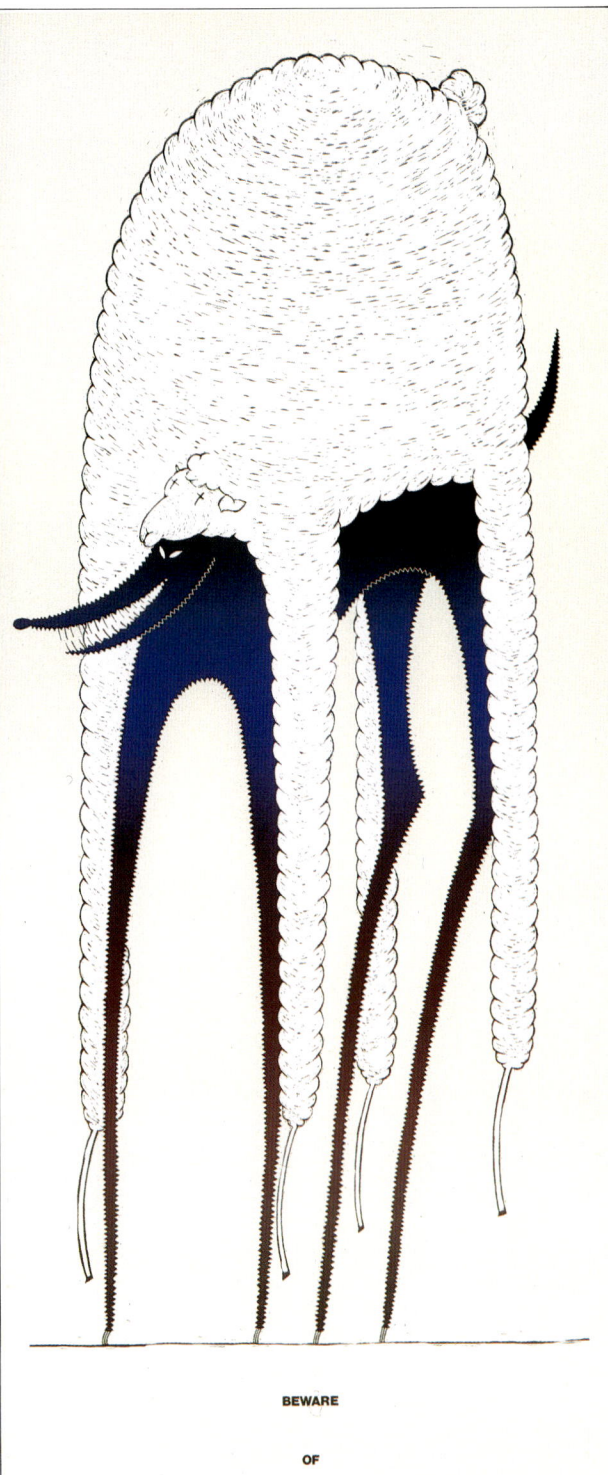

Peter Rosler's Card
1976
Jim Jacobs
Art Director, Designer, Copywriter
Jim Jacobs' Studio
Design Firm
Peter Rosler
Client

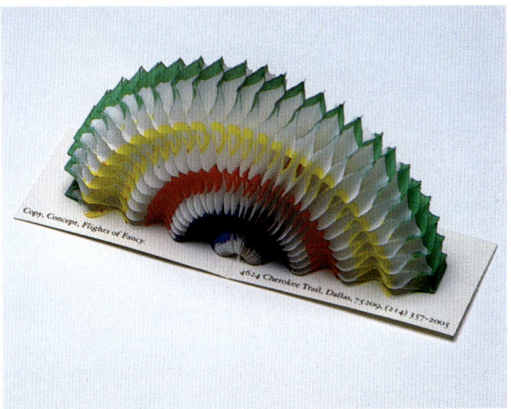

Cults Poster
1983
Chris Rovillo
Art Director, Designer, Illustrator
Mark Perkins
Copywriter
Richards, Sullivan, Brock & Associates
Design Firm
The Richards Group
Agency
Young Presidents Organization
Client

Miller Outdoor Theatre
1979

Ann Pitts
Art Director, Designer

John Katz
Photographer

Ogilvy & Mather
Design Firm, Agency

Miller Outdoor Theatre
Client

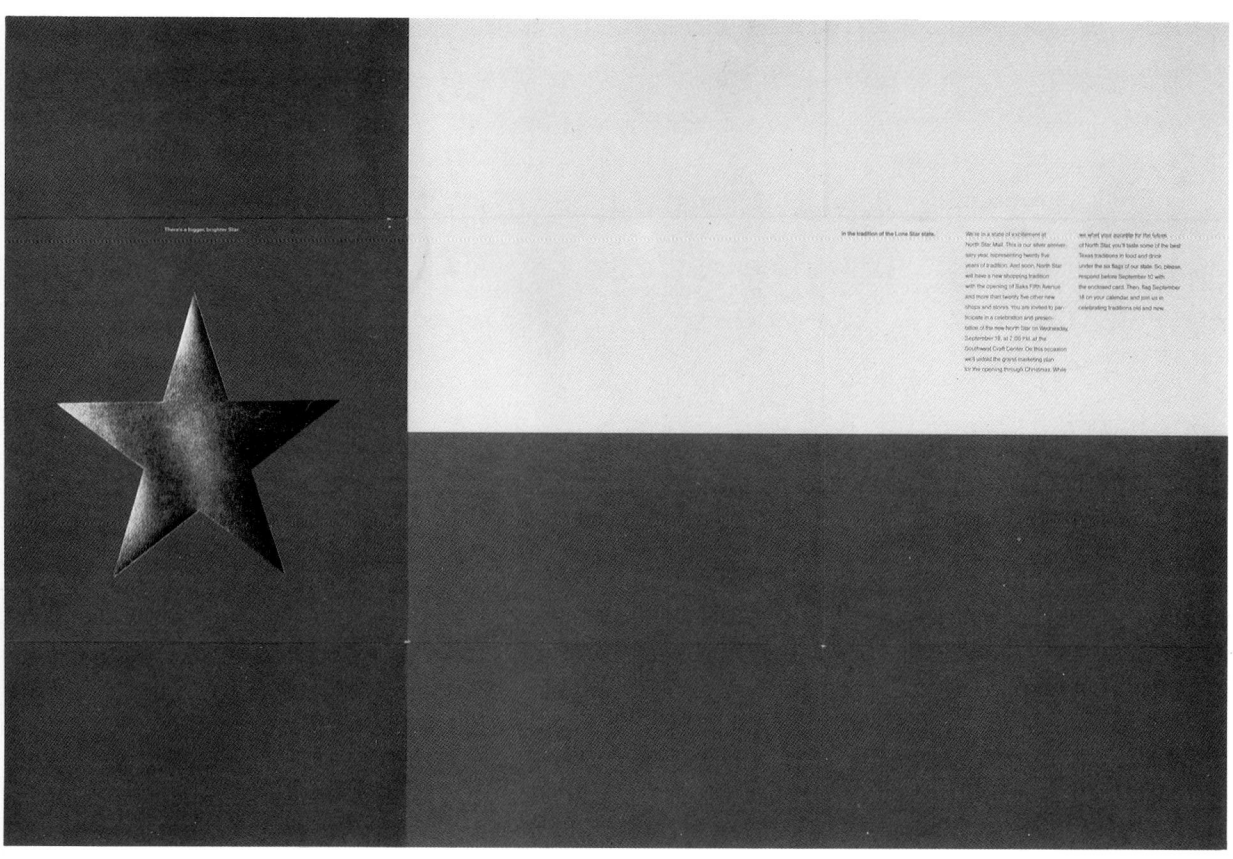

North Star Invitation
1985
Ron Sullivan
Art Director
Ann Rust, Diana McKnight
Designers
Mark Perkins
Copywriter
Sullivan Perkins
Design Firm
The Rouse Company/
North Star Mall
Client

Collage
1971
Jim Jacobs
Art Director, Designer
Jim Jacobs' Studio
Design Firm
Collage Systems Inc.
Client

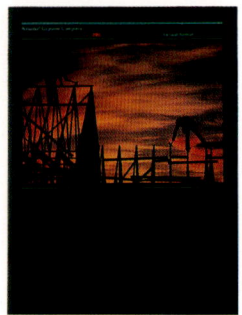

National Gypsum
Annual Report
1981

Woody Pirtle
Art Director, Designer

Arthur Meyerson
Photographer

Lee Sneath
Copywriter

Pirtle Design
Design Firm

National Gypsum Company
Client

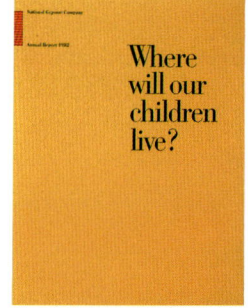

National Gypsum
Annual Report
1982

Woody Pirtle
Art Director, Designer

Arthur Meyerson
Photographer

Lee Sneath
Copywriter

Pirtle Design
Design Firm

National Gypsum Company
Client

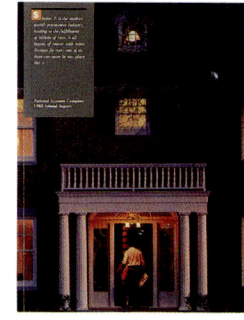

National Gypsum
Annual Report
1983

Woody Pirtle
Art Director

Woody Pirtle, Kenny Garrison
Designers

Arthur Meyerson
Photographer

Steve Barnhill
Copywriter

Pirtle Design
Design Firm

National Gypsum Company
Client

National Gypsum
Annual Report
1984

Woody Pirtle
Art Director

Woody Pirtle, Kenny Garrison
Designers

Arthur Meyerson,
Ron Scott, Mike Haynes
Photographers

Steve Barnhill
Copywriter

Pirtle Design
Design Firm

National Gypsum Company
Client

Gary Goodwin Mailer
1985

Jim Jacobs
Art Director, Designer, Copywriter, Illustrator

Gary Goodwin
Photographer

Jim Jacobs' Studio
Design Firm

Gary Goodwin
Client

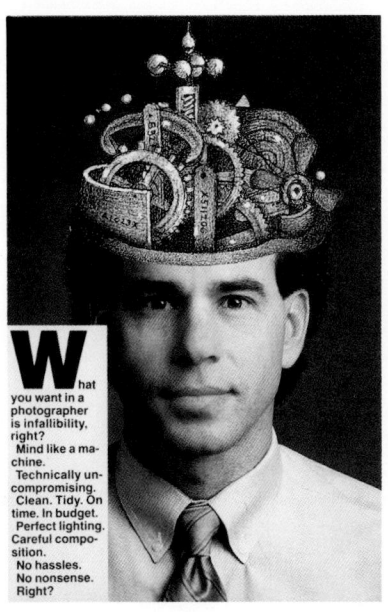

Halloweenophobia
1984

Chris Hill, Jeffrey McKay
Art Directors, Designers

Regan Dunnick
Illustrator

Mary Langridge
Copywriter

HILL/A Marketing Design Group
Design Firm

Lisa & Dennis Thrasher
Client

A Pressing Engagement
Invitation
1975

John Heck
Art Director

Jerry Herring, Woody Pirtle
Designers

Woody Pirtle
Illustrator

Jim Sanders
Copywriter

Herring & Pirtle, Inc.
Design Firm

Weekley & Penny
Agency, Client

STUD1O

Studio 10 Productions
1968

Stan Richards
Art Director, Designer

Stan Richards & Associates
Design Firm, Agency

Studio Ten Productions
Client

Handweavers Mark
1977

Woody Pirtle, Don Grimes
Art Directors

Don Grimes
Designer, Illustrator

Don Grimes Design Inc.
Design Firm

The Richards Group
Agency

Handweavers Assoc.
Client

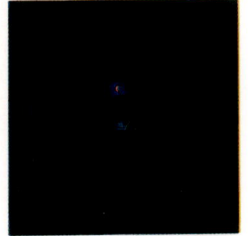

Moonlight Beach Brochure
1984

Walter Horton
Art Director, Designer

Ann Eklund Phillips
Copywriter

Sibley/Peteet Design, Inc.
Design Firm

The Williams Group
Agency

Moonlight Beach Development
Client

PBA Champagne Bottle Invitation
1980

Rex Peteet, Bob Dennard
Art Directors

Rex Peteet
Designer, Illustrator, Copywriter

Dennard Creative
Design Firm

Paul Broadhead & Associates
Client

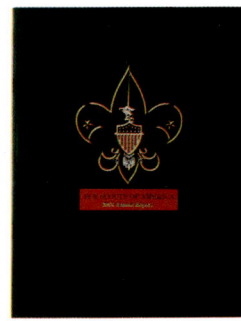

Boy Scouts
Annual Report
1983

Woody Pirtle, Alan Colvin
Art Directors

Alan Colvin
Designer

Alan Colvin,
Mike Schroeder, Woody Pirtle
Illustrators

Boy Scouts
Copywriters

Pirtle Design
Design Firm

Boy Scouts of America
Client

Lakewood Theatre Poster
1984

Woody Pirtle
Art Director, Copywriter

Alan Colvin, Woody Pirtle
Designers

Alan Colvin
Illustrator

Pirtle Design
Design Firm

Lakewood Theatre
Client

85

Shakespears Poster
1980
Jim Jacobs
Designer, Illustrator
Jim Jacobs' Studio
Design Firm
Dallas Public Library
Client

Coulson Tough: Coulson is an architect and executive of a remarkable "planned community" development north of Houston. It is expected to house a self-contained population of 150,000 upon completion in 1994, and like many such community developments, will have a balance of industrial, commercial and residential components — all created from scratch from raw land in conformity with an integrated economic, social and environmental plan. Coulson comments: "A metropolitan area growing as fast as Houston offers some of the best and the worst in real estate development. I believe that a forward-looking, well-capitalized developer can meet the needs of people at all socio-economic levels."

Mercantile Texas Corp.
1979

Dick Mitchell
Designer

Greg Booth
Photographer

Richards, Brock,
Miller, Mitchell & Associates
Design Firm

Mercantile Bank
Client

A ssociate Memberships are available to those who wish only to use the Club's social facilities. And Corporate Sponsored Memberships entitle one or more individuals to full or Associate Club privileges under the auspices of their corporation.

Initiation fees and monthly dues are very competitive for the area, and Lakewood Yacht Club's sound professional management safeguards that financial stability while allowing for facilities expansion in the years ahead.

The membership of Lakewood Yacht Club has found a protected harbor for their boats, in a geographic area shielded from the hazards of wind and weather. They have found a secure waterfront setting, patrolled 24 hours a day by trained security personnel. They have found a wide range of athletic, social and boating programs for every member of their family to enjoy.

But most of all, they have found the camaraderie and sense of community that is fostered when many diverse people share a common interest: the pleasures of good friends made and challenges met, a relaxed pace of living and a love of the sea.

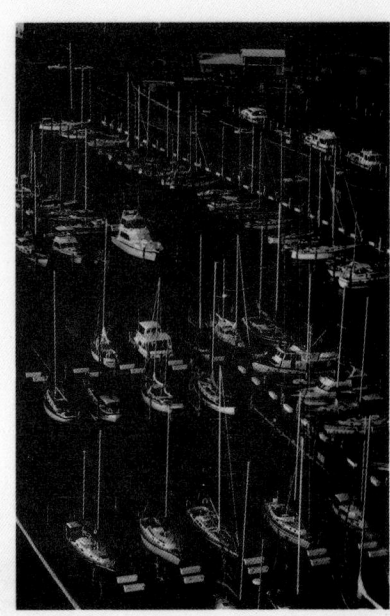

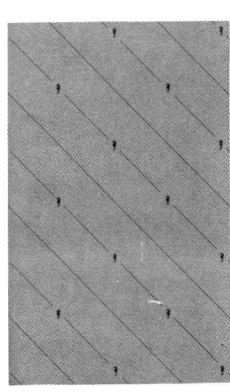

Lakewood Yacht Club
Facilities Brochure
1985

Lowell Williams
Art Director

Lowell Williams,
Bill Carson, Denise Pollack
Designers

Ron Scott, Marc St. Gill
Photographers

Lee Herrick
Copywriter

Lowell Williams Design, Inc.
Design Firm

Lakewood Yacht Club
Client

Texas Primer
1985
Fred Woodward, Suzi Sands
Art Directors
David Kampa
Designer
Texas Monthly
Client

The Two-step

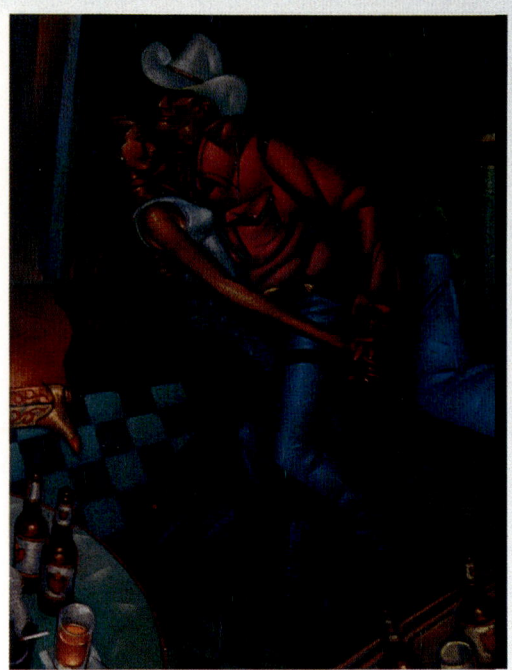

Legal Assistant/
Big 12 Year Old
1984
Jim Jacobs
Art Director, Designer, Illustrator
Katherine Sheehy Hussey,
Jim Jacobs
Copywriter
Jim Jacobs' Studio
Design Firm
Legal Assistant Today
Client

Pencil Poster
1979
Rex Peteet, Woody Pirtle
Art Director
Rex Peteet
Designer
Rex Peteet, Mike Schroeder
Illustrators
Mary Keck
Copywriter
Pirtle Design
Design Firm
Dallas Society of
Visual Communications
Client

Texas Special Olympics
1983

Mark Geer, Richard Kilmer
Art Directors, Designers

Jim Sims
Photographer

Beth Baker/Steve Barnhill & Co.
Copywriter

Kilmer/Geer Design
Design Firm

Texas Special Olympics
Client

Lost Increments
1983

Tom Zielinski
Art Director, Designer

Terry Widener
Illustrator

James Sallis
Copywriter

Dallas Life Magazine
Design Firm

The Dallas Morning News
Agency, Client

Williamson Printing
100-Year Anniversary Poster
1984
Brian Boyd
Art Director, Designer
Robert Forsbach, Dianna McKnight
Illustrators
Richards, Brock,
Miller, Mitchell & Associates
Design Firm
The Richards Group
Agency
Williamson Printing Corporation
Client

Texas/New York
1983
Chris Hill
Art Director

Chris Hill, Joe Rattan
Designers

Regan Dunnick
Illustrator

HILL/A Marketing Design Group
Design Firm

Art Directors Club of New York
Client

Protocol Letterhead Kit
1985
Woody Pirtle, Kenny Garrison
Art Directors
Kenny Garrison
Designer
Pirtle Design
Design Firm
Simpson Paper Company
Client

Grape Menu
1979
Rex Peteet, Woody Pirtle
Art Directors
Rex Peteet
Designer, Illustrator
Mike Schroeder
Calligrapher
Mary Keck
Copywriter
Pirtle Design
Design Firm
The Grape
Client

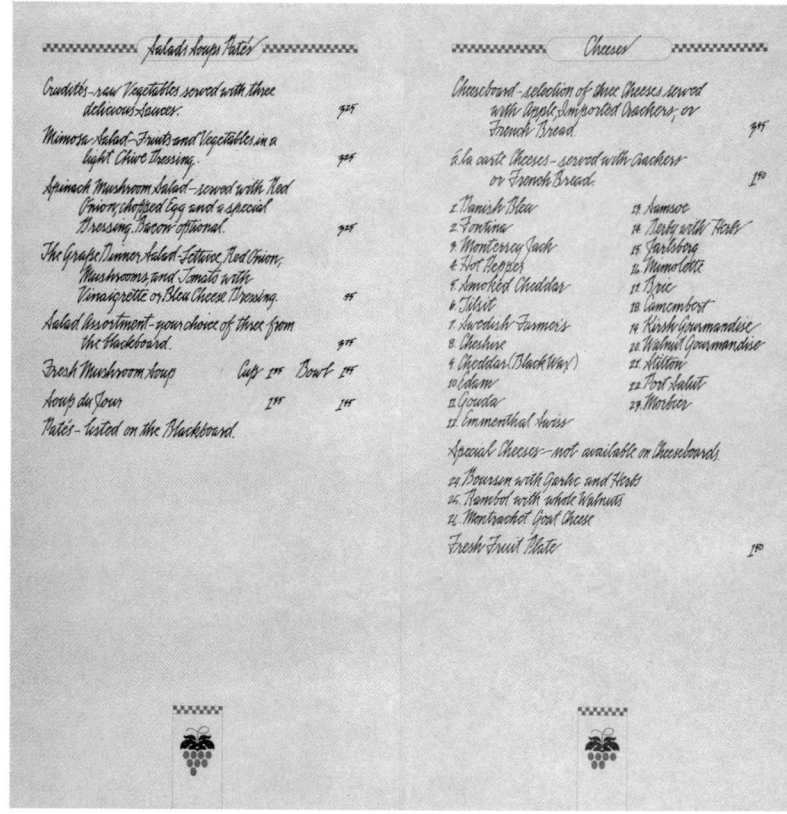

Emily Dimperio Birth Announcement
1985
Mike Schroeder
Art Director, Designer, Illustrator
Woody Pirtle, Mike Schroeder
Copywriters
Pirtle Design
Design Firm
Mr. & Mrs. Dimperio
Client

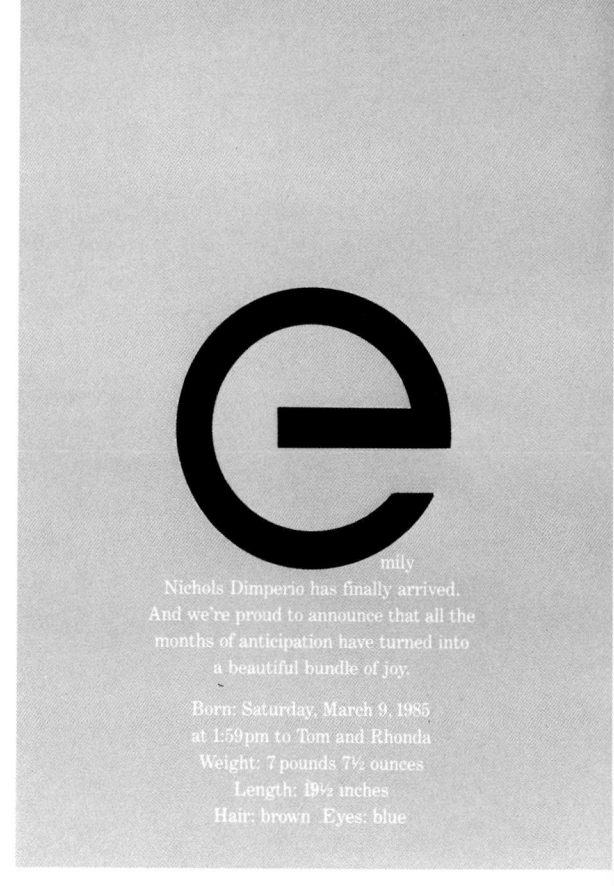

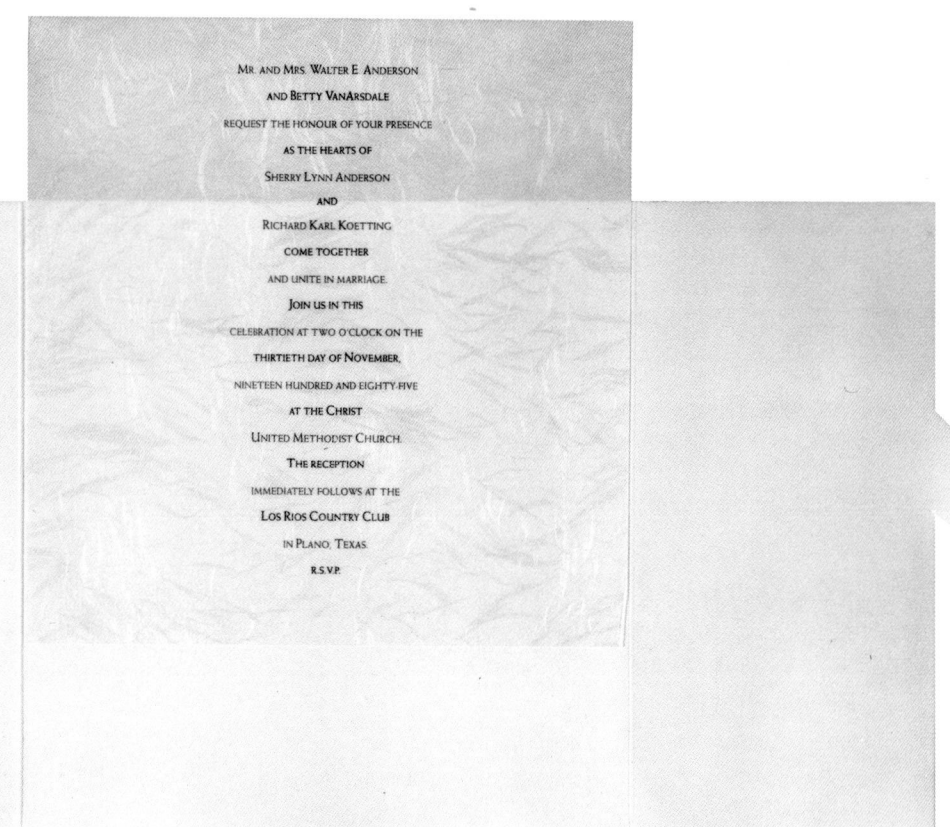

Anderson Koetting
Announcement
1985

Judy Dolim
*Art Director, Designer,
Illustration, Copywriter*

Sibley/Peteet Design, Inc.
Design Firm

Sherry Anderson,
Richard Koetting
Clients

Zoom Thud
1984

Bob Dennard,
Chuck Johnson, David Martin
Art Directors

Chuck Johnson
Designer, Illustrator

David Martin
Copywriter

Dennard Creative, Inc.
Design Firm

Dallas Society of
Visual Communications
Client

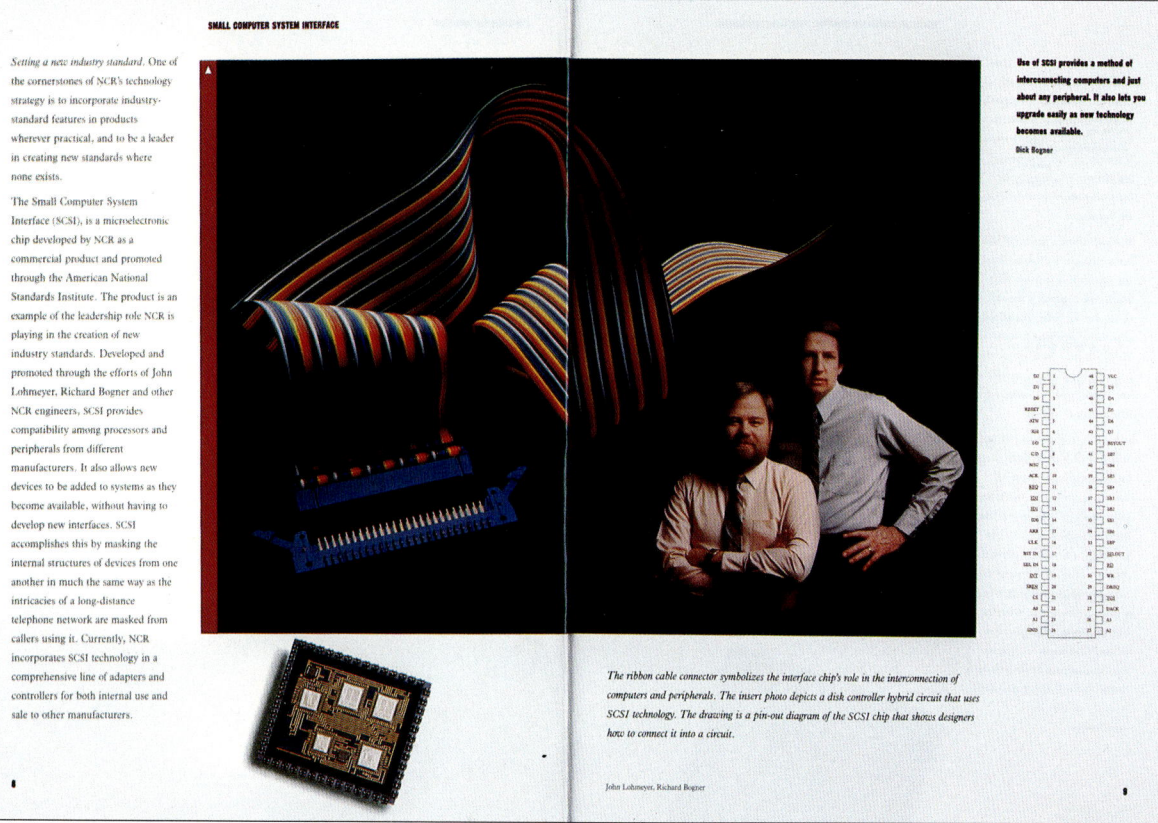
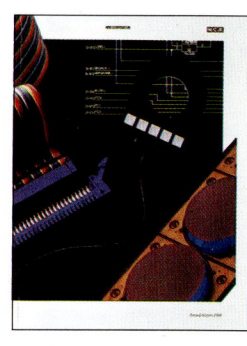

NCR Corporation
Annual Report
1984

Woody Pirtle
Art Director

Luis Acevedo
Designer

Joe Baraban
Photographer

NCR Corporation
Copywriter

Pirtle Design
Design Firm

NCR Corporation
Client

Hill Stationery
1981

Chris Hill
Art Director

Chris Hill, Joe Rattan
Designers

HILL/A Marketing Design Group
Design Firm, Client

Eraser Book
1979
Rex Peteet
Art Director, Designer, Copywriter
Rex Peteet, Luis Acevedo
Illustrators
Pirtle Design
Design Firm
Dallas Society of Visual Communications
Client

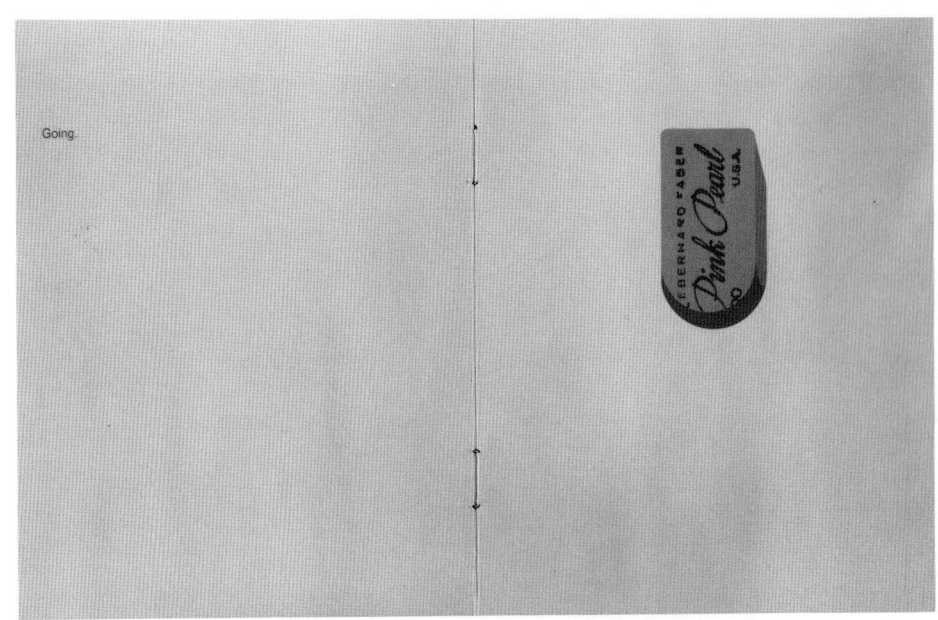

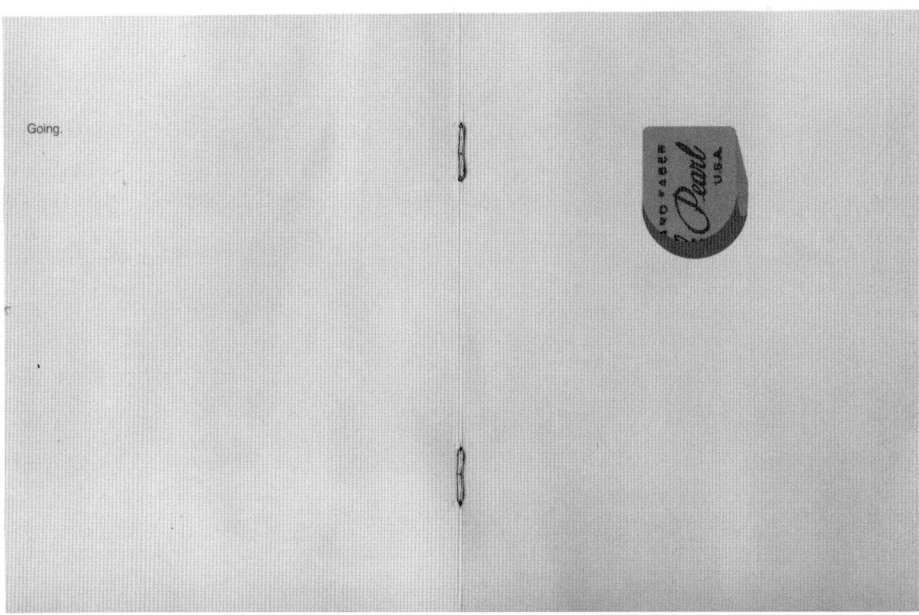

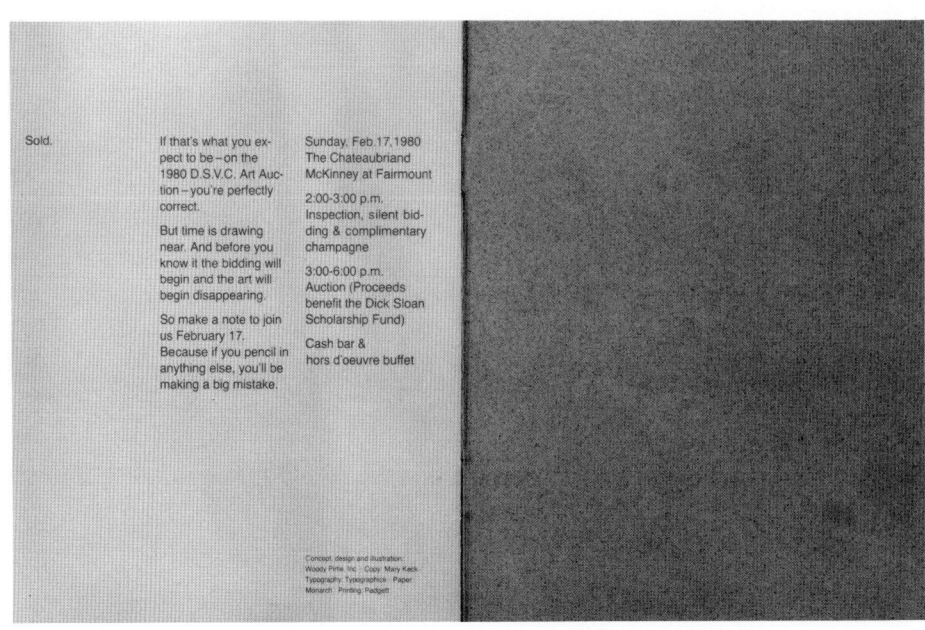

After a brief interruption in a partnership, Jerry Herring is again doing business as Herring Design. Not wanting to relaunch my business ill advised, I have sought out some of the best advisors that could be found.

Palmistry Reader
1975
Jerry Herring
Art Director, Designer, Copywriter
Herring Design
Design Firm, Client

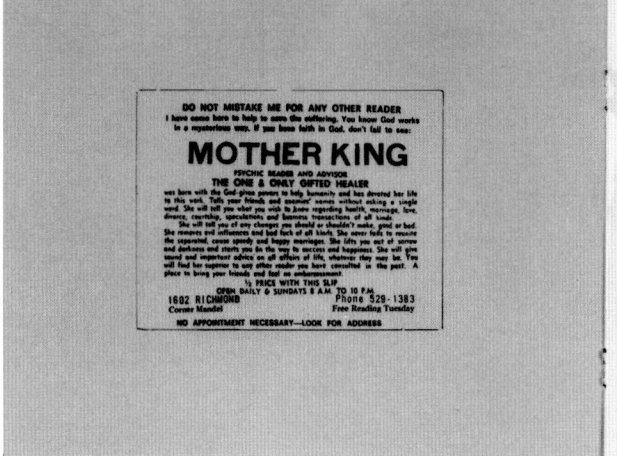

One Realty Corporation
1986
Paul Black
Designer, Illustrator
Sibley/Peteet Design
Design Firm
One Realty Corporation
Client

Dalt's Drink Menu
1983
Woody Pirtle
Art Director, Designer
Woody Pirtle, Mike Schroeder
Illustrators
T.G.I. Friday's
Copywriter
Pirtle Design
Design Firm
T.G.I. Friday's Inc.
Client

Dalts To Go Menu
1982
Woody Pirtle
Art Director, Designer
T.G.I. Friday's
Copywriter
Pirtle Design
Design Firm
T.G.I. Friday's Inc.
Client

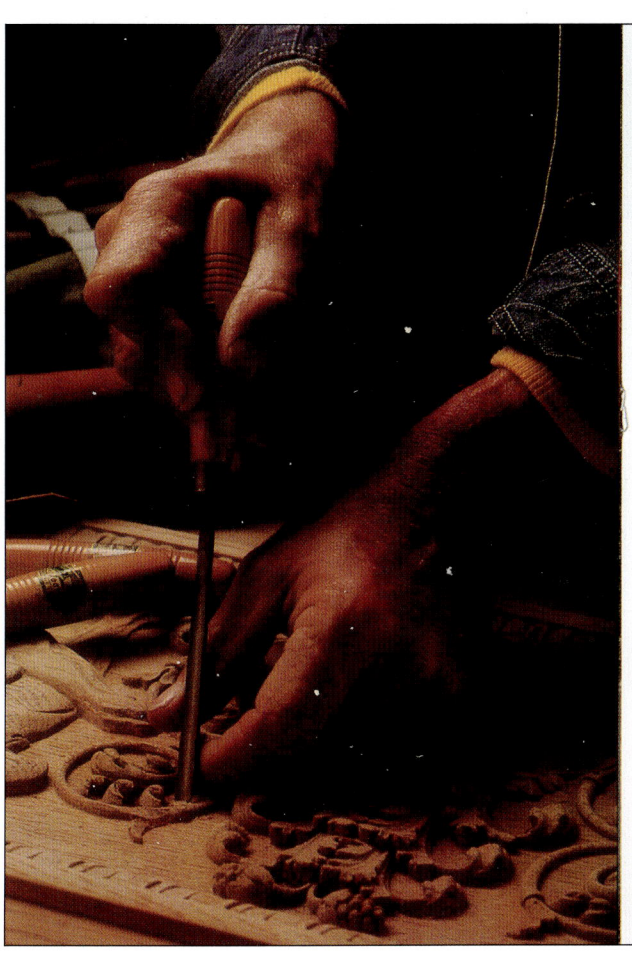

Steven Interiors
1982
Chris Hill
Art Director
Chris Hill, Joe Rattan
Designers
Arthur Meyerson
Photographer
Mary Langridge
Copywriter
HILL/A Marketing Design Group
Design Firm
Media Communications
Agency
Stevens Interiors
Client

PBA Crystal Ball Invitation
1981
Rex Peteet, Bob Dennard
Art Directors
Rex Peteet
Designer, Copywriter
Rex Peteet, Don Sibley
Illustrators
Dennard Creative
Design Firm
Paul Broadhead & Associates
Client

67,455
Solid Reasons
to Lease in
City Post
Oak.

City Post Oak Brochure
1984
Jerry Herring
Art Director, Designer
Steve Brady,
Richard Payne, Rick Gardner
Photographers
Lee Herrick
Copywriter
Herring Design
Design Firm
Gerald D. Hines Interests
Client

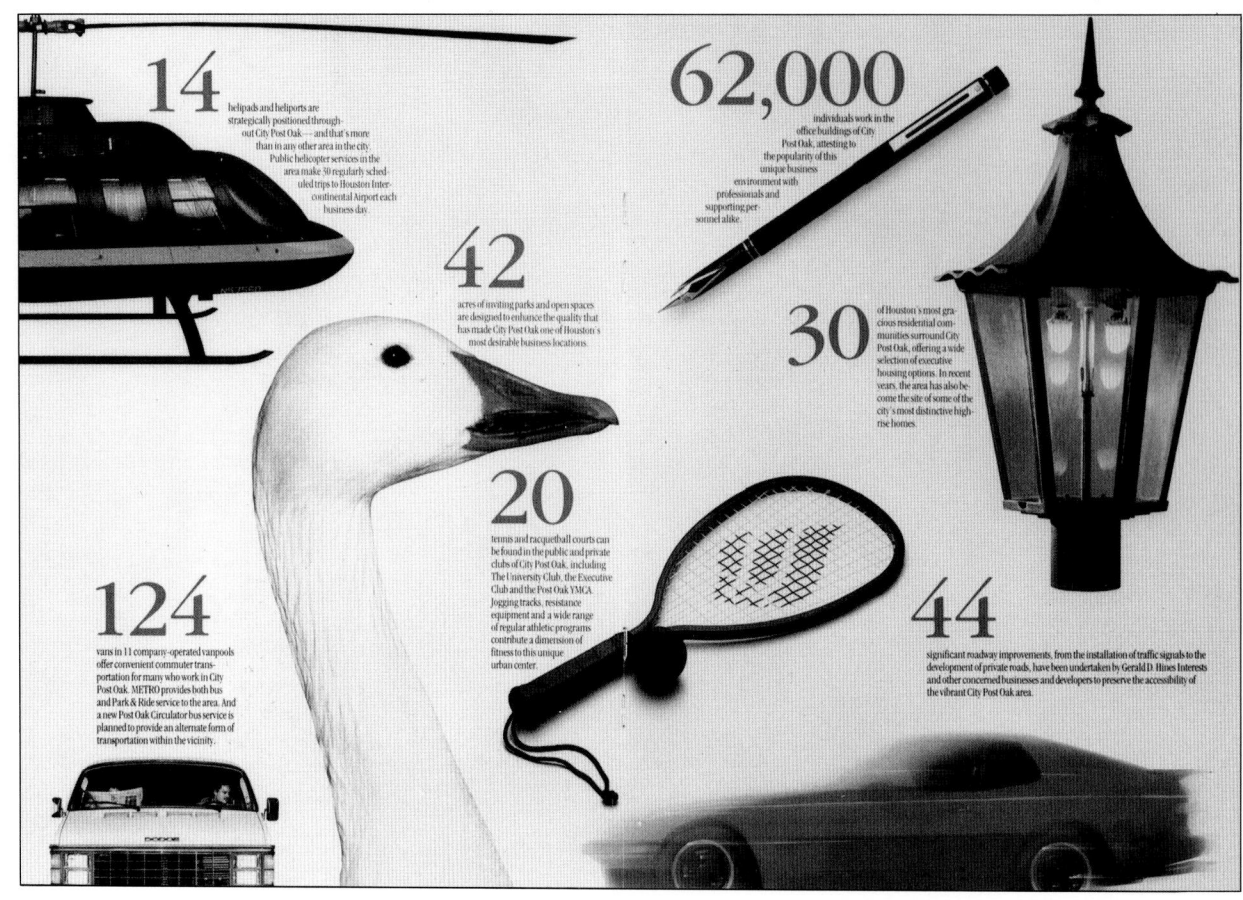

Helvetica
1979
Jack Summerford
Art Director, Designer
Summerford Design, Inc.
Design Firm
Southwestern Typographics
Client

102

Construction Party Poster
1983
Woody Pirtle
Art Director
Woody Pirtle, Mike Schroeder
Designers, Copywriters
Mike Schroeder
Illustrator
Pirtle Design
Design Firm
Gerald D. Hines Interests
Client

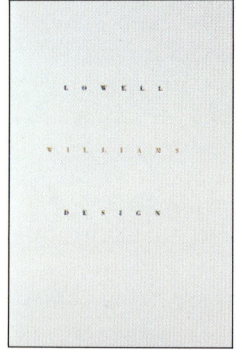

Lowell Williams Design
1985
Lowell Williams
Art Director, Copywriter
Lowell Williams, Bill Carson
Designers
Ron Scott
Photographer
Lowell Williams Design, Inc.
Design Firm, Agency, Client

Martha Vansyckle
1986
Carol Burke
Art Director, Designer
Melinda Marcus
Copywriter
Martha Vansyckle
Client

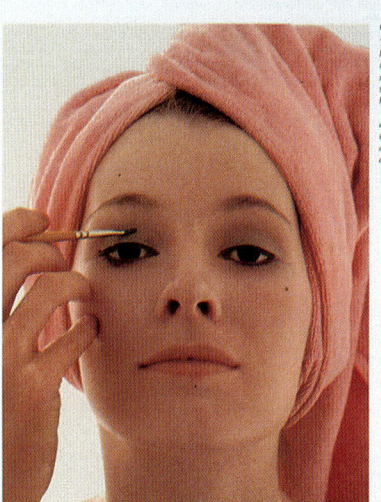
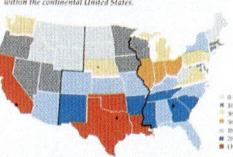

The Company

In the short span of seven years, Mary Kay Cosmetics, Inc. has evolved from a small regional cosmetics firm to a fully-integrated manufacturer and international distributor of an exclusive line of skin care products. There are currently over 8,000 Beauty Consultants actively selling and demonstrating Mary Kay products throughout the United States, its territories, and Australia.

The Company's basic product line originated from a unique process developed many years ago by a hidetanner. This process was later obtained from the tanner's descendants by our founder and Chairman of the Board, Mary Kay Ash, and subsequently became the basis for the Mary Kay Beauty Program.

Prior to forming the Company, Mary Kay was active in the direct selling industry for over twenty years. During her career, she earned a nationwide reputation as a leading saleswoman and an accomplished motivator. Mary Kay organized the Company and developed a special marketing plan based on her experience and expertise in direct sales. This plan incorporates a sophisticated marketing concept, with built-in incentives designed to afford the same opportunities for economic rewards to all of the Company's Beauty Consultants.

In January 1968, an ambitious and aggressive expansion program was conceived and launched. This program was designed to accelerate corporate growth through selected acquisitions and development of internal resources. Under the direction of Richard R. Rogers, President, the Company established long-term objectives to develop new market opportunities within the burgeoning cosmetics industry.

Thus far, this program has resulted in the acquisition of two subsidiary companies, Cosmetic Creations, Inc. and Mary Kay Cosmetics Pty. Ltd. (formerly Rachel York Pty. Ltd.) of Melbourne, Australia; the establishment of regional distribution and training centers in Atlanta and Los Angeles; and the completion of a modern $3 million manufacturing and distribution facility in Dallas, Texas. Land has also been acquired in anticipation of future development needs and expansion requirements. These accomplishments have considerably enlarged our cosmetic manufacturing capabilities, expanded our marketing resources and provided efficient services to support our rapidly growing organization.

Our Australian subsidiary is presently undergoing a complete changeover to the Mary Kay product line, to be completed by the first quarter of 1971. The transition from Rachel York to Mary Kay Cosmetics Pty. Ltd. was a planned program to provide a springboard for introducing the Mary Kay product line into the rapidly growing far-eastern market.

The management team, headed by Graeme McDougall, President and founder, maintains corporate headquarters in Melbourne, and has over 500 Beauty Consultants throughout Australia.

Marketing

Mary Kay Cosmetics markets skin care and glamour items for women and men under the tradenames of "Mary Kay" and "Mr. K". These products are merchandised solely through a marketing organization composed of specially trained, self-employed sales representatives called Beauty Consultants.

These Beauty Consultants market our product through professionally conducted "Beauty Shows" held in the privacy of the

Mary Kay Annual Report
1970
Bob Dennard
Art Director, Designer
Jerry Abramowitz
Photographer
David Russel, Gerald Allen
Copywriters
The Richards Group
Design Firm
Mary Kay Cosmetics
Client

Fresh
1978
Jack Summerford
Art Director, Designer, Copywriter
Andy Post
Photographer
Summerford Design, Inc.
Design Firm, Client

Party On The Green
1985

David Wesko
Art Director, Designer, Illustrator

Peggy Olson, David Wesko
Copywriters

McBride, Dealey & Day
Design Firm, Agency

Lincoln Property Company
Client

cultural terms, be seen as an eerie anticipation of the annihilation of the one thousand-year-old Romanov dynasty by firing squad in 1918—all acted out in advance by art, as art so often does. Or, again: It is fascinating and significant that while Diego Rivera was painting his damning vision of Detroit's automobile industry by presenting American workers as dehumanized cogs in the conveyor belt of mass production, George Grosz, with mordant line and wit, was depicting the post-war German laborers of the 1930s as mindless worker ants, and Margaret Bourke-White was producing art photographs of inescapable social implications and irony. "I am simply satisfied for my art to have a purpose," said Käthe Kollwitz. The concerns and expressions of her great heart found full artistic realization in her eloquent *form*, and yet she went further: With her *content* she admonished and enriched the world, broadcasting universal messages of compassion, tolerance, and love. I think of her adversaries during the seven long decades she spent on this planet—the bellicose Kaiser Wilhelm II, who plunged us into World War I, and who personally vetoed the awarding of a gold medal to Kollwitz for her *A Weavers' Revolt* cycle because of its supposedly subversive social content. I think of the megalomaniac Adolf Hitler, perpetrator of World War II and personal enemy of the stubborn woman pacifist who insisted on depicting the consequences of war in an unheroic light. And then I think of Kollwitz's message, "Never Again War," and I feel obliged to pass that message on, even though I am teaching ostensibly only about art.

We are not politicians, but we are educators—we can present the lessons of history. Students and teachers can participate in shaping the autobiography of our century. Only when confronted with the awesome task of passing knowledge on to others do we truly come to grips with knowledge and the responsibilities it engenders. I am simply content to be part of this teaching chain.

Alessandra Comini is University Distinguished Professor of Art History in the Meadows School of the Arts. Her mother, Megan Laird Comini, also taught at SMU and founded the Italian Department.

MAKING THE GRADE: STUDENTS ON TEACHING

Breaking Classroom Barriers
BY ROBERT JOFFE ('86)

In my field, broadcast news, it's particularly important for a teacher to have a strong professional as well as academic background. In teaching television production, for instance, you need experience in that area. The field is always changing. It's important that we are kept up to date on what's going on in the industry and are not merely taught something that was put into a book seven years ago.

It is very satisfying to me that my instructors teach and practice their craft as well. One of my professors, for example, not only teaches writing and television news, he does both every day for one of the papers and for a local television station. His work goes into the makeup of his knowledge, and he shares it with us. Teachers like this understand the value of practical experience and don't begrudge you for trying to accumulate it.

Along the same lines, the interaction you have outside of the classroom is sometimes more academically enriching than what you have in the classroom. When I sit and talk with one of my professors, I get more out of that than anything else. There are two types of instructors. Some think we don't care (and admittedly there are some students who don't). But there are also professors who know many of us are as interested in the material we're studying as they are. The teachers who approach the classroom with that attitude are the ones I value most.

Robert Joffe is a senior from Louisville, Kentucky, majoring in broadcast news.

Spirit and Sanctity
BY SHANNON SMITHEY ('87)

I choose a class by who's teaching it, because I'm interested in what they're interested in, but also because I'm interested in what I think they, as individuals, can bring to the class. The very best are those who act as though all of human history is still before us. Every semester at SMU I have had one class which I term "magic"—it's fascinating, it's scholastically important, it moves me, it changes me emotionally, spiritually, intellectually, professionally. It is a unique combination of the material, the questions addressed, and the individual teaching it.

One of my history classes in particular was a moving spiritual experience. It sounds a little funny, I know. But in that class we dealt with questions about the sanctity of individuals and their responsibility to find some sense of themselves and the world, and not to be swept up in mass movements and trends like fascism or communism. It's the responsibility to remain an individual and not become part of the faceless mob, but at the same time to maintain a sense of humanity and compassion. It's important to try to strike that balance.

We talked about the "engaged intellectual." It's all well and good that you're smart and can think, but if you just sit in your ivory tower and don't get involved in things, what good is it to you? That class was important to me because I'm concerned about many different world issues, and I feel I make some kind of commitment and contribution. It sounds terribly idealistic, but I know it's not right to wash your hands of the world's problems.

Good teachers have to be committed to their students, to care about the impact they're having on them and what sort of development they're encouraging in them. That means being interested in them personally as well as academically.

Shannon Smithey is a junior from Duncanville, Texas, majoring in political science and history.

Giving Form to Fascination
BY JOHN SARE ('86)

THE BEST TEACHERS GIVE FORM TO OUR FASCINATION AND SUGGEST PERSUASIVELY WHAT WE OUGHT TO BE FASCINATED WITH.

The best teachers are vital people who come into class not as though they're bored with the world, or as though it's going to end any minute. The very best are those who act as though all of human history is still before us. They may even talk occasionally about apocalypse, but they don't let their fears or political bias ruin their enthusiasm.

In an art history class one day, for instance, we learned less about art than we did about World War II and Nazi Germany. There were slides of horrible images from Nazi Germany, things all of us had seen before, and they seemed a little odd in an art history class. But they did relate to the art the professor was showing us.

Energy makes good teachers—the sense that when they come into the room, they are in command of what's going on because they've invested so much in learning about the subject and so much in learning how to present it. The best professors come in loaded with knowledge and present it with a great sense of importance. You find yourself looking at something you at first thought was trivial, yet learning that there is a meaning that makes it important.

The best teachers give form to our fascination and suggest persuasively what we ought to be fascinated with.

John Sare is a senior from Bartlesville, Oklahoma, majoring in English and news editorial journalism.

LOOKING BACK: ALUMNI RECALL THE TEACHERS AND TOPICS THAT CHANGED THEIR LIVES

Lessons on Living
BY PATRICIA ANN LA SALLE

However distressing and familiar the slides were, they didn't depress or bore us because the professor presented them with great energy and passion, as if to say, "These are things you really need to know about, and I'm going to do everything I can to make sure you do." You look at Hitler and think, "My God, human beings are capable of that," and then you look at her and think, "But she is capable of something else." She demonstrated a good side of human possibility while talking about a bad one. Her teaching was playing the same role as some of the art she talked about that day.

Dancer Kay Quisenberry ('73) lived with the aborigines of Australia for 19 months to find out "why people have the urge and necessity to express themselves through stylized movement."

While working in Kenya, Zambia, and Zaire for 11 years, Leta Gorham ('59, '60) used to sit in the dirt of primitive villages teaching women how to read. She feels equally at home "sharing a meal at a banquet table with my own country's elite."

Other alumni may have crossed few geographic boundaries in their lives after college. But even before they left the SMU campus, they had sampled other cultures, probed the minds of the great philosophers, watched powerful empires rise and fall, witnessed the birth of new concepts, and immersed themselves in the art, literature, and music of the world. "The insights have enabled me to move within all walks of life and social status," says salesman Ben Morton ('73).

All this because of the liberal arts classes they took at SMU—courses they still remember as forces that changed their lives.

SMU Mustang Magazine
1985

Bryan L. Peterson
Art Director, Designer

Patti La Salle
Copywriter

Peterson & Company
Design Firm

Southern Methodist University
Client

| 30 | ANDEAN CONDOR *Vultur gryphus* | In its iron coffin it dwells among the rusty stones feeding on horseshoes. |

In the mountains the north wind
whistles and howls like a missile
and the condor leaves its casket,
sharpens its talons on the rocks,
spreads its mystical plumage,
flies to the end of the sky,
gallops the concave heights
with its iron wings,
and pecks at the sky's zinc,
waiting for a sign of blood:
a motionless speck,
the heartbeat that prepares
to die and be devoured.

The black cyclone planes down
and falls like a cruel fist:
death waited down below.

Above, cruel cordilleras,
like bloodstained cacti,
and the bitter-colored sky.
It soars back to its dwelling,
folds its imperious wings
and again stretches out to sleep
in its abominable coffin.

Art of Birds
1985

George Lenox
Art Director, Designer

Jack Unruh
Illustrator

University of Texas Press
Client

580 California
1984

Lowell Williams
Art Director

Lowell Williams, Bill Carson
Designers

Tom McNeff
Illustrator

Ron Scott, Bob Harr
Photographers

Lee Herrick
Copywriter

Lowell Williams Design, Inc.
Design Firm, Agency

Gerald D. Hines Interests
Client

Rising directly across the street from the Bank of America world headquarters, 580 California recalls the richness of another age. At street level, granite archways mark the entrances to a two-story arcade. Ornamental lanterns and metal grillwork lend an air of old-fashioned charm to this pedestrian walkway.

The granite facade, with its regular window pattern, is reminiscent of solid masonry design. Corner towers support rows of bay windows, long a hallmark of San Francisco architecture. The rounded columns separating the bays reinforce the sculptural quality of the stone facade and carry the eye upward to the classic French mansard roof with its cresting and finials. Here, highlighted against the two-story roofline of slate grey glass, statues crown the columns on all four sides of the building.

While greatly influenced by classical precedents, 580 California is very much a product of the present. Dual pane grey glass in all windows greatly enhances the building's energy efficiency. In the two rooftop office levels, dark grey insulating glass keeps heat transfer to a minimum while providing panoramic views of the Bay Area.

To the south, the building overlooks the dynamic California Street corridor and the activity on the Bank of America Plaza. To the north and northwest stretch broad vistas of Russian Hill, Telegraph Hill, Coit Tower, San Francisco Bay, and the foothills of Marin County.

"In designing 580 California, we focused on a number of details that add to the sculptural quality of the building. Solid granite piers on the tower's four corners support walls of curved bay windows. And the round granite columns are capped by statues in the classical style. Such decorative sculptures have graced rooflines through the ages, from the palace at Versailles to the great Bernini arcade at St. Peter's in Rome."
    John Burgee

**Paul Leon, DPM
Letterhead**
1978

Mike Schroeder
Art Director, Designer

Eisenberg, Pannell
Design Firm

Paul Leon, DPM
Client

IABC Call For Entries
Poster
1985
Rex Peteet
Art Director, Designer, Illustrator
Sharon Larkin
Copywriter
Sibley/Peteet Design, Inc.
Design Firm
International Association of Business Communicators
Agency

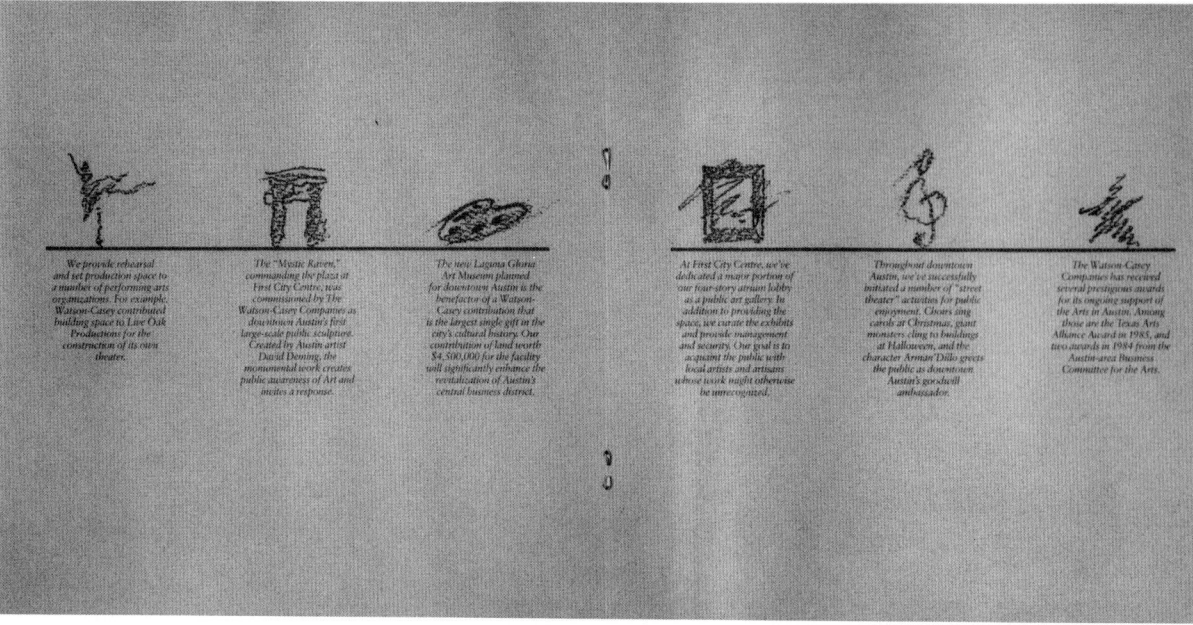

Watson-Casey Arts
Brochure
1985

Tom Poth, Mike Hicks
Art Directors

Mike Hicks
Designer

Patti Bishop
Illustrator

Hixo, Inc.
Design Firm

The Watson-Casey Companies
Client

77 Good Books
1977

Richard Hendel
Art Director

Richard Hendel, Ed Lindlof
Designers

Ed Lindlof
Illustrator

University of Texas Press
Design Firm, Client

USA Film Festival Poster
1983
Jill Hawkins
Art Director, Designer
Kent Kirkly
Photographer
Jill Hawkins Design
Design Firm
USA Film Festival
Client

Pet Potato Giveaway
Promotion
1981
Rex Peteet, Bob Dennard
Art Directors
Rex Peteet
Designer, Illustrator
Bob Dennard,
George Toomer, Rex Peteet
Copywriters
Dennard Creative
Design Firm
Bennigan's
Client

Bennigan's Winter Drink Menu
1982
Don Sibley, Bob Dennard
Art Directors
Don Sibley
Designer
Jerry Jeanmard
Illustrator
Bob Dennard,
Don Sibley, Cody Calhoun
Copywriters
Dennard Creative
Design Firm
Bennigan's
Client

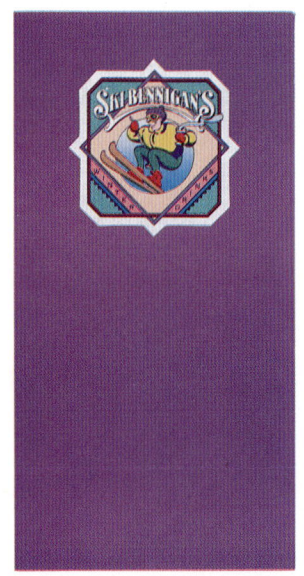 

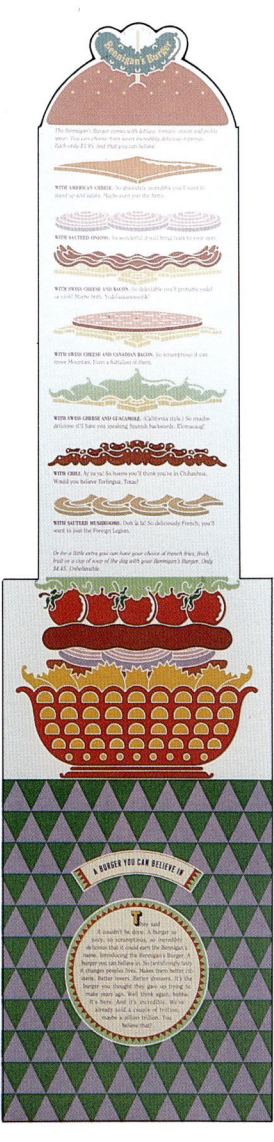

Bennigan's Hamburger Menu
1981

Rex Peteet, Bob Dennard
Art Directors

Rex Peteet
Designer, Illustrator

Bob Dennard,
Rex Peteet, Glyn Powell
Copywriters

Dennard Creative
Design Firm

Bennigan's
Client

Bennigan's Hamburger
Promo Poster
1981

Rex Peteet, Bob Dennard
Art Directors

Rex Peteet
Designer, Illustrator

Bob Dennard
Copywriter

Dennard Creative
Design Firm

Bennigan's
Client

Merry Christmas,
Happy Hanukah
1982
Don Crum
Art Director

Don Crum, Amy Werfel
Designers

Don Crum & Co.
Design Firm, Client

Yellow Pages
1983
Dick Mitchell
Art Director, Designer, Illustrator

Mark Perkins
Copywriter

Richards, Sullivan,
Brock & Associates
Design Firm

The Richards Group
Agency

Dallas Society of
Visual Communications
Client

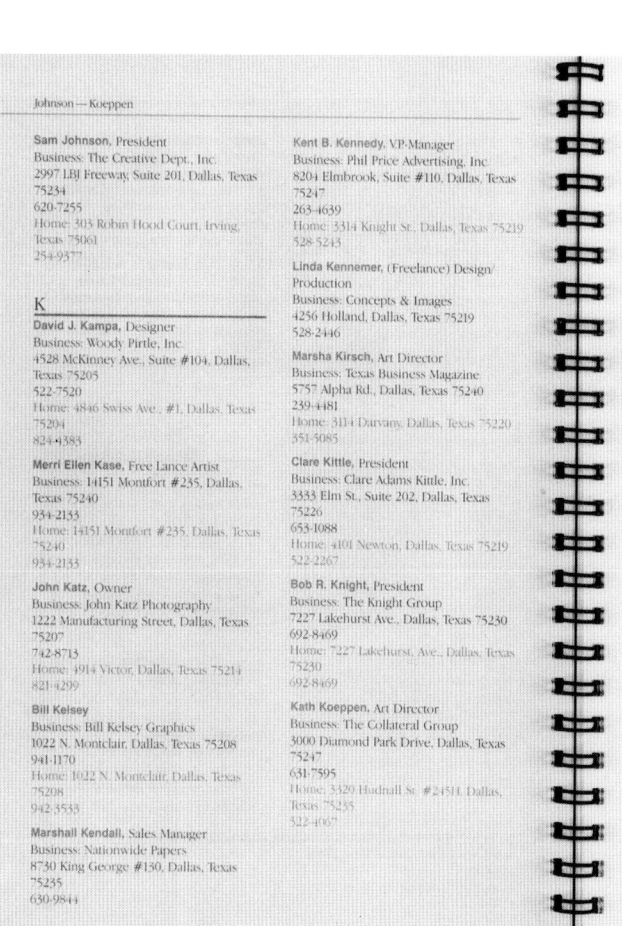

114

Cheers/Cherri
1985
Steve Connatser
Art Director, Designer
Connatser & Co.
Design Firm
Dallas Advertising League
Client

The Richards Group
Christmas Card
1983
D.C. Stipp
Art Director, Designer
D.C. Stipp, Stan Richards
Copywriters
Richards, Sullivan,
Brock & Associates
Design Firm
The Richards Group
Agency, Client

1st Annual Chili Poster
1981
Rex Peteet
*Art Director, Designer,
Illustrator, Copywriter*
Dennard Creative
Design Firm
Dallas Designers' Chili Cookoff
Client

Williamson Printing Brochure
1981

Woody Pirtle
Art Director, Designer

Mary Keck
Copywriter

Pirtle Design
Design Firm

Williamson Printing Company
Client

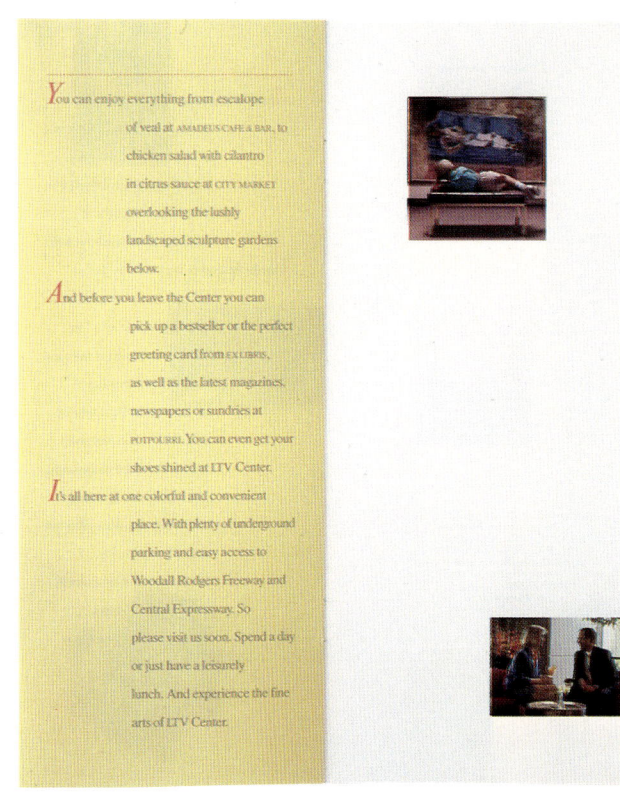

LTV Center Retail Directory
1985

Rex Peteet
Art Director, Designer, Copywriter

Joe Aker
Photographer

Sibley/Peteet Design, Inc.
Design Firm

Trammell Crow Company
Client

How To Become Texan
1983

Scott Eggers
Art Director, Designer

Jim Jacobs
Illustrator

Mark Perkins, Charlie Allen
Copywriters

Richards, Sullivan,
Brock & Associates
Design Firm

The Richards Group
Agency

Texas Monthly
Client

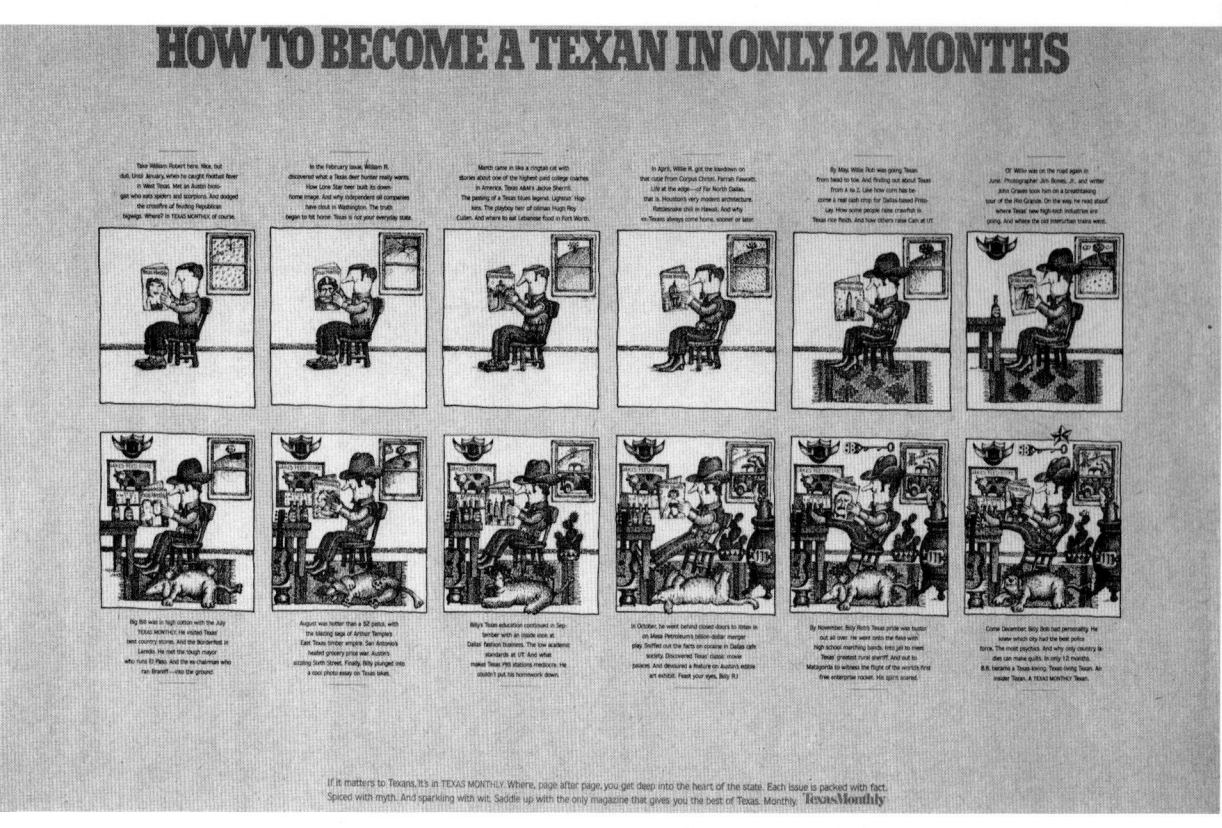

End Construction Poster
1983

Rex Peteet
*Art Director, Designer,
Copywriter*

Rex Peteet, Walter Horton
Illustrators

Sibley/Peteet Design, Inc.
Design Firm

Tom & Cynthia Pharr
Client

Images for Survival
1985
Alan Lidji
Art Director, Designer

Alan Lidji, Charlie Freeman
Illustrators

Alan Lidji Design
Design Firm

The Shoshin Society
Client

Katz & Dogs
1981

John Katz
Art Director, Photographer

Woody Pirtle
Designer, Copywriter

Pirtle Design
Design Firm

John Katz Photography
Client

LINE. It is like the framework of art. And line work can appear in as many forms as there are hairs on your head. There are curly lines, frizzy lines, zig-zag lines and lines as straight as an arrow. In the painting "Egyptian Triptych" the artist paints all kinds of lines. Try our line board and see what types of lines you can create. Even if you can't draw a straight one.

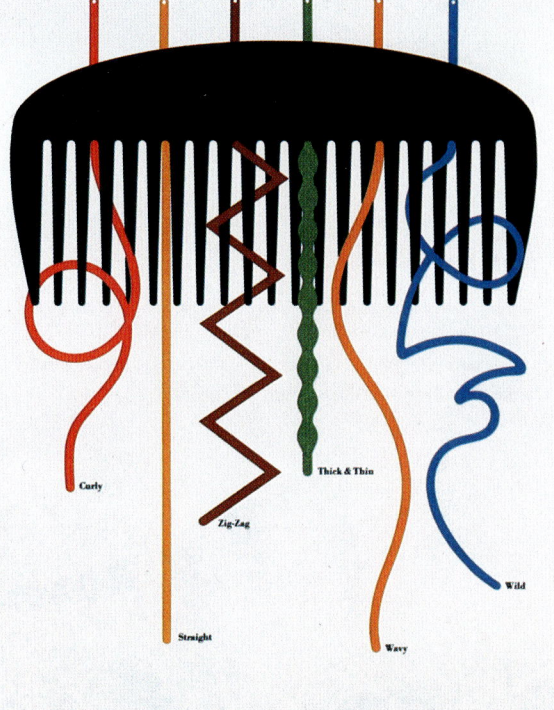

Egyptian Triptych by Alan Davie, 1965.

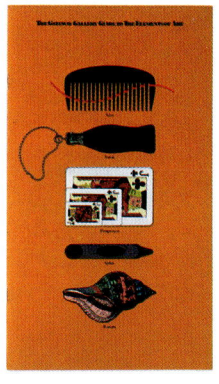

Gateway Gallery Brochure
1985

Rex Peteet
Art Director

Rex Peteet, Paul Black
Designers, Illustrators, Copywriters

Gary McCoy
Photographer

Sibley/Peteet Design, Inc.
Design Firm

Dallas Museum of Fine Art
Client

Sit Up & Take Notice
1982

Steve Connatser
Art Director

Judy Connatser
Copywriter

Connatser & Co.
Design Firm

Texas Homes Magazine
Client

121

Dallas Ad League
1978
Don Crum
Art Director, Designer

Wayne Gary
Illustrator

Connatser & Crum
Design Firm

Dallas Advertising League
Client

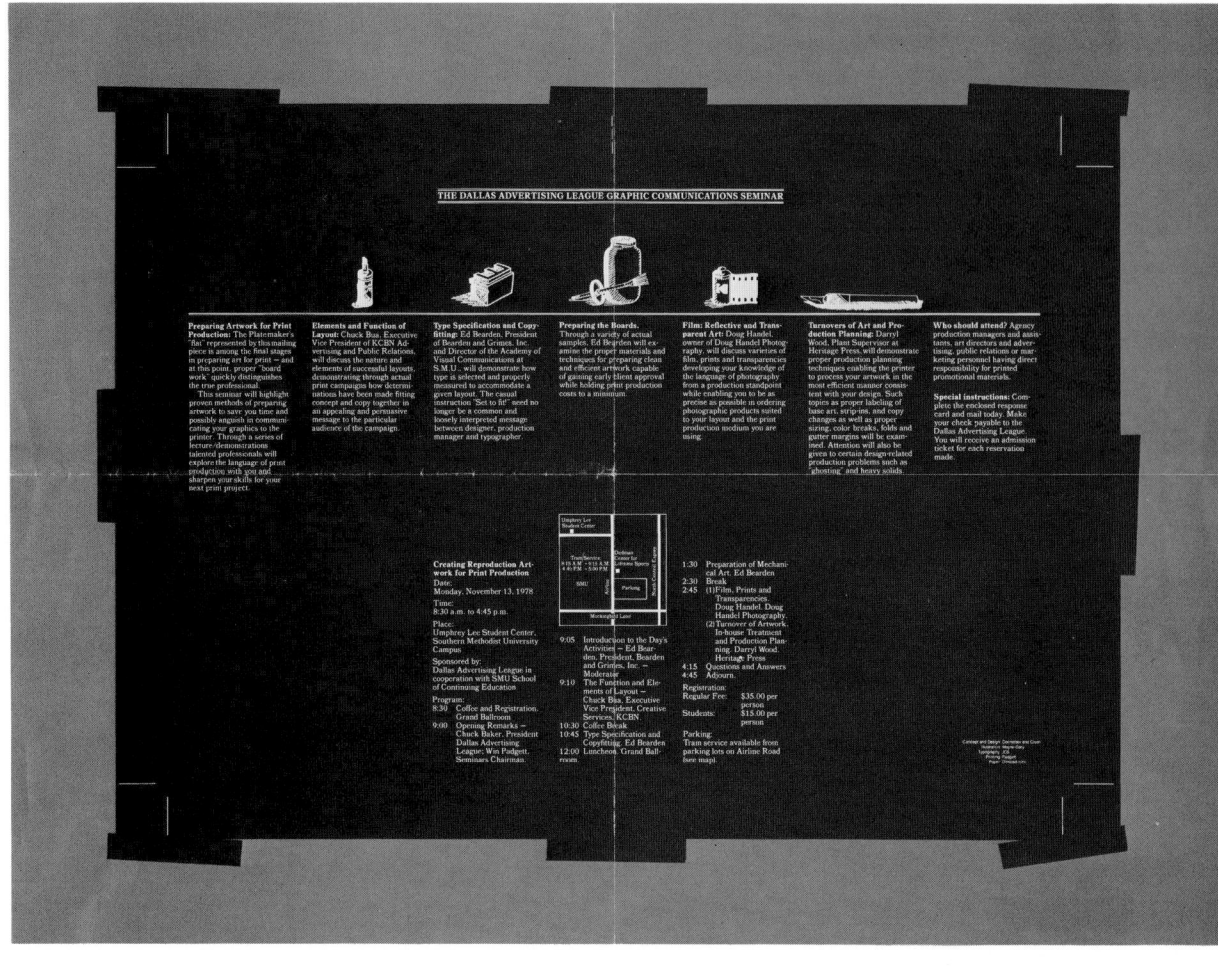

Texas Weather
1983
George Lenox
Art Director

George Lenox, Ed Lindlof
Designers

Ed Lindlof
Illustrator

University of Texas Press
Design Firm, Client

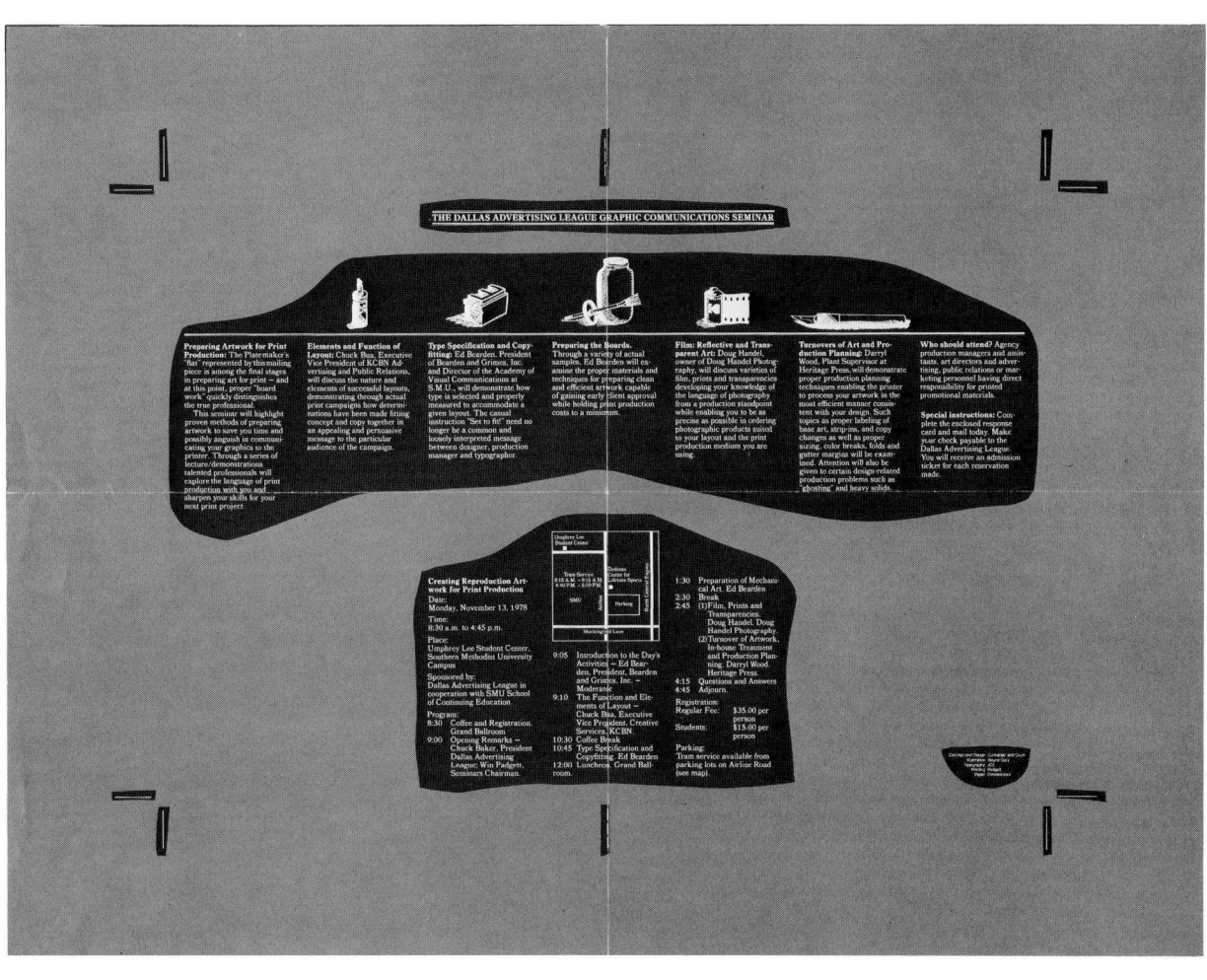

Jeff Copp Stationery
1975

Chris Hill
Art Director, Designer

Loucks Atelier Inc.
Design Firm

Jeff Copp
Client

Twenty Years of
Summerford Design
1985

Jack Summerford
*Art Director, Designer
Copywriter*

Summerford Design, Inc.
Design Firm, Client

Thom Liddell Letterhead
1975

Woody Pirtle
Art Director, Designer

Stan Richards & Associates
Design Firm

Thom Liddell, Interior Designer
Client

Change Poster
1979

Chris Rovillo
Art Director, Designer, Illustrator

Gary Gibson
Copywriter

Richards, Sullivan, Brock & Associates
Design Firm

The Richards Group
Agency

Richards, Sullivan, Brock & Associates
Client

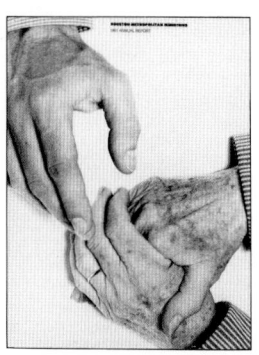

Houston Metropolitan Ministries
Annual Report
1981

Jerry Herring
Art Director, Designer

Jim Sims
Photographer

Linda Bradford, Steve Barnhill
Copywriters

Herring Design
Design Firm

Houston Metropolitan Ministries
Client

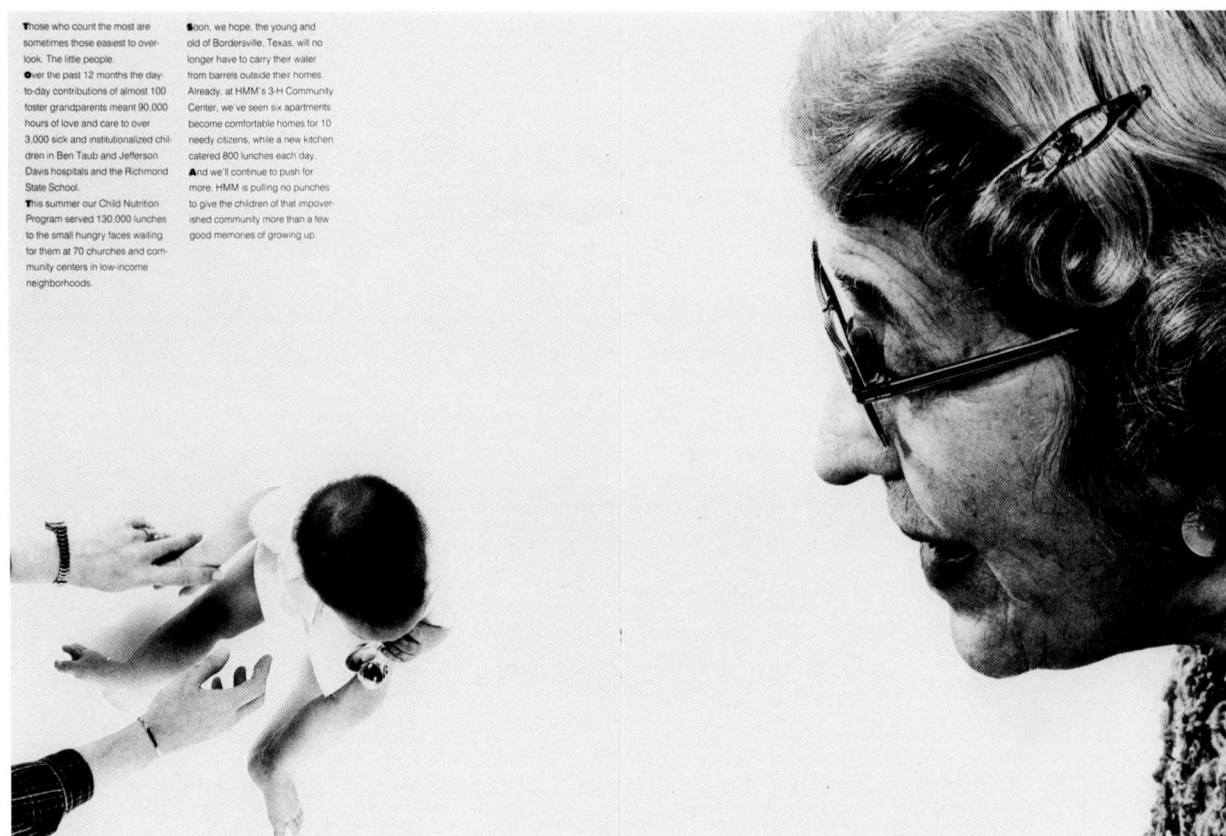

Serve-Rigs Brochure
1980

Lowell Williams
Art Director

Lowell Williams, Bill Carson
Designers

Jim Sims
Photographer

Lee Herrick
Copywriter

Lowell Williams Design, Inc.
Design Firm, Agency

Serve-Rigs
Client

Design in Texas
A Retrospective Exhibition
AIGA Texas
1986

AIGA-Texas Poster
1986

Jim Jacobs, Cap Pannell
Art Directors, Designers

Shel Hershorn
Photographer

Carol St. George
Copywriter

Chimayo
Design Firm

AIGA-Texas
Client

Dallas Symphony
1812 Poster Invitation
1983

Brian Boyd
Art Director, Designer, Illustrator

Mark Perkins
Copywriter

Richards, Sullivan, Brock & Associates
Design Firm

The Richards Group
Agency

Dallas Symphony Orchestra
Client

Dewey Square Brochure
1983
Lowell Williams
Art Director
Lowell Williams, Bill Carson
Designers
Bob Harr
Photographer
Lee Herrick
Copywriter
Lowell Williams Design, Inc.
Design Firm, Agency
Rose Associates
Client

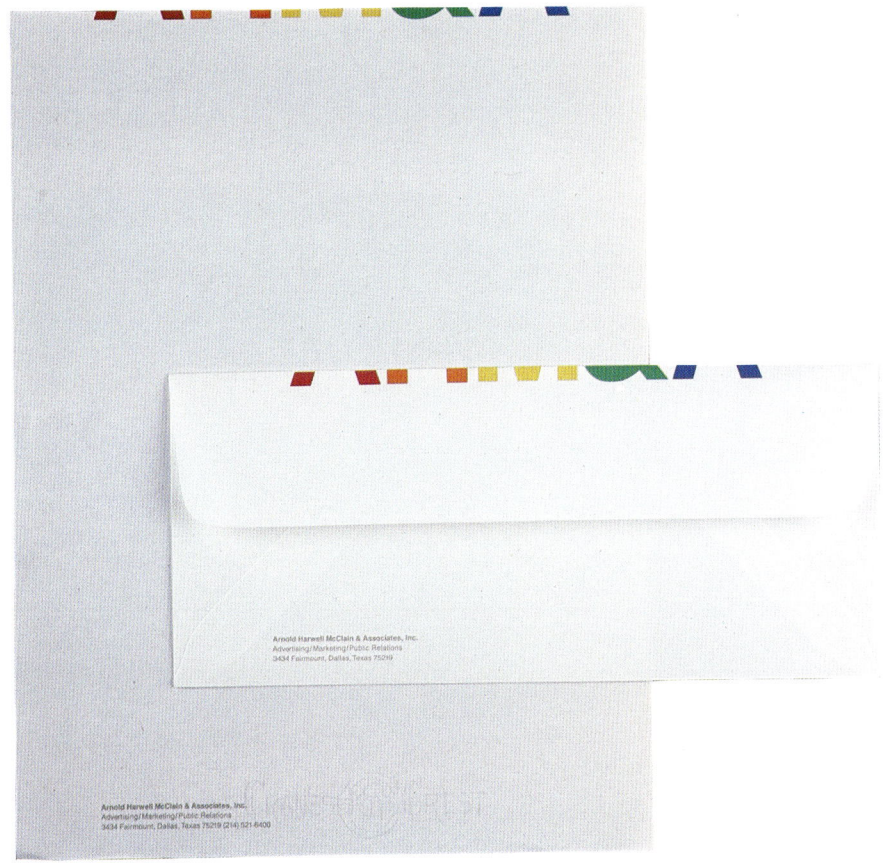

Arnold, Harwell, McClain Assoc.
Letterhead
1980
Woody Pirtle
Art Director
Frank Nichols
Designer, Illustrator
Pirtle Design
Design Firm
Arnold, Harwell, McClain Assoc.
Client

Calls
1975
Woody Pirtle, Jerry Herring
Art Directors, Designers, Illustrators
Jerry Herring
Copywriter
Herring & Pirtle, Inc.
Design Firm
Art Director's Club of Houston
Client

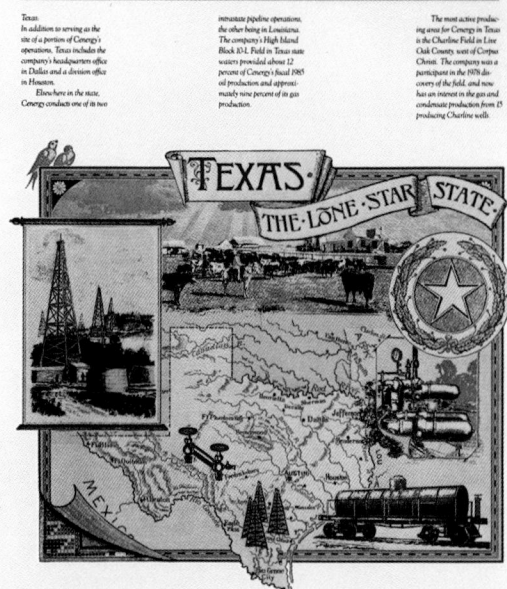

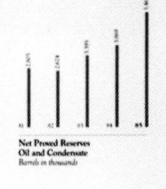

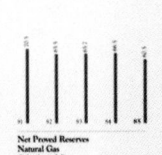

Cenergy Annual Report
1984

Woody Pirtle, Joe Rattan
Art Directors

Joe Rattan
Designer

John Craig
Illustrator/Photographer

Cenergy
Copywriter

Pirtle Design
Design Firm

Cenergy Corporation
Client

Cenikor Annual Report
1978

Jerry Herring
Art Director, Designer

Joe Baraban
Photographer

Steve Barnhill
Copywriter

Herring Design
Design Firm

Cenikor Foundation, Inc.
Client

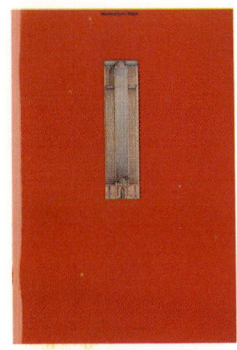

Momentum Place Brochure
1985

Lowell Williams
Art Director

Lowell Williams, Bill Carson
Designers

Andy Dearwater
Illustrator

Ron Scott, Bob Harr
Photographers

Jo Ann Stone
Copywriter

Lowell Williams Design, Inc.
Design Firm, Agency

Cadillac Fairview
Client

U.S. West
Annual Report
1984

Woody Pirtle,
Alan Colvin, Joe Rattan
Art Directors

Alan Colvin, Joe Rattan
Designers

Fallon McElligott Rice
Copywriter

Pirtle Design
Design Firm

U.S. West
Client

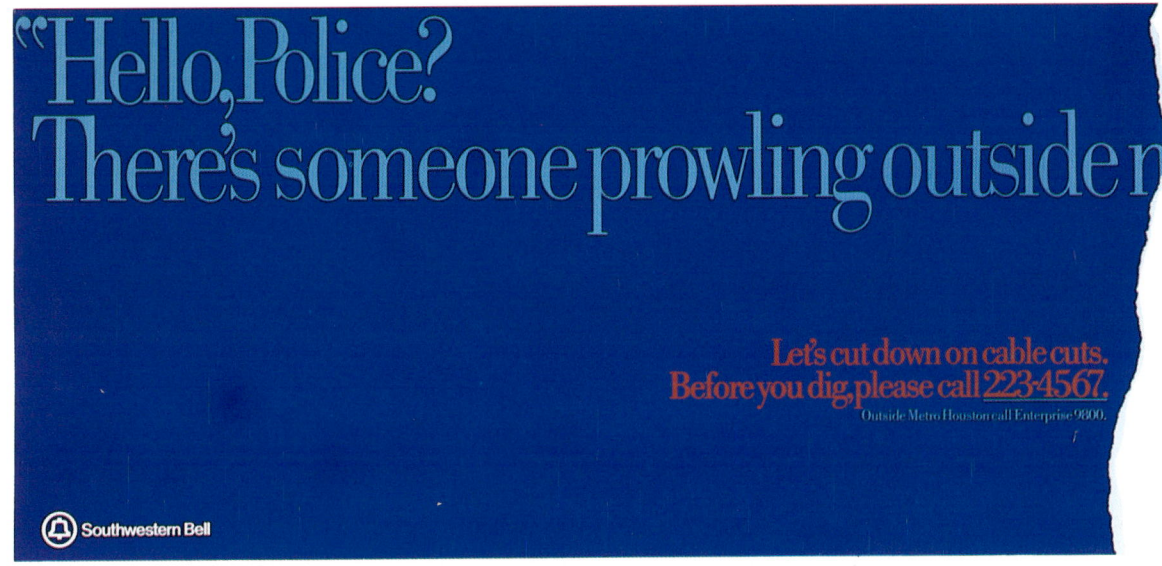

S. W. Bell Cable Cuts
1983
Cap Pannell
Art Director, Designer, Copywriter
Pannell/St. George
Design Firm
Southwestern Bell
Client

Houston Metropolitan Ministries
Annual Report
1980

Jerry Herring
Art Director, Designer

Jim Sims
Photographer

Steve Barnhill
Copywriter

Herring Design
Design Firm

Houston Metropolitan Ministries
Client

Simpson Paper Sequences
. Poster
1986

James Cross, Rex Peteet
Art Directors

Rex Peteet
Designer, Illustrator, Copywriter

Sibley/Peteet Design, Inc.
Design Firm

Cross Associates
Agency

Simpson Paper Co.
Client

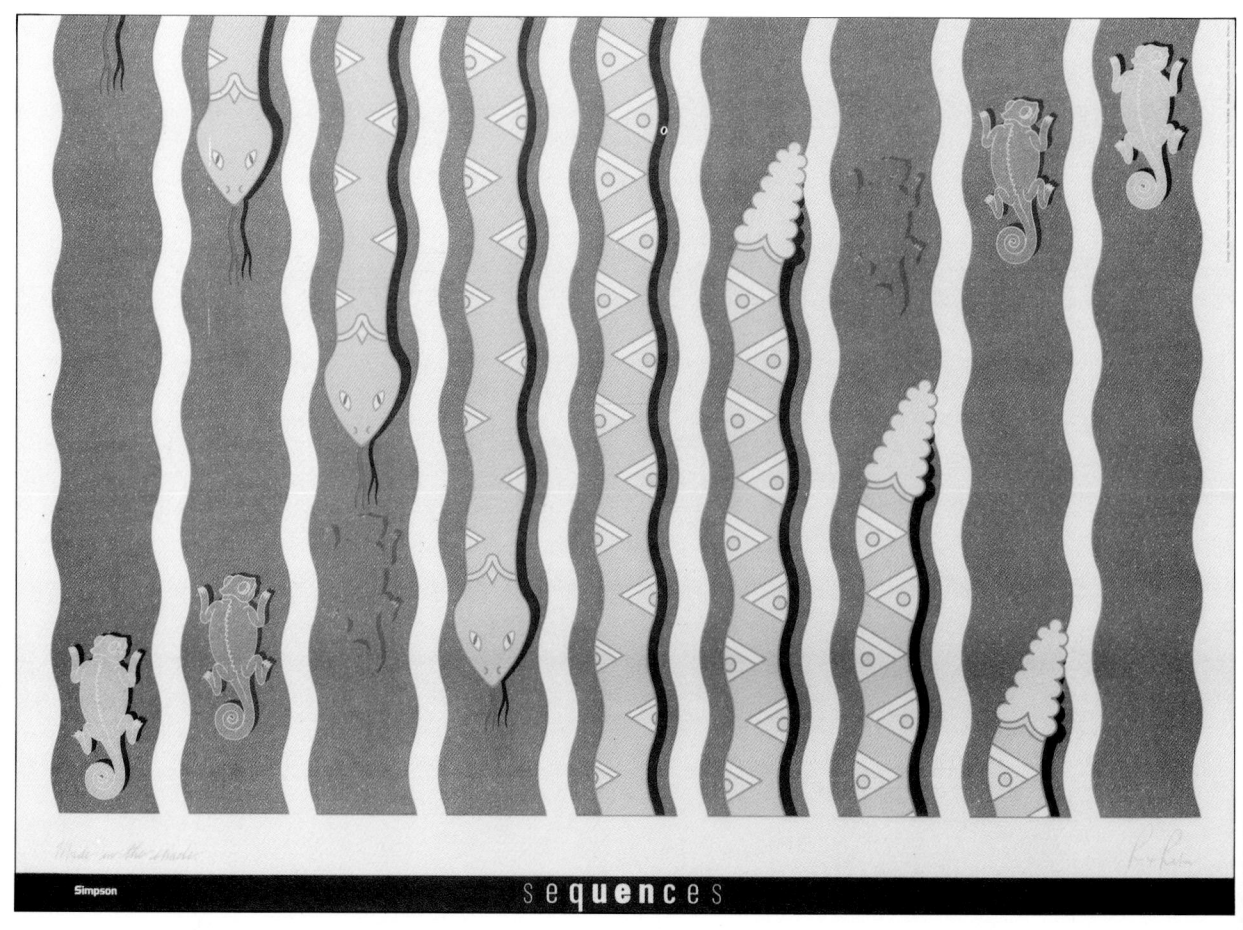

LTV Center Opening
Invitation
1984

Don Sibley, Steve Gibbs
Art Directors

Steve Gibbs
Designer, Illustrator

Sibley/Peteet Design, Inc.
Design Firm

Trammell Crow Company
Client

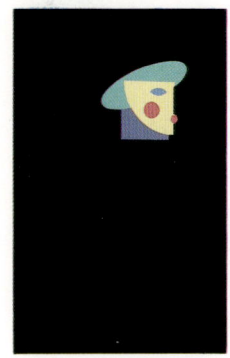

Neiman Marcus
Beauty Notebook
1985

Don Sibley, Steve Gibbs
Art Directors, Designers

Thom Jackson, John Parrish
Photographers

Kelly Stribling
Illustrator

Laura Rivers
Copywriter

Sibley/Peteet Design, Inc.
Design Firm

Neiman-Marcus
Client

White Marsh Mall
1981

Ron Sullivan
Art Director, Designer

Ron Sullivan,
Nancy Hoefig, Dick Mitchell
Illustrators

Mark Perkins
Copywriter

Richards, Sullivan,
Brock & Associates
Design Firm

The Richards Group
Agency

The Rouse Company
Client

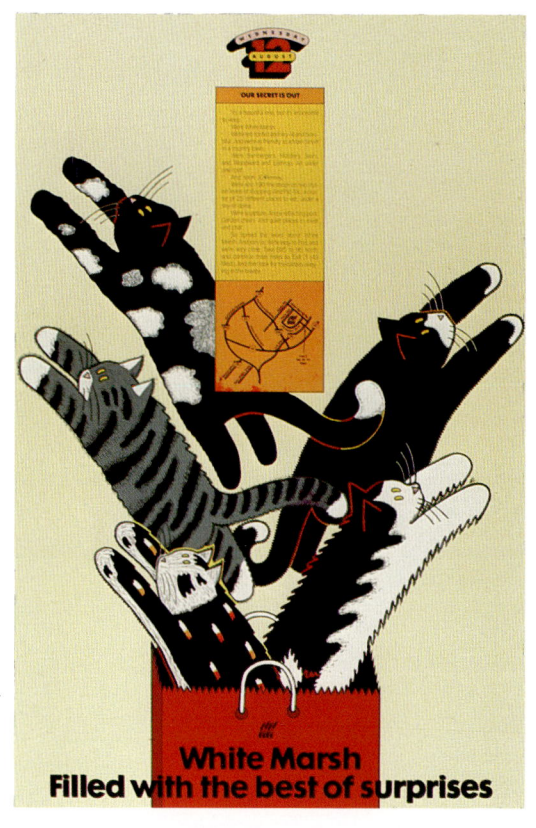

Rise & Shine
1980
Bob Dennard, Don Sibley
Art Directors, Copywriters
Don Sibley
Designer
Jerry Jeanmard
Illustrator
Dennard Creative, Inc.
Design Firm
Paul Broadhead & Associates
Client

4th USA Film Festival
1974
Cap Pannell
Art Director, Designer
The Richards Group
Illustrator, Design Firm
USA Film Festival
Client

Hats Off
1982
Cap Pannell
Art Director, Designer, Writer
Cap Pannell, Cerita Smith
Illustrators
Pannell/St. George
Design Firm
Riverside Square/
JMB Federated
Client

It's Willie, western boots and white-collared executives. It's long necks, longhorns and loads of new activity. It's cowboys, Cadillacs and construction galore. It's the west. The new west. Full of new people, new ideas and new retail opportunities. A place Paul Broadhead and Associates thinks you should be. How? It's easy. Join us during the ICSC Convention in New Orleans, May 17-21. We'll tell you about three of the biggest, most beautiful shopping malls west of the Mississippi. All to open in 1981. So drop by and see us at the New Orleans Marriott, Suite 3630, and we'll introduce you to a west that was never wilder. Paul Broadhead and Associates, Inc.

Head West Poster
1981
Bob Dennard, Don Sibley
Art Directors
Don Sibley
Designer
Jack Unruh
Illustrator
Bob Dennard
Copywriter
Dennard Creative, Inc.
Design Firm
Paul Broadhead & Assoc.
Client

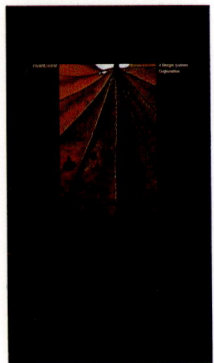

Compendium
1980
Jay Loucks
Art Director
Chris Hill, Mark Geer
Designers
Gary Braasch
Photographer
Loucks Atelier Inc.
Design Firm
Compendium
Client

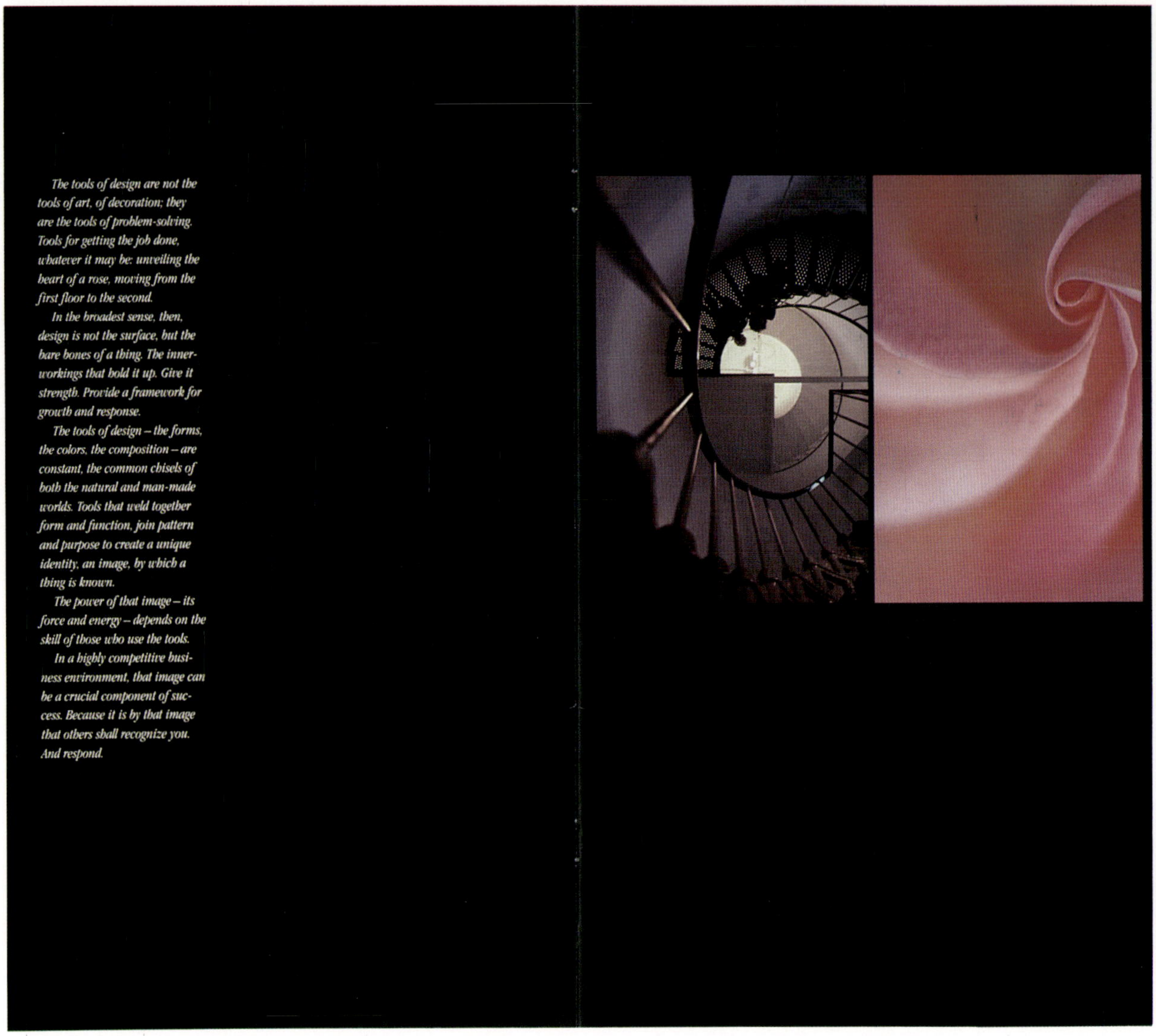

After the Phoenix Merger
1982
Richard Kilmer
Art Director, Designer, Illustrator
Russell Burget
Copywriter
Ben Carter & Associates
Design Firm
Texas International Company
Client

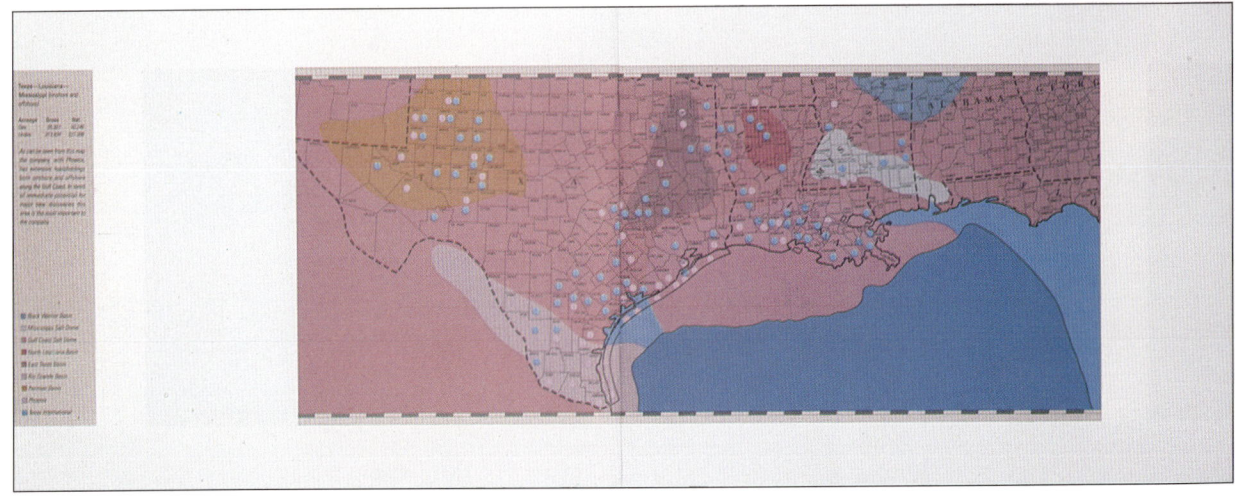

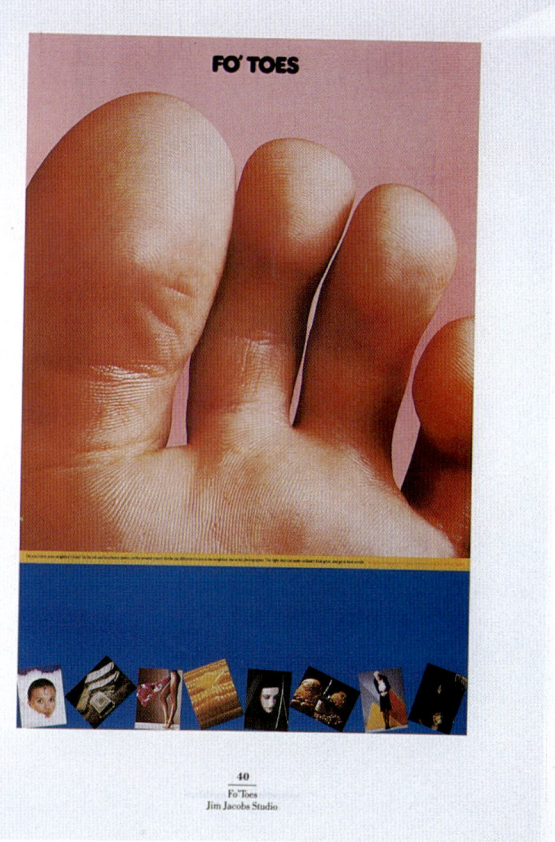
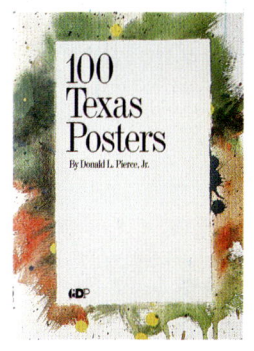

100 Texas Posters
1985

Jerry Herring
Art Director, Designer

Donald L. Pierce, Jr.
Copywriter

Herring Design
Design Firm

Graphic Design Press
Client

Pirtle Calendars
1984, 1985, 1986

Woody Pirtle
Art Director

Woody Pirtle,
Kenny Garrison, Jeff Weithman
Designers

Woody Pirtle,
Joe Rattan, Brian Kagan
Copywriters

Pirtle Design
Design Firm, Client

141

Tootsies Ads
(Series)
1979
Paula Savage
Art Director, Designer
Total Picture
Photographer
Mickey Rosemarin
Copywriter
Savage Design Group, Inc.
Design Firm, Agency
Tootsies
Client

Tootsies
(Series)
1978
Paula Savage
Art Director
Total Picture
Photographer
Savage Design Group, Inc.
Design Firm, Agency
Tootsies
Client

Anniversary 5
1981
Cap Pannell
Art Director
Cap Pannell, Cerita Smith
Designer
Carol St. George
Copywriter
Pannell/St. George
Design Firm
Tele-Image
Client

McGilvray Buick Mailer
1982

Jim Jacobs
Designer, Illustrator, Copywriter

Jim Jacobs' Studio
Design Firm

Anne McGilvray & Company
Client

Christmas Book
1977

Ann Barrington
Art Director

Olivette Hubler, Diane Chasey
Designers

Greg Booth and Assoc.
Photographer

Pat Steak
Copywriter

Hubler Roseburg & Assoc.
Design Firm

Neiman Marcus
Client

143

Redbird Mall Ad Series
1981

Woody Pirtle
Art Director, Designer, Illustrator

Mary Keck
Copywriter

Pirtle Design
Design Firm

Redbird Mall
Client

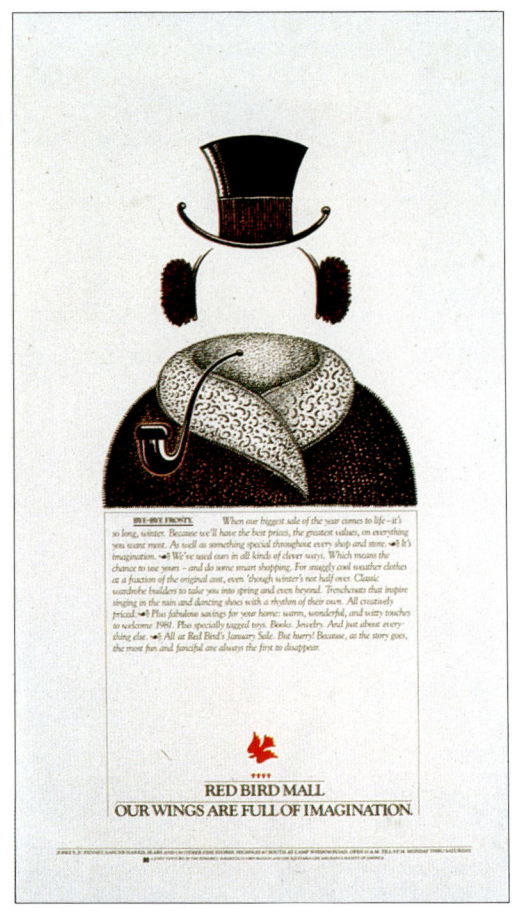
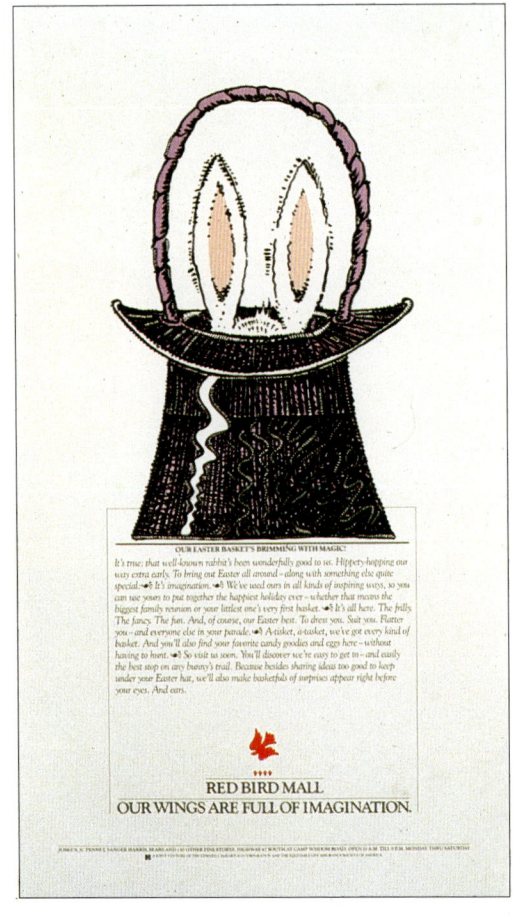
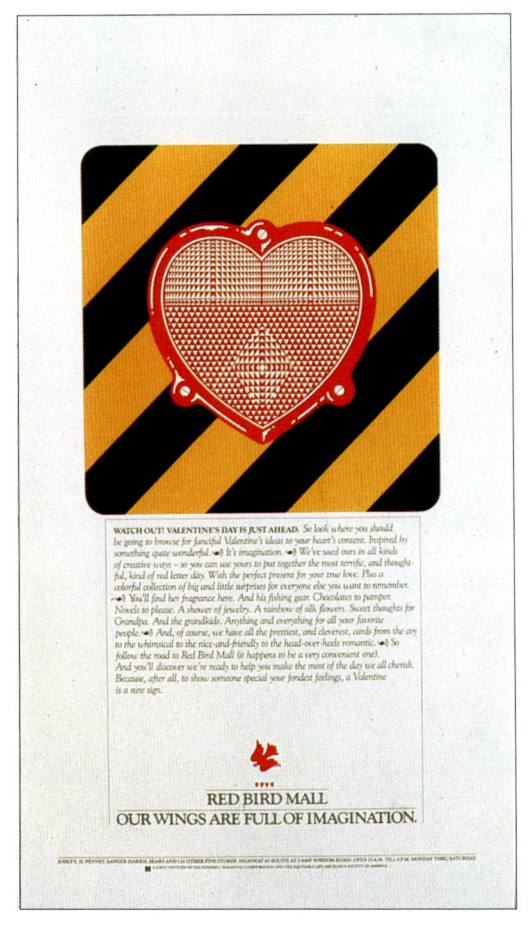

A.I.A. Houston
Poster
1982

Woody Pirtle
Art Director

Alan Colvin, Woody Pirtle
Designers

Arthur Meyerson, Joe Baraban
Photographers

Pirtle Design
Design Firm

Taylor Inc.
Agency

A.I.A. Houston
Client

Don Pierce Stationery
1976

Chris Hill
Art Director, Designer

Loucks Atelier Inc.
Design Firm

Don Pierce
Client

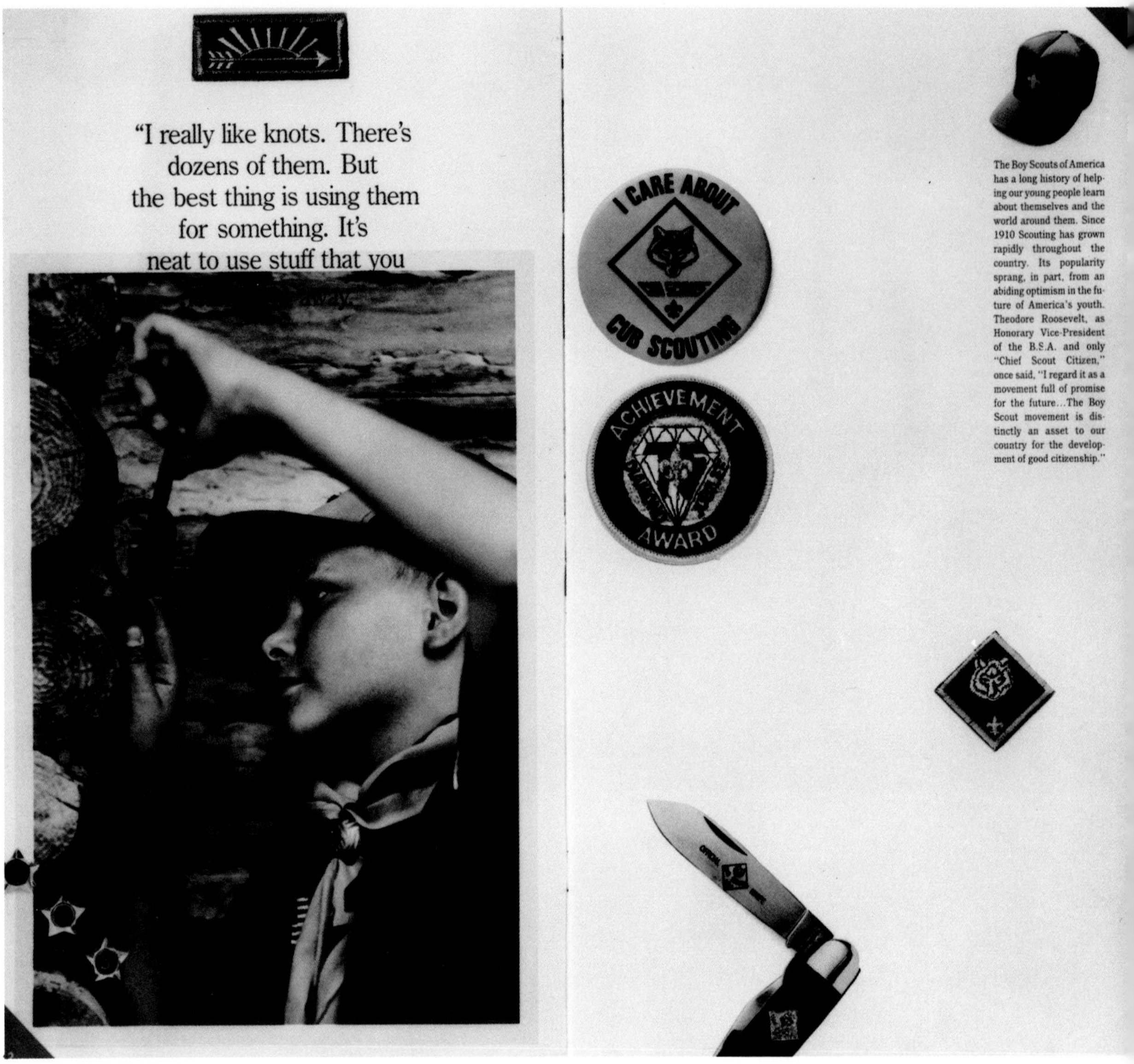

Boy Scouts
Circle 10 Council Brochure
1984
Brian Boyd
Art Director, Designer

Jim Sims
Photographer

Owen Page
Copywriter

Richards, Brock,
Miller, Mitchell & Associates
Design Firm

The Richards Group
Agency

Boy Scouts, Circle 10 Council
Client

The Bae
1974

Woody Pirtle
Designer

Greg Booth
Photographer

Stan Richards & Associates
Design Firm

Braniff International
Client

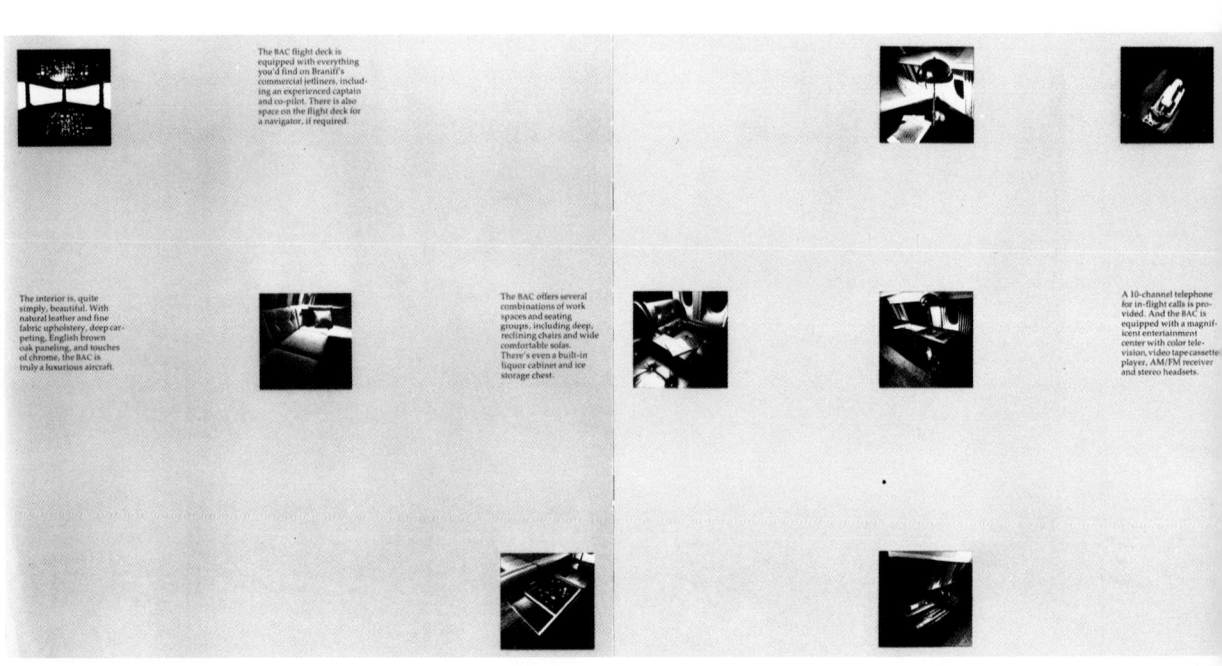

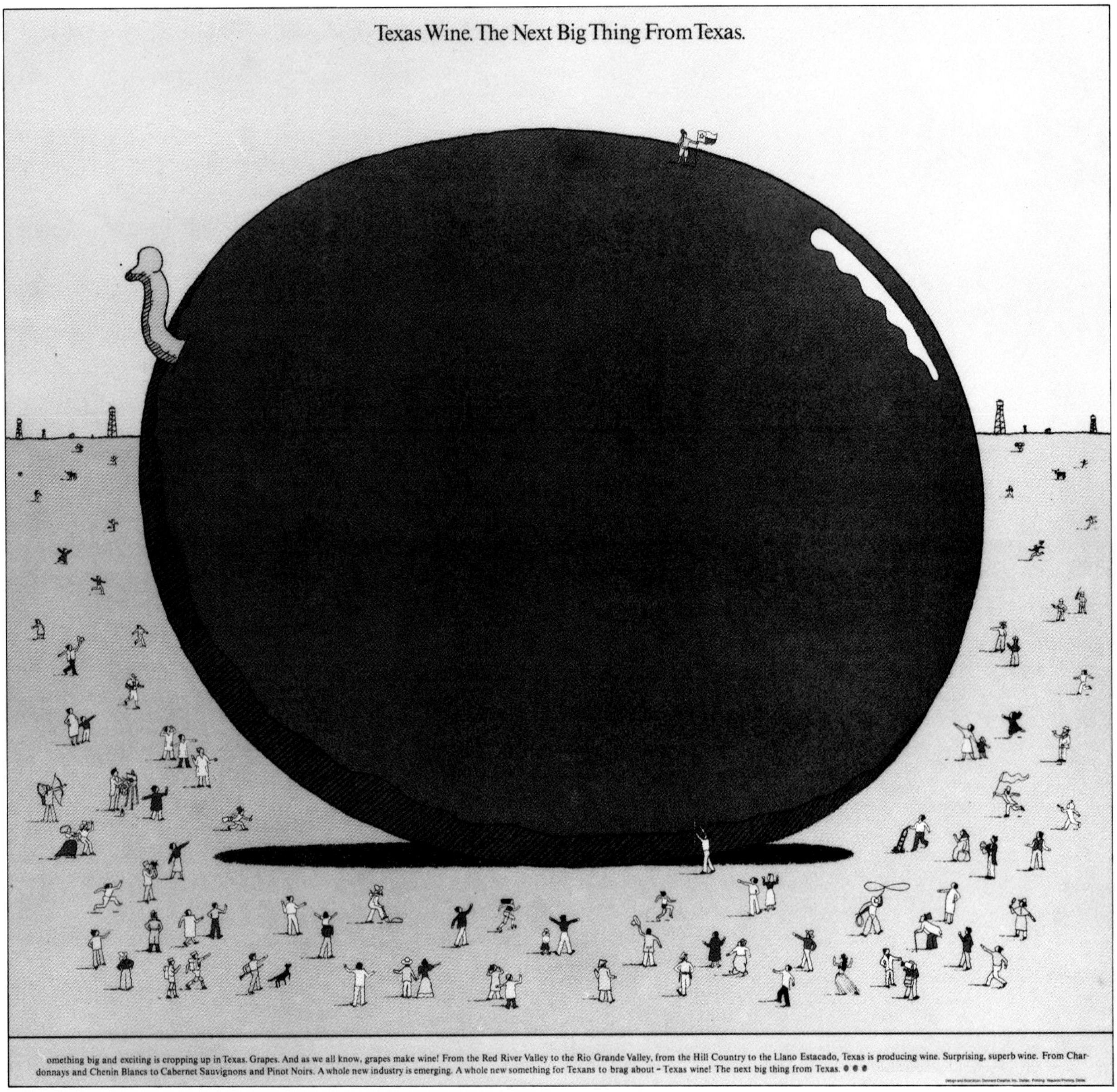

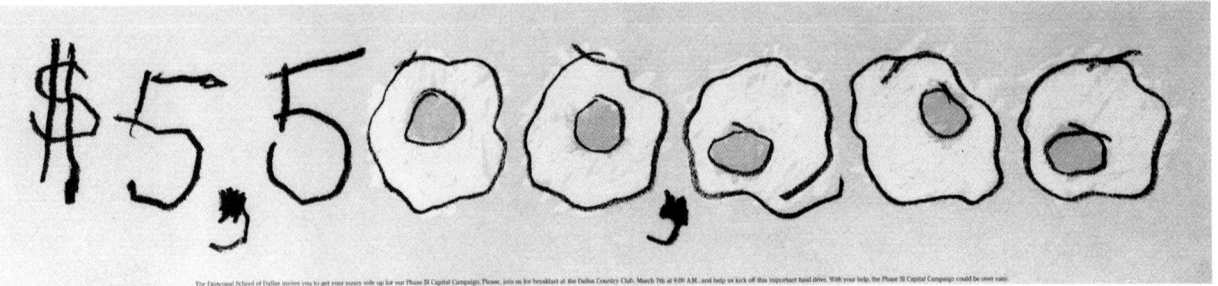

**Texas Wine
The Next Big Thing From Texas
1983**

Bob Dennard, Ken Koester
Art Directors

Ken Koester
Designer, Illustrator

John Crawley,
Bob Dennard, Jim Hightower
Copywriters

Dennard Creative, Inc.
Design Firm

Texas Department of Agriculture
Client

**5,500,000 Eggs
1984**

Doug May
Art Director, Designer

Chris Rovillo
Illustrator

Owen Page
Copywriter

Richards, Brock,
Miller, Mitchell & Associates
Design Firm

The Richards Group
Agency

Episcopal School of Dallas
Client

Cowboy Clock
1985
Neil L. Chavigny Jr.
Art Director
Neil L. Chavigny, Cathy Brown
Designers
Cathy Brown
Illustrator/Photographer
Argus Clock
Design Firm
Cotton Club/
Terrall Akers
Client

Pic Talkers
1983
Bob Dennard, Jan Wilson
Art Directors
Jan Wilson
Designer, Illustrator
Bob Dennard, Liza Orchard
Copywriters
Dennard Creative, Inc.
Design Firm
Pizza Inn
Client

 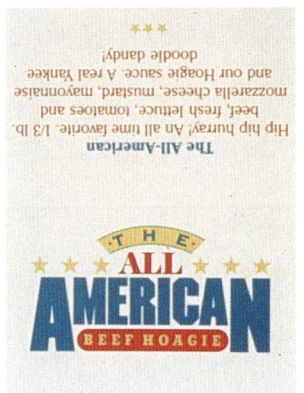 

US Film Festival Poster
1973

Cap Pannell
Art Director, Designer, Writer

Ron Sullivan
Illustrator

The Richards Group
Design Firm

US Film Festival
Client

Past Due
1982
Dean Narahara
Art Director, Designer
The Chaucer Group
Illustrators
Bruce Henry Davis
Copywriter
The Chaucer Group
Agency, Client

Acadiana Symphony
1985
Willie Baronet
Art Director, Designer
Acadiana Symphony Orchestra
Client

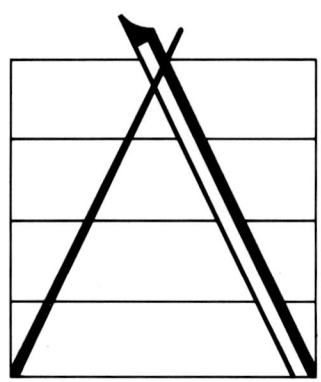

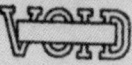

That's right.
We decided that a party was
desperately overdue to fill the

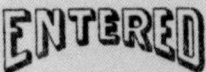

of social events between Halloween
and Christmas. So we

the kitchen
where the calendar is and

FINALly
NOTICEd

that absolutely nothing was happening
on Friday,

NOV 1 2 1982

So come on over
to 5512 Chaucer after work and have
some beer and wine

FOR INTERNAL USE ONLY

and more of the food that was so well

at our last party.
We'll have live music by the Shuffle Brothers,
who are a

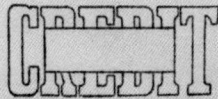

to their profession.
The only thing we ask is that you

DO NOT BEND

everybody's ears with boring business chatter.
And, if you wish to pay any compliments
to your party hosts,

PAY TO THE ORDER OF
THE CHAUCER GROUP
5512 CHAUCER DR.

*Steve Collier, Bruce Henry Davis, Mike Dean, Dee Dee Hunter,
Janice Mataya, Peggy McDaniel, Dean Narahara, Mary Reilly*

KVIL Album Cover Vol. 2
1983
Brian Boyd
Art Director, Designer

Andy Post
Photographer

Ron Chapman
Copywriter

Richards, Brock,
Miller, Mitchell & Associates
Design Firm

The Richards Group
Agency

KVIL Radio
Client

Moses Olmos Business Card
1969
Jerry Herring, Stan Richards
Art Directors

Jerry Herring
Designer

Stan Richards & Associates
Design Firm

Moses Olmos Photographer
Client

Infoworks Poster
1985

Woody Pirtle
Art Director, Designer

Jeff Weithman
Illustrator

Pirtle Design
Design Firm

Dallas Market Center/
Infoworks
Client

Infoworks Campaign
1985
Woody Pirtle
Art Director
Woody Pirtle,
Mike Schroeder, Jeff Weithman
Designers
Jeff Weithman, Mike Schroeder
Illustrators
Dana Collins
Copywriter
Pirtle Design
Design Firm
Dallas Market Center/
Infoworks
Client

153

Mental Health Law
1981
Steve Gibbs, Nancy Hoefig
Art Directors
Steve Gibbs
Designer
Terry Widener
Illustrator
Mary Keck
Copywriter
Richards, Sullivan,
Brock & Associates
Design Firm
The Richards Group
Agency
Mental Health Associates of Texas
Client

The Other Texas Frontier
1984
George Lenox
Art Director, Designer
Ed Lindlof
Illustrator
University of Texas Press
Client

Rules
1981

Jack Summerford
Art Director, Designer, Illustrator

Jack Summerford, Larry Sons
Copywriters

Summerford Design, Inc.
Design Firm

Typographers International Association
Client

Lone Star Donuts
1985

Rex Peteet
Art Director, Designer

John Evans
Illustrator

Sibley/Peteet Design
Design Firm

Saunders, Lubinski & White
Agency

Lone Star Donuts
Client

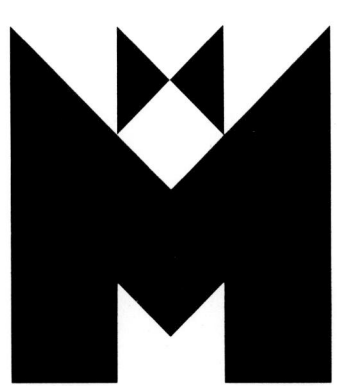

Manhattan Laundry & Dry Cleaning
1985

Arthur Eisenberg, Don Arday
Art Directors

Don Arday
Designer, Illustrator

Eisenberg Inc.
Design Firm

Manhattan Laundry & Dry Cleaning
Client

Town Center Campaign/
Ice Cream Ad
1980

Rex Peteet, Woody Pirtle
Art Directors

Rex Peteet
Designer

Rex Peteet, Luis Acevedo,
Woody Pirtle
Illustrators

Mary Keck
Copywriter

Pirtle Design
Design Firm

Federated Stores Realty, Inc.
Client

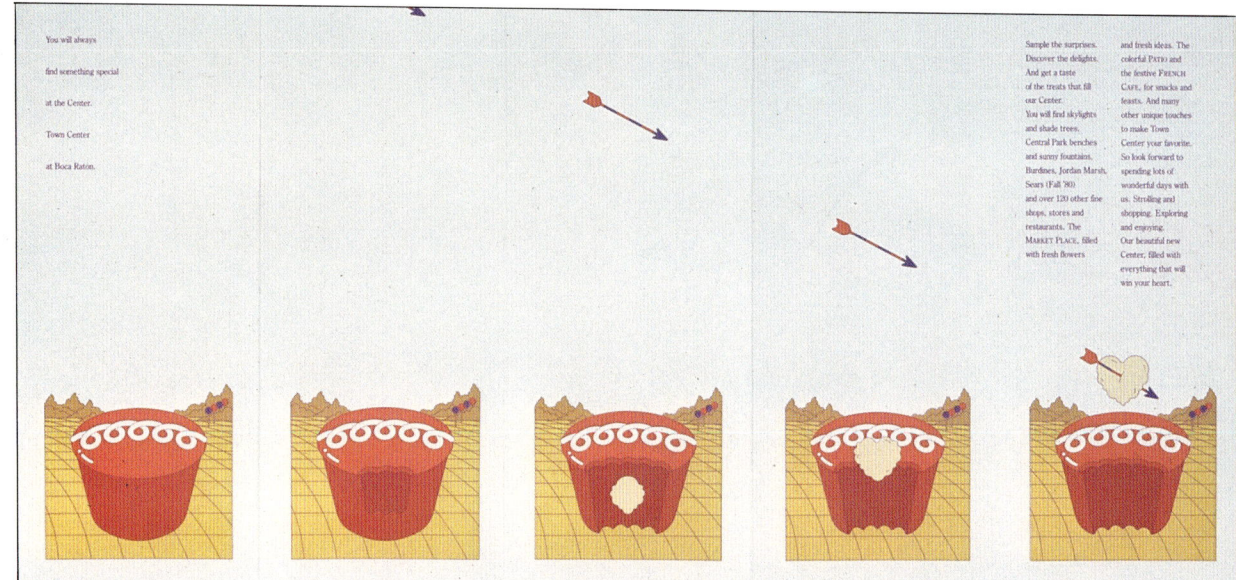

Jay Silverman Talks Business
1984
Jim Jacobs
Art Director, Designer, Copywriter
Jay Silverman
Photographer
Jim Jacobs' Studio
Design Firm
A.S.M.P.
Client

Villa Linda Mall
Grand Opening Posters
(Series)
1985
Don Sibley
*Art Director, Designer,
Illustrator, Copywriter*

Sibley/Peteet Design, Inc.
Design Firm

The Herring Group/
Villa Linda Mall
Client

Whispering Words
1981
Alan Lidji
Art Director, Designer

Mary Keck
Copywriter

Alan Lidji Design
Design Firm

The Dallas Morning News
Client

Washing the Cow's Skull
1981

Jim Jacobs
Designer

Jim Jacobs' Studio
Design Firm

Prickly Pear Press
Client

North Park Legend Campaign
1978
Ron Sullivan, Rex Peteet
Art Directors

Rex Peteet
Designer, Illustrator

Mary Keck
Copywriter

The Richards Group
Design Firm

The Nasher Co./
North Park
Client

Dallas Society of
Visual Communications
Letterhead
1973
Woody Pirtle
Art Director, Designer

Don Grimes
Illustrator

Stan Richards & Associates
Agency

Dallas Society of
Visual Communications
Client

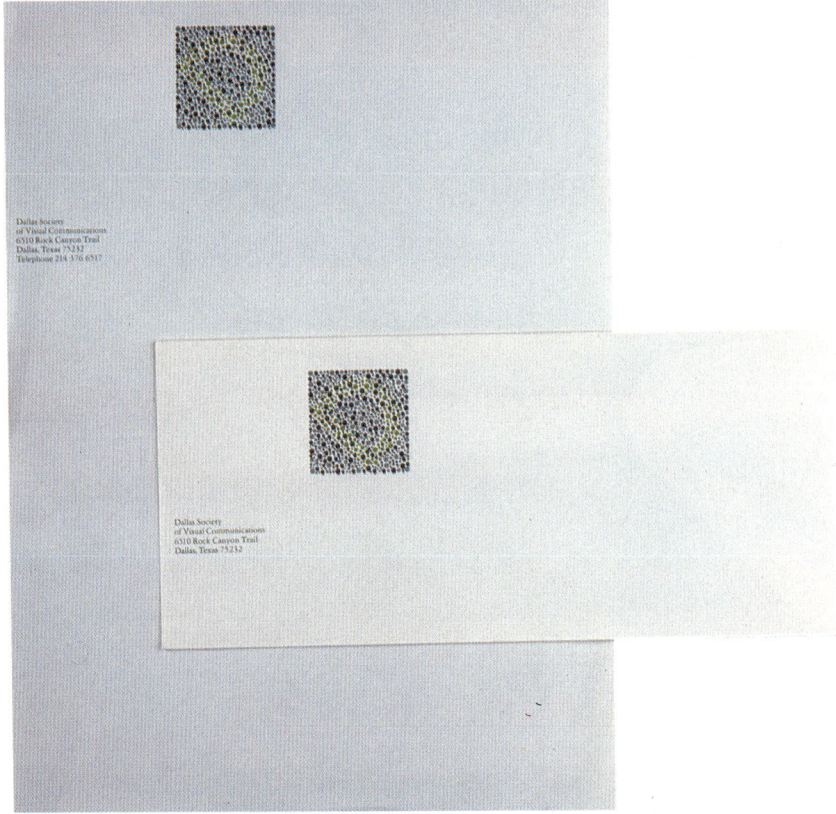

Heritage Press
Christmas Rudolph
1980
Woody Pirtle, Mike Schroeder
Art Directors, Designers
Mike Schroeder
Illustrator
Woody Pirtle
Copywriter
Pirtle Design
Design Firm
Heritage Press
Client

Good Earth Restaurant
Breakfast Menu
1984
Rex Peteet
Art Director, Designer

Rex Peteet, Jerry Jeanmard
Illustrators

Sibley/Peteet Design, Inc.
Design Firm

Good Earth Restaurants
Client

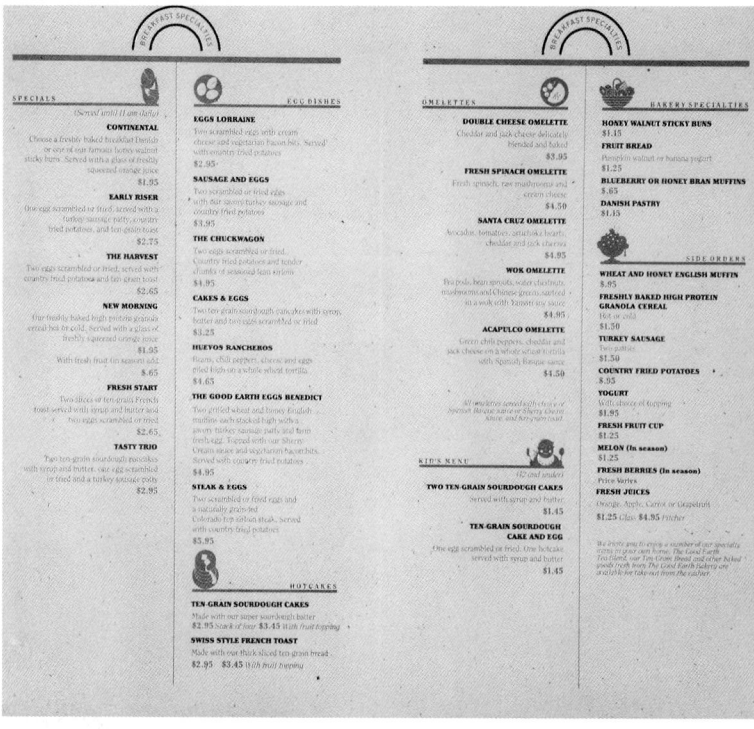

Bread & Butter Client Party
Invitation
1968
John Heck
Art Director, Designer

Anna Jane Wingfield
Copywriter

Goodwin Dannenbaum,
Littman & Wingfield
Agency, Client

 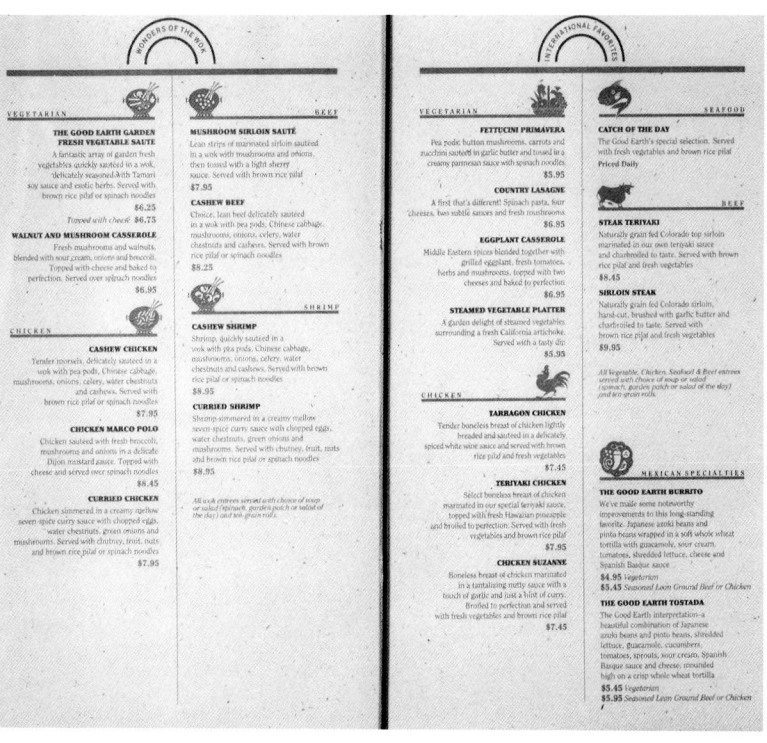

Good Earth Restaurant Menu
1984
Rex Peteet
Art Director, Designer
Rex Peteet, Jerry Jeanmard, Don Sibley, Ken Shafer
Illustrators
Sibley/Peteet Design, Inc.
Design Firm
Good Earth Restaurants
Client

Priore Tiny Ad
1984
Jim Jacobs
Art Director, Designer, Illustration, Copywriter
Jim Jacobs' Studio
Design Firm
Priore BMW Autocare
Client

Omnibus Ad
(Series)
1985

Ron Sullivan
Art Director

Linda Helton, Diana McKnight,
Jon Flaming
Designers

Mark Perkins
Copywriter

Sullivan Perkins
Design Firm

The Rouse Company/
St. Louis Union Station
Client

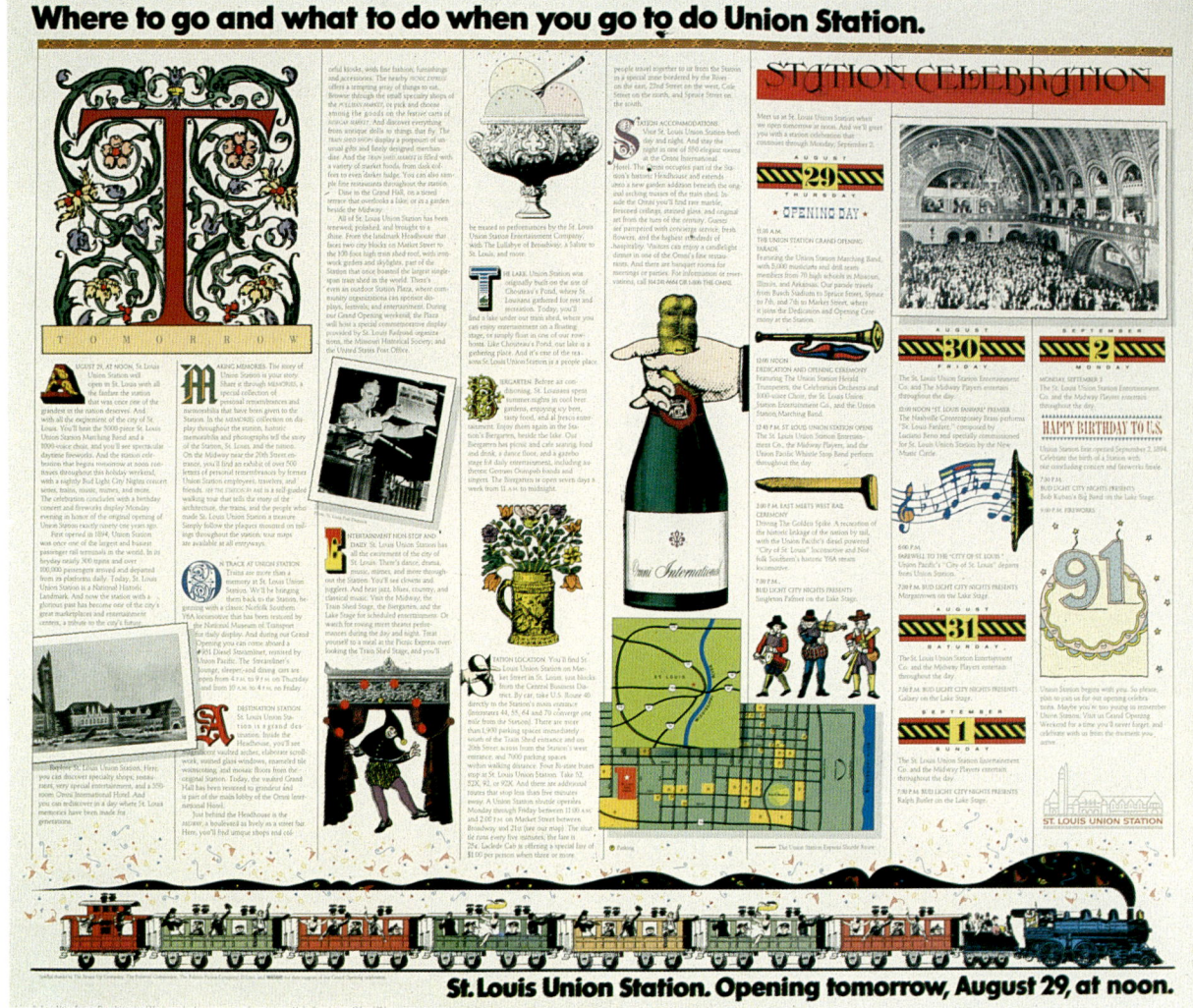

Beachwood Place Ads
1978

Woody Pirtle
*Art Director, Designer,
Illustrator*

Jim Hradecky
Copywriter

The Richards Group
Design Firm, Agency

The Rouse Company
Client

164

Crackerjack Poster
1985

Bob Dennard,
Glyn Powell, Judy Dolim
Art Directors

Judy Dolim
Designer

Judy Dolim, Glyn Powell,
Chuck Johnson, Bryan Collins,
Steve Chambers, Greg King,
Ken Koester
Illustrators/Photographers

David Martin
Copywriter

Dennard Creative, Inc.
Design Firm

Dallas Society of
Visual Communication
Client

165

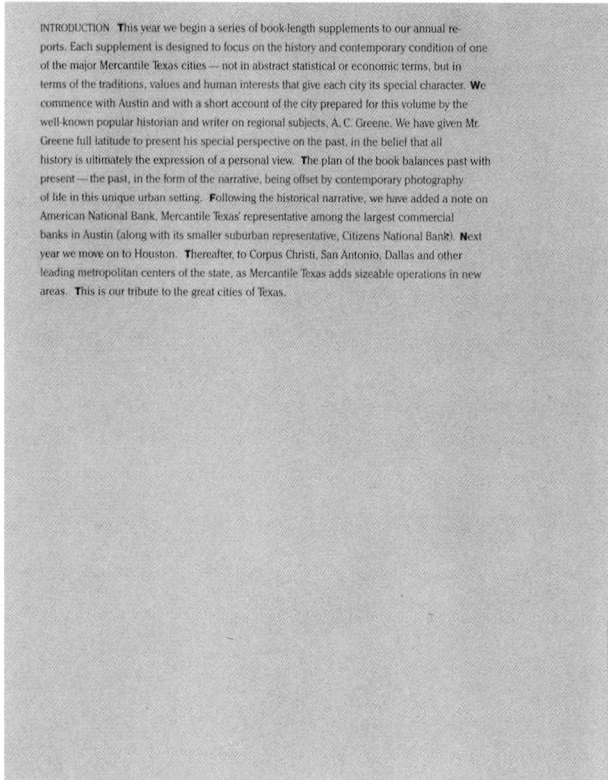

Austin Commerative Book
1981
Dick Mitchell
Art Director, Designer
Greg Booth
Photographer
A.C. Green
Copywriter
Richards, Sullivan,
Brock & Associates
Design Firm
The Richards Group
Agency
Mercantile Texas Corporation
Client

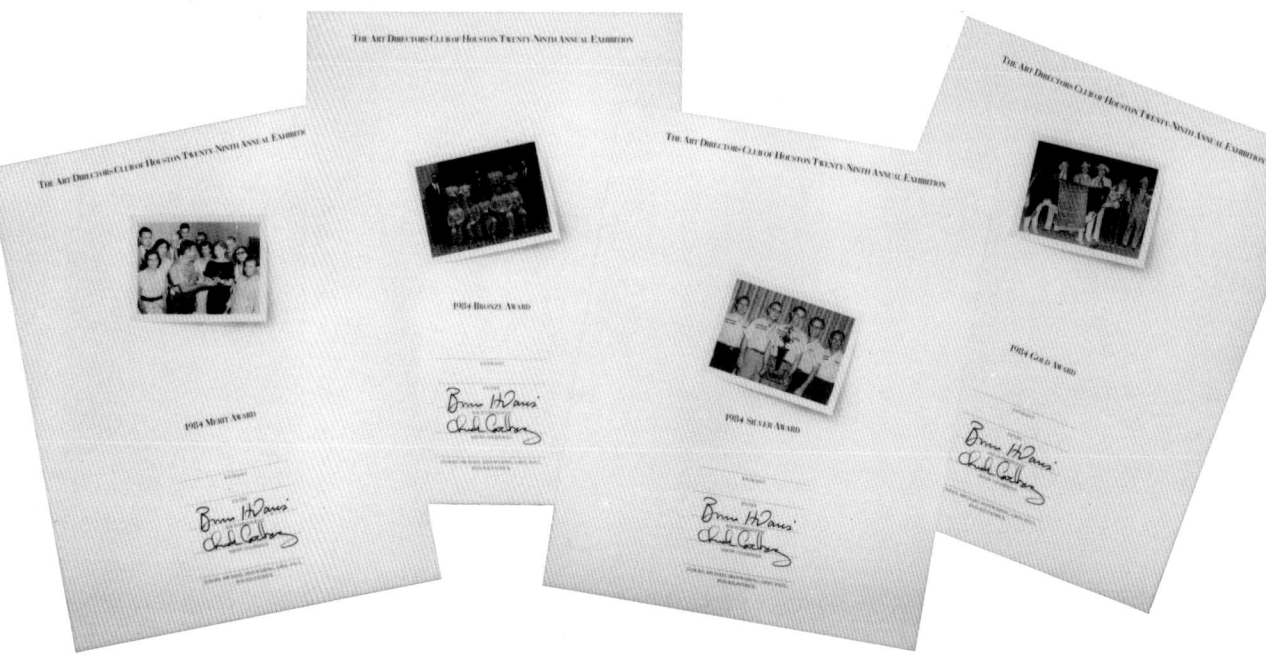

ADCH Award Certificates
(Series)
1985
Richard Kilmer, Mark Geer
Art Directors, Designers
Kilmer/Geer Design
Design Firm
Art Directors Club of Houston
Client

AIGA-Texas Magazine Design
1986
Duana Gill, Mike Hicks
Art Directors
Mike Hicks, Melinda Williams
Designers
Mike Hicks,
Duana Gill, Melinda Williams
Copywriters
Hixo, Inc.
Design Firm
AIGA-Texas
Client

Northern Telecom Comtel
Convention Invitation
1986
Brian Boyd
*Art Director, Designer,
Illustrator*

Melinda Marcus
Copywriter

Richards, Brock,
Miller, Mitchell & Associates
Design Firm

The Richards Group
Agency

Northern Telecom
Client

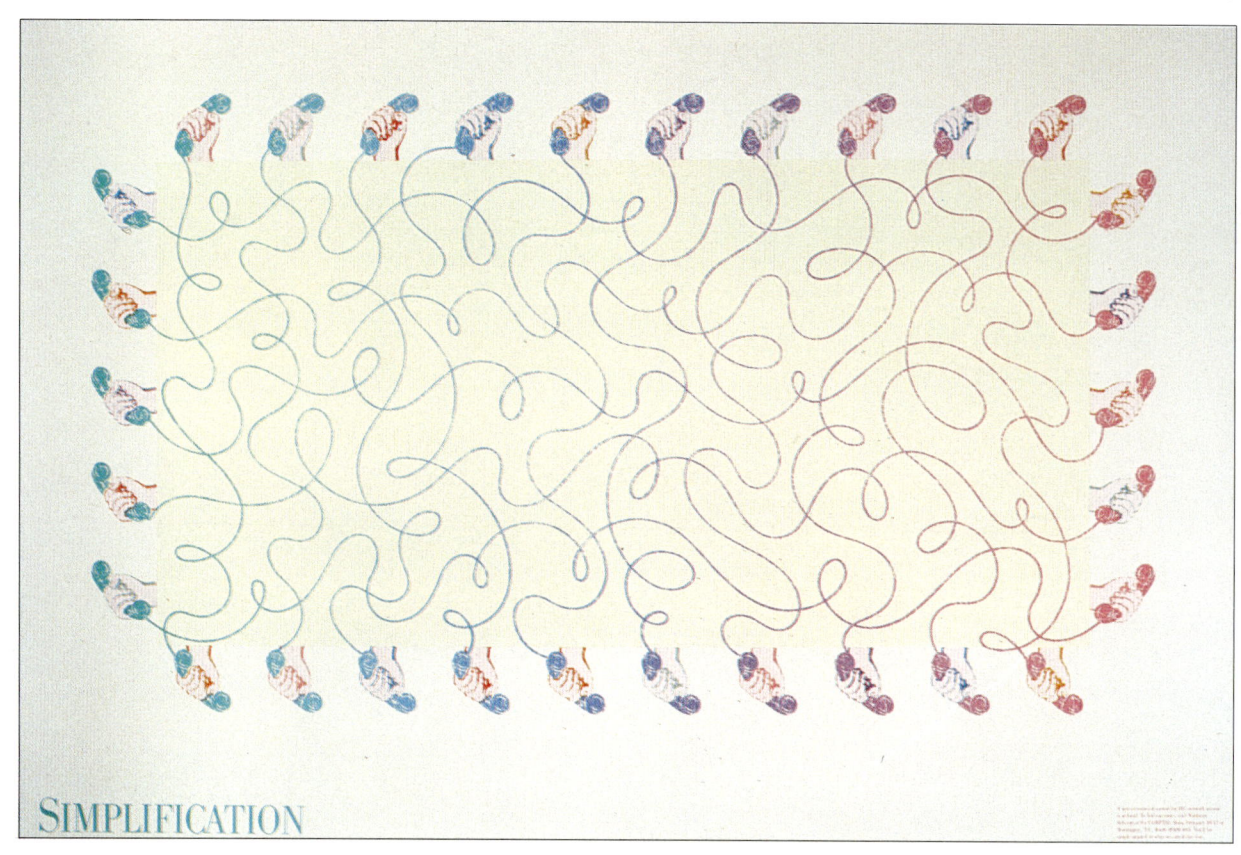

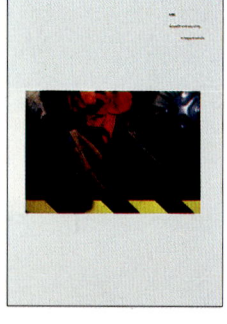

RMI
1985
Steven Sessions
Art Director, Designer

Jim Sims
Photographer

Greg Bolton
Copywriter

Steven Sessions Design
Design Firm

RMI
Client

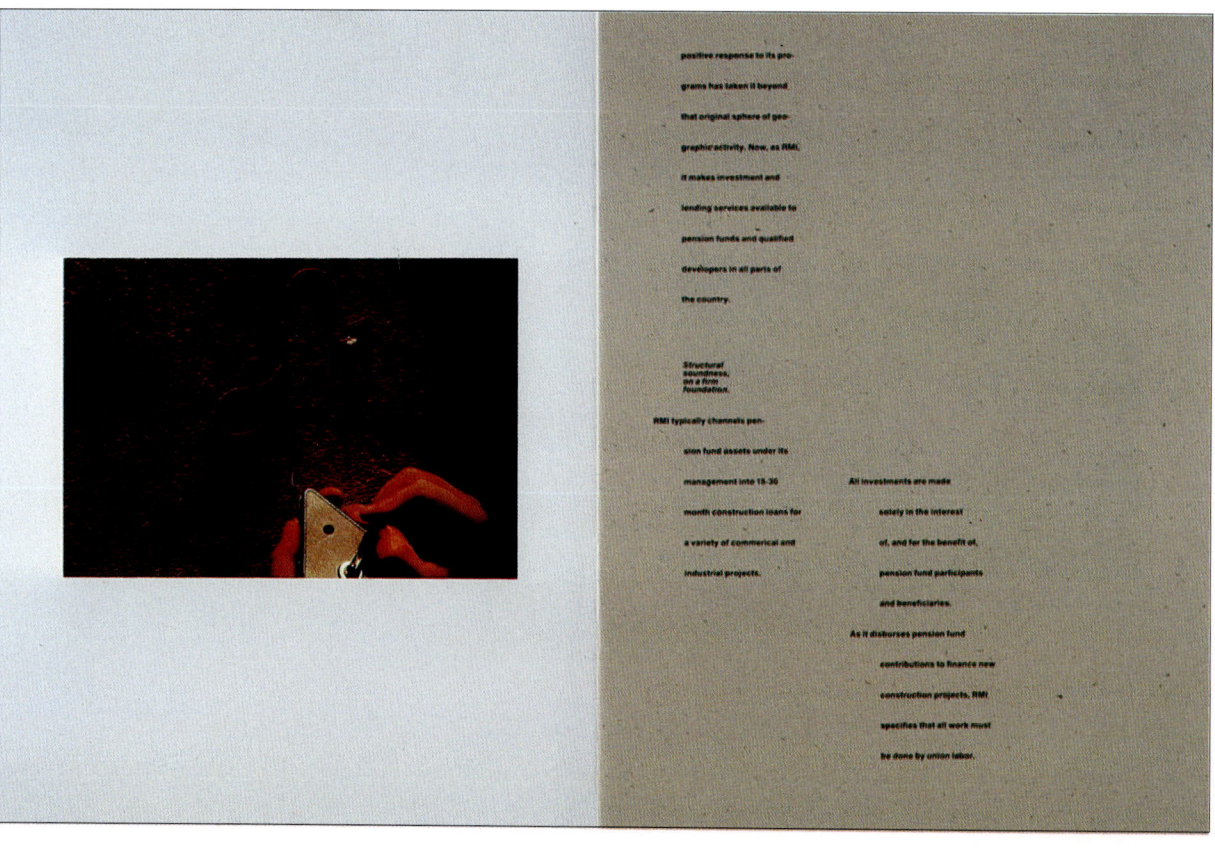

Cobb & Friend Poster
1985
Luis Acevedo
Art Director, Designer, Illustrator

Luis Acevedo, Woody Pirtle
Copywriters

Pirtle Design
Design Firm

Cobb & Friend
Client

Oops Poster
1981
Mike Schroeder
Art Director, Designer, Illustrator
Mike Schroeder, Carol St. George
Copywriters
Pirtle Design
Design Firm
Olmsted-Kirk Paper Co./ Scott Towel
Clients

The Killdeer Crying
1977
Jim Jacobs
Art Director, Designer
Jack Unruh
Illustrator
William Barney
Copywriter
Jim Jacobs' Studio
Design Firm
Prickly Pear Press
Client

Praise for a Honey Locust

So cruel a tree, a stiff defiant cock
plucking his gaffed grim heel from the dun sand:
look how his wattles blow in hard lake wind,
gleaming of late-spilled blood, a ribald wake
of battle. Tree fashioned also an altar,
where the priest-shrike can immolate, impale
his penitents, mark us the sparrow's fall,
wren's bier, grasshopper's fatal shelter.

A tree so cruel none can forage,
what comeliness can quicken in my eye
to catch and hang upon the harsh riposte
of thorns that prick the heart's thin purse –
that sac of hope too tender for much storage
riddles, the lean wealth is drained away?
Praise for the caltrop fangs, bleak bitter spikes
aglitter in a gray day ungently. So
let me put on the rowels of raw larks,
lunge at a fat world till it draw
back from my foot, give me room to sun.
Or howl at my approach, seeing me spined,
calamitous as some churlish saint
crying repentance by a burning bank.

Praise for the honey locust: belligerent,
his desert precedent I thank.
Stark wood piercing air with an outrage
against all sleek felicity,
in a made world gives no harborage
for bookish bleat or pious formula.
On keen excrescences like these have hung
lizards of quickest foot, peddlers of song,
those agonized who cried in God's grave tongue.

On Greer Island a Copperhead Lies Slain

One of the owners of this isle
lies here, head clipped from slaughtered corse,
lies here, for all reputed guile,
tricked into stiffness, shorn of force.
    Assassin, while he trod his fief,
    you struck his angry armor off.

This jack of diamonds dull and smooth,
this copper-coopered smoldering band,
thicket will never again soothe
him sleeping in sleek ampersand.
    The spice of peril shall be gone
    from fallen log, from flaggy stone.

What easy thing now shall we say
for sentiment, a small rebate
to salve with pardon? Rather pray
for your enemy in his strait.
    This Ichabod has left us poorer.
    Where shall we turn for simple terror?

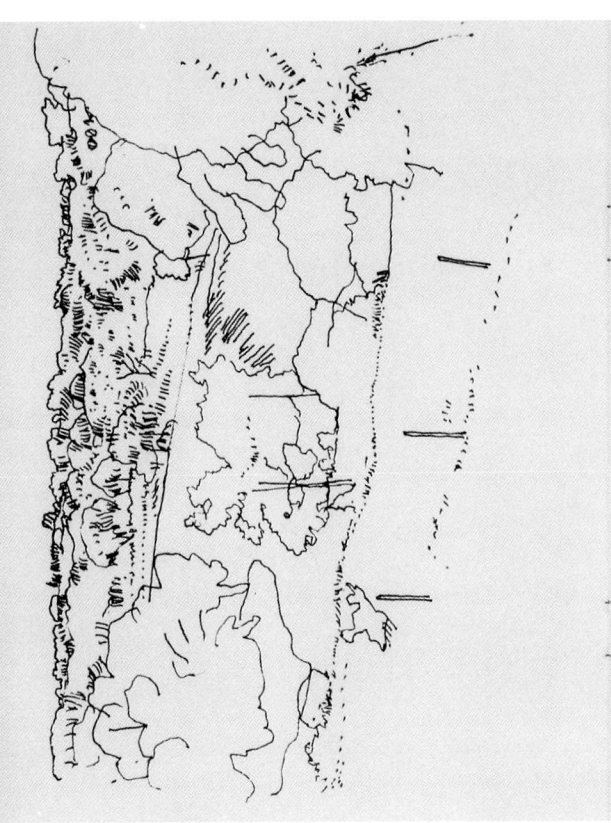

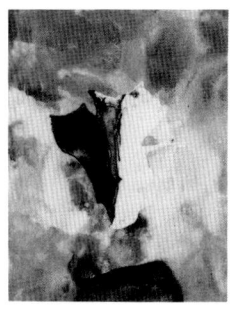

Drawings & Notes II
1983
Jerry Herring
Art Director, Designer
Charles Schorre
Illustrator, Designer, Copywriter
Herring Design
Design Firm
Seashore Press
Client

If you are sick, they'll care for you here.

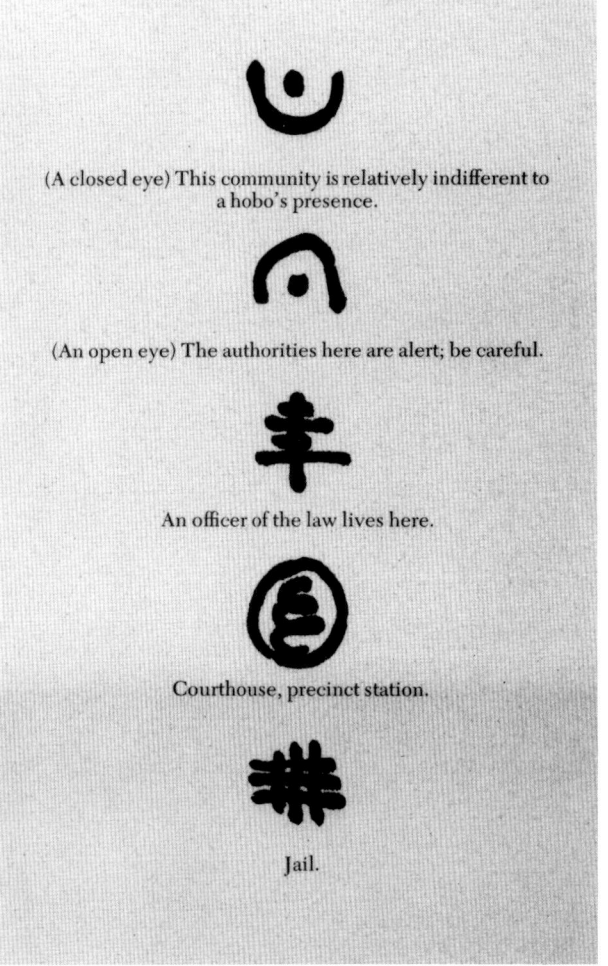

(A closed eye) This community is relatively indifferent to a hobo's presence.

(An open eye) The authorities here are alert; be careful.

An officer of the law lives here.

Courthouse, precinct station.

Jail.

Hobo Book
1966
Stan Richards
Art Director
Jim Jacobs
Designer, Illustrator, Copywriter
Stan Richards & Associates
Design Firm
Canterbury Press
Client

Milton Glass Poster
1985
Woody Pirtle
Art Director

Woody Pirtle, Jeff Weithman
Designers, Illustrators, Copywriters

Pirtle Design
Design Firm

Dallas Society of Visual Communications
Client

172

Picnic in the Park
1985
Pete Madrulli, Beth Secker
Designers
Beth Secker
Illustrator
RTKL Associates, Inc.
Design Firm
The Lehndorff Group/
Park Central, Phoenix
Client

Big Day Poster
1983

Chris Rovillo
Art Director, Designer

Mark Perkins
Copywriter

Richards, Sullivan,
Brock & Associates
Design Firm

The Richards Group
Agency

Dallas Society of
Visual Communications
Client

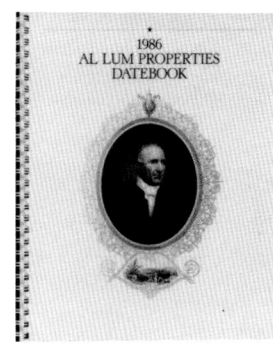

Al Lum Properties Datebook
1985

Jerry Herring
Art Director

John Heck
Designer

Rick Gardner
Photographer

Jim McElgunn
Copywriter

Herring Design
Design Firm

Al Lum Properties
Client

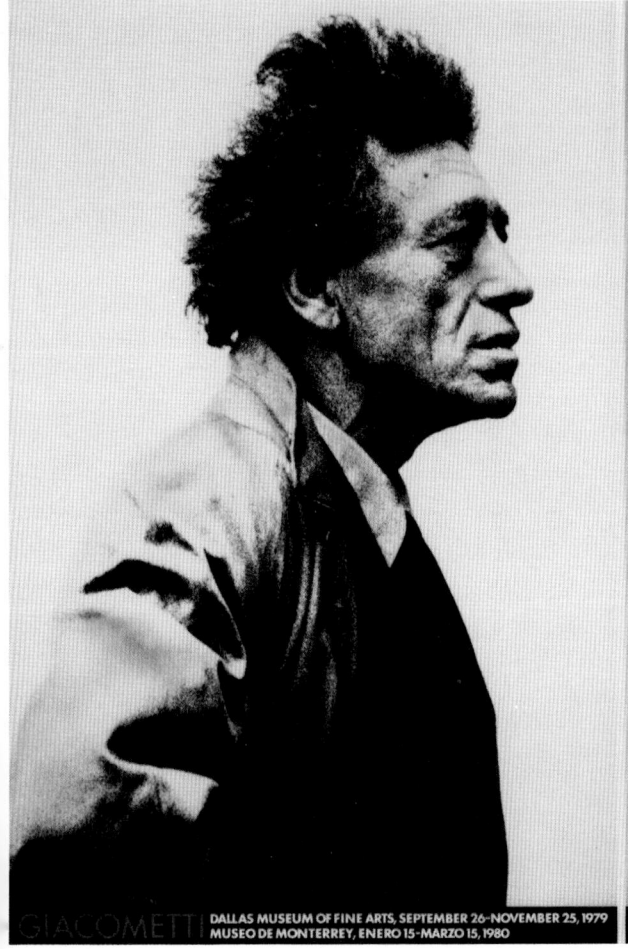

DMFA Giacometti Poster
1979

Jim Jacobs
Designer

Dick Jones
Retoucher

Jim Jacobs' Studio
Design Firm

Dallas Museum of Fine Art
Client

Zapf Poster
1983

Jay Loucks
Art Director

C. Randall Sherman
Designer

Hermann Zapf
Illustrator

Don Pierce
Copywriter

Loucks Atelier, Inc.
Design Firm

Palmer Paper Co.
Client

Shakespearean Nights
1980
Woody Pirtle
Art Director, Designer, Illustrator

Mike Schroeder
Copywriter

Pirtle Design
Design Firm

Shakespeare Festival of Dallas
Client

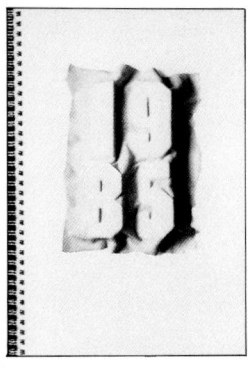

1985/Trompe L'oeil
1984
Alan Lidji
Art Director, Designer

John Eickmeyer
Copywriter

Alan Lidji Design
Design Firm

Webb & Sons
Client

No Clowning Around
1986
Cap Pannell
Art Director, Designer, Illustrator

Gary Goodwin
Photographer

Carol St. George
Copywriter

Pannell/St. George
Design Firm

Learning Technologies, Inc.
Client

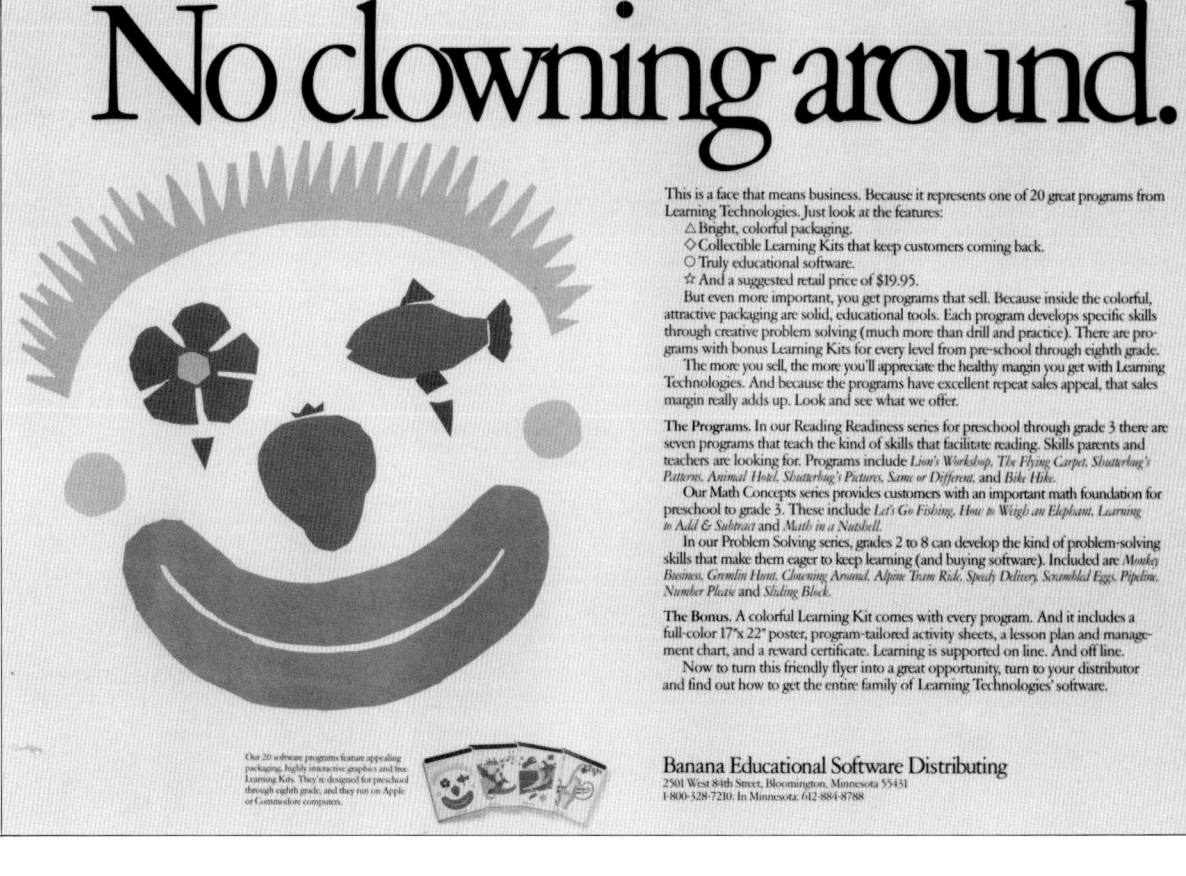

State Fair of Texas Poster
1976
Dennis Benoit
Art Director, Designer
Jack Unruh
Illustrator
Benoit Rutter, Inc.
Design Firm
State Fair Texas
Client

The Market
1985
Jim Sailor, Beth Secker
Designers
Jim Busby, Beth Secker
Illustrator/Photographer
RTKL Associates, Inc.
Design Firm
Bramalea Texas, Inc./
InterFirst Building
Client

Grand Opening Ads
1976
Bob Dennard
Art Director, Designer
Woody Pirtle,
Ron Sullivan, Larry Sons
Illustrators
Bob Dennard
Copywriter
The Richards Group
Design Firm
The Nasher Company
Client

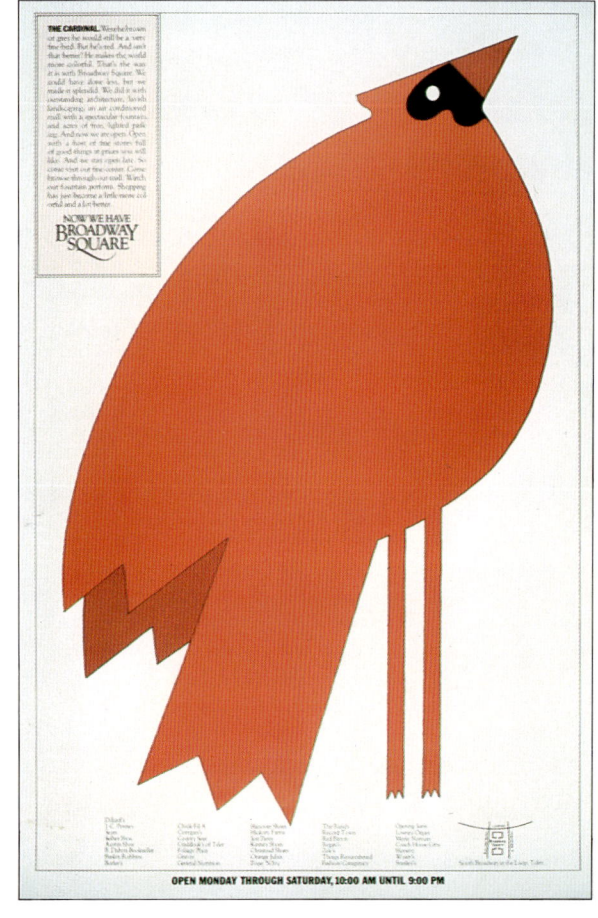 

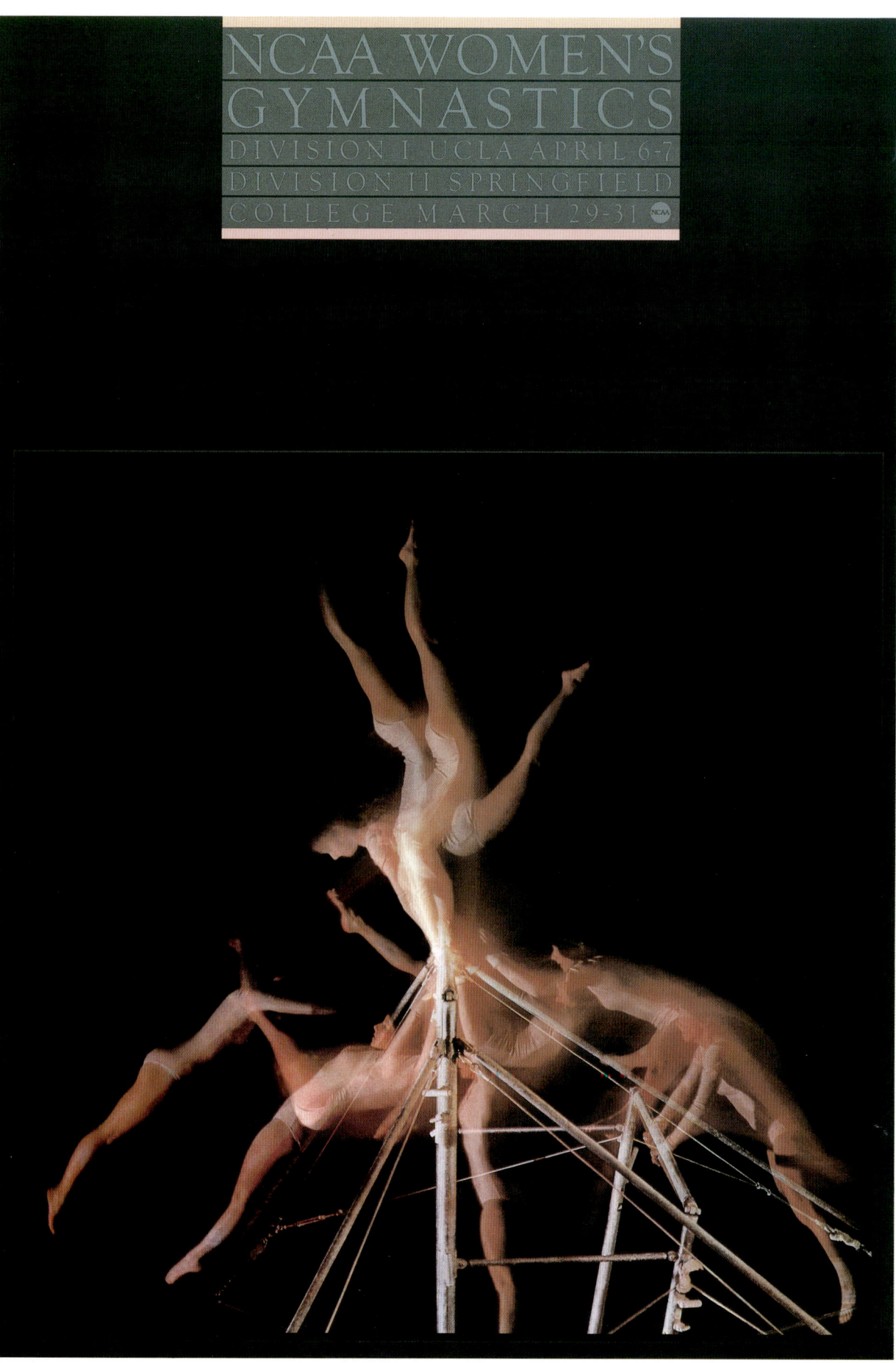

NCAA Women's Gymnastics
Championship
1984
Chris Hill
Art Director
Chris Hill, Joe Rattan
Designers
Steve Brady
Photographer
HILL/A Marketing Design Group
Design Firm
NCAA
Client

Houston Art Directors Club
Student Show
1984

Chris Hill, Jeffrey McKay
Art Directors, Designers

Mary Langridge
Copywriter

HILL/A Marketing Design Group
Design Firm

Houston Art Directors Club
Client

Art Investors Gallery
1983

Cap Pannell
Art Director, Designer

Carol Burke
Illustrator

Pannell/St. George
Design Firm

Sunwest Communications
Agency

Art Investors Gallery
Client

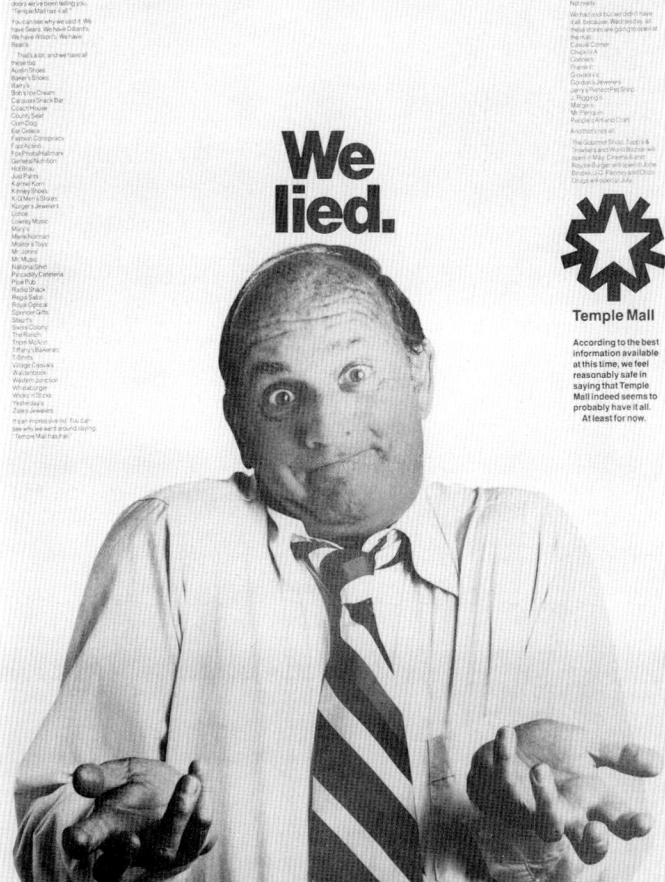

Cherry On Top Ad
1977
Rex Peteet
Art Director, Designer, Illustrator
Rex Peteet
Copywriter
The Richards Group
Design Firm
The Rouse Company
Client

Santas Ad
1977
Rex Peteet
Art Director, Designer, Illustrator
Larry Sons
Copywriter
The Richards Group
Design Firm
Paul Broadhead & Associates
Client

We Lied
1979
Jim Jacobs
Art Director, Designer, Copywriter
Jim Jacobs' Studio
Design Firm
Ad Works
Agency
Temple Mall
Client

D Magazine Best & Worst
1979
Rex Peteet, Woody Pirtle
Art Directors
Rex Peteet
Designer
Tom Curry
Illustrator
Pirtle Design
Design Firm
D Magazine
Client

Dallas Judges Cover
1979
Woody Pirtle, Carol Burke
Art Directors
Woody Pirtle
Designer
Robert Latorre
Photographer
Pirtle Design
Design Firm
D Magazine
Client

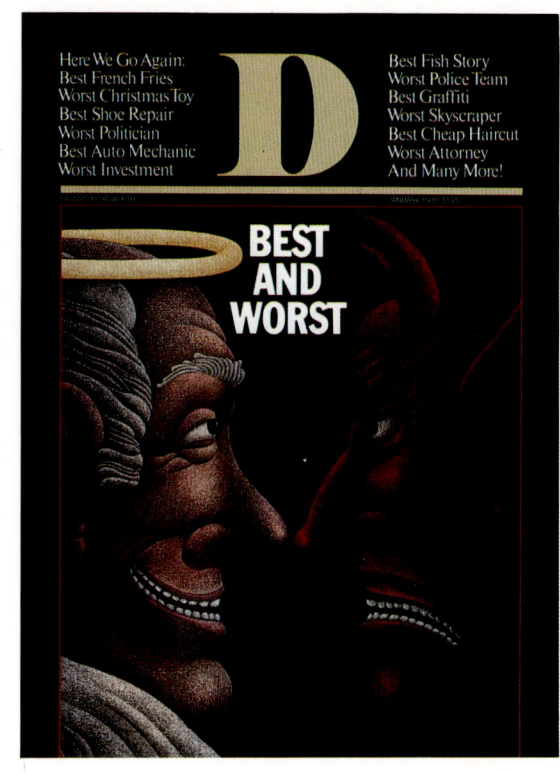

Cardiology Spread
1979
Woody Pirtle, Carol Burke
Art Directors
Woody Pirtle
Designer
Pirtle Design
Design Firm
D Magazine
Client

High Rollers Spread
1979
Woody Pirtle
Art Director, Designer
Pirtle Design
Design Firm
D Magazine
Client

Yard Art Spread
1979
Woody Pirtle, Carol Burke
Art Directors
Woody Pirtle
Designer, Illustrator
Pirtle Design
Design Firm
D Magazine
Client

Bayou City Oyster Co. Menu
1982
Lowell Williams
Art Director, Designer
Jim Sims
Photographer
Lowell Williams Design, Inc.
Design Firm, Agency
Bayou City Oyster Co.
Client

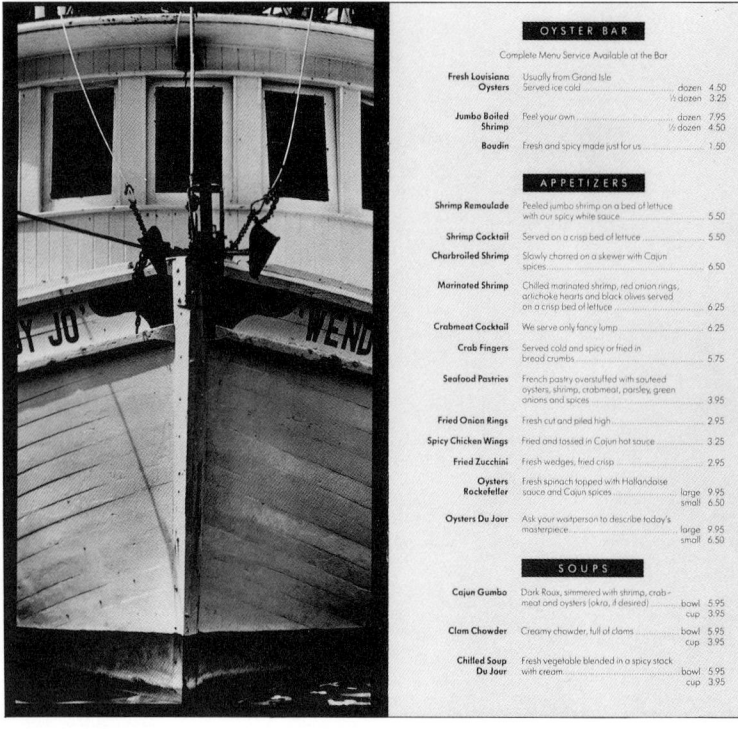

Superb Litho Brochure
1983
Chris Hill
Art Director
Chris Hill, Joe Rattan
Designers
Gary Braasch
Photographer
Robert Frost
Copywriter
HILL/A Marketing Design Group
Design Firm
Superb Litho
Client

Stock Trade Marks
1977
Jerry Herring
Art Director, Designer, Copywriter
Herring Design
Design Firm, Client

Tom Thumb Produce Campaign
1978
Don Sibley
Art Director, Designer
The Bettman Archive
Photographer
Don Sibley, Barbara Harwell
Copywriter
KCBN Advertising
Agency
Tom Thumb-Page
Client

Birthday Cake Poster
1981

Woody Pirtle
Art Director, Designer, Illustrator

Pirtle Design
Design Firm

Shakespeare Festival of Dallas
Client

188

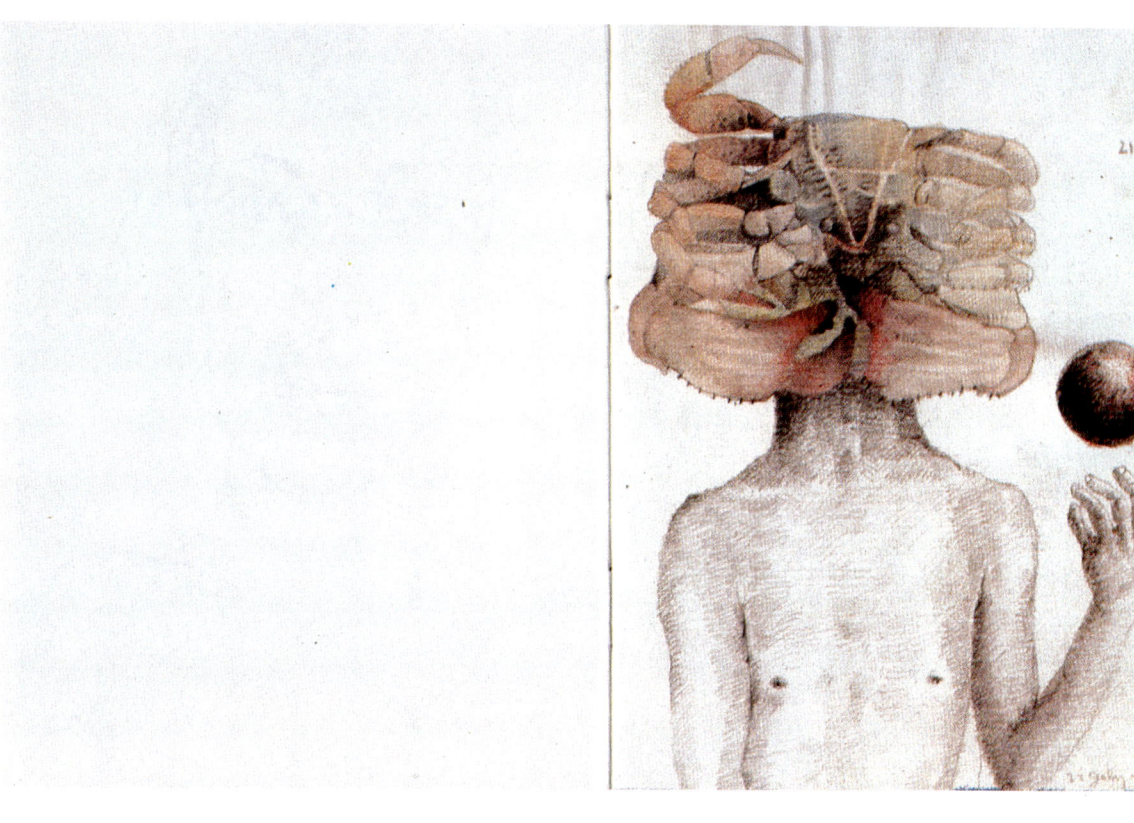

Alan Cober's Sketch Book
1979
Chris Hill
Art Director, Designer
Alan Cober
Illustrator
HILL/A Marketing Design Group
Design Firm
Art Directors Club of Houston
Client

North Hills Banners
1985
Beth Secker
Art Director
Bart Chambers,
Beth Secker, Theo Kondos
Designers
Beth Secker
Illustrator
RTKL Associates, Inc.
Design Firm
JMB Federated/
North Hills Mall
Client

Texas Guide Book
1979
Mike Hicks
Art Director, Designer, Copywriter
Hixo, Inc.
Design Firm
Texas Monthly
Client

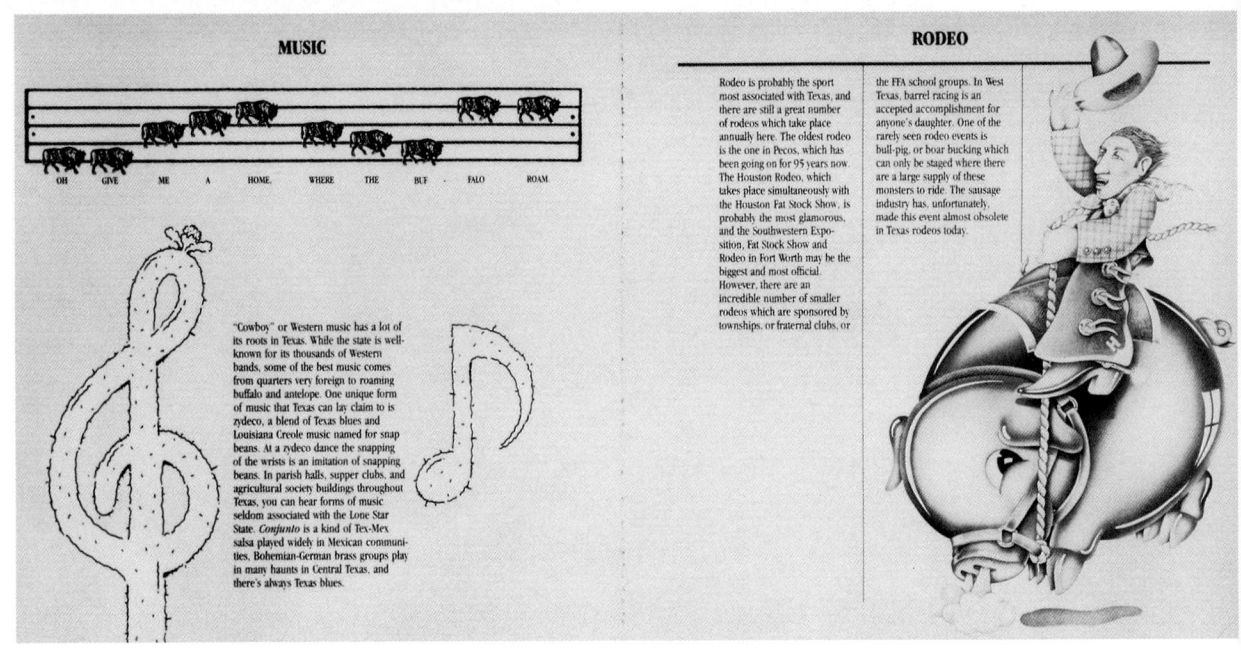

How To Be Texan
1982
Tom Poth, Mike Hicks
Art Directors
Mike Hicks
Designer, Copywriter
Hixo, Inc.
Design Firm
Texas Monthly Press
Client

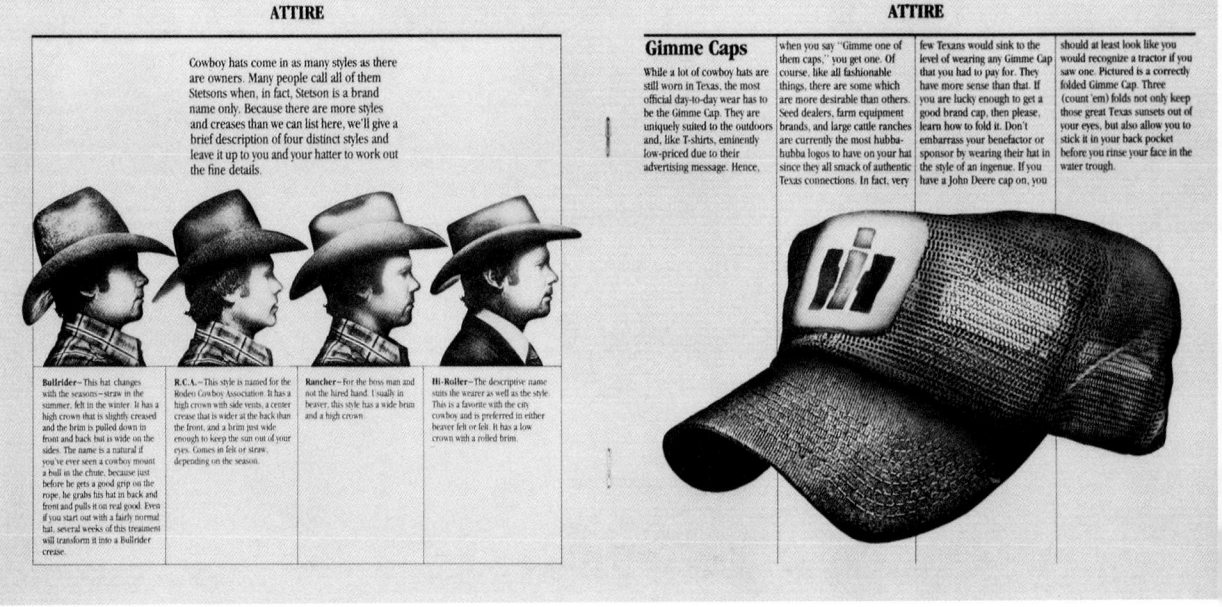

The South Made Simpler
1982
Tom Poth, Mike Hicks
Art Directors, Designers
Mike Hicks
Copywriter
Hixo, Inc.
Design Firm
Texas Monthly Press
Client

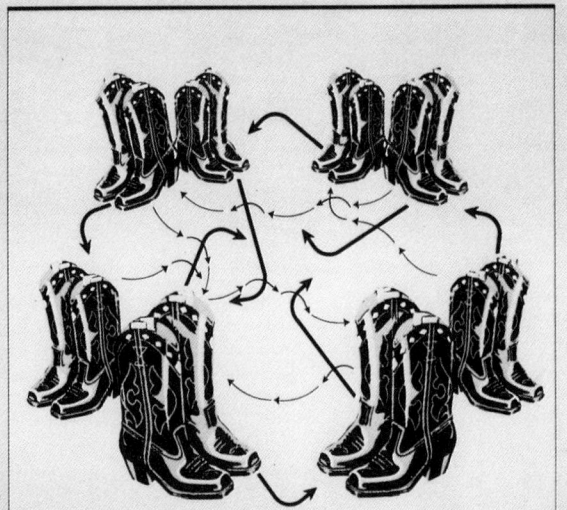
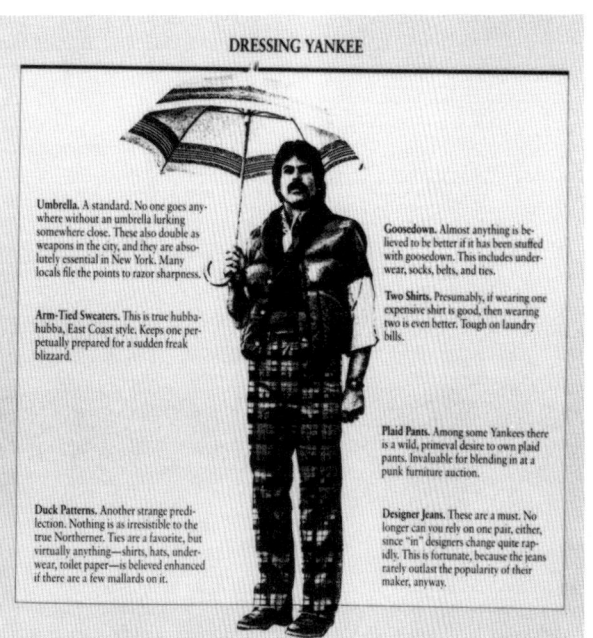

Mother Hixo's Chili
1984
Tom Poth, Mike Hicks
Art Directors, Designers

Melinda Bordelon
Illustrator

Mike Hicks
Copywriter

Hixo, Inc.
Design Firm, Client

The Heralds
(Series)
1984–1986
Bob Dennard,
Ken Koester, Jan Wilson,
Glyn Powell, Chuck Johnson
Art Directors, Designers

Glyn Powell, Chuck Johnson,
Ken Koester, Terry Widener,
Lee Lee Brazeal, Jan Wilson
Illustrators

Cheryl Kotarski-McCue, David Martin
Copywriters

Dennard Creative
Design Firm

The Herring Group
Client

Pearl Bailey Poster
1985
Bryan L. Peterson
Art Director, Designer, Illustrator
Peterson & Co.
Design Firm
Southern Methodist University
Client

Rodeo
1978

Woody Pirtle
Art Director

Woody Pirtle, Rex Peteet,
Don Grimes
Designers

Carl Cannedy, Eric Lindstrom
Photographers

The Richards Group
Design Firm

Dallas Society of
Visual Communications
Client

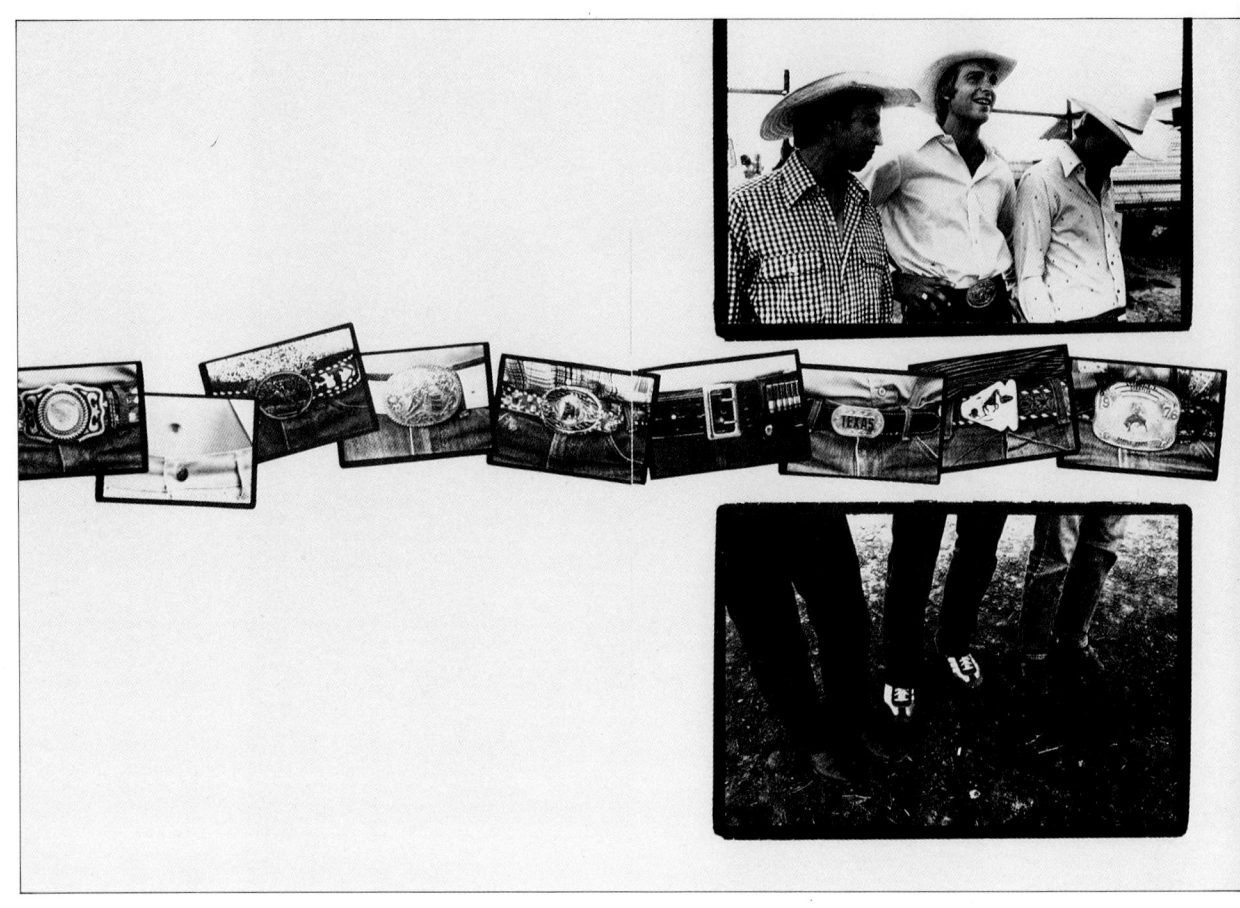

Culinary Workshop
1982

Tom Poth
Art Director, Designer

Larry McEntire
Illustrator

Guy Bommarito
Copywriter

Hixo, Inc.
Design Firm

St. David's Hospital
Client

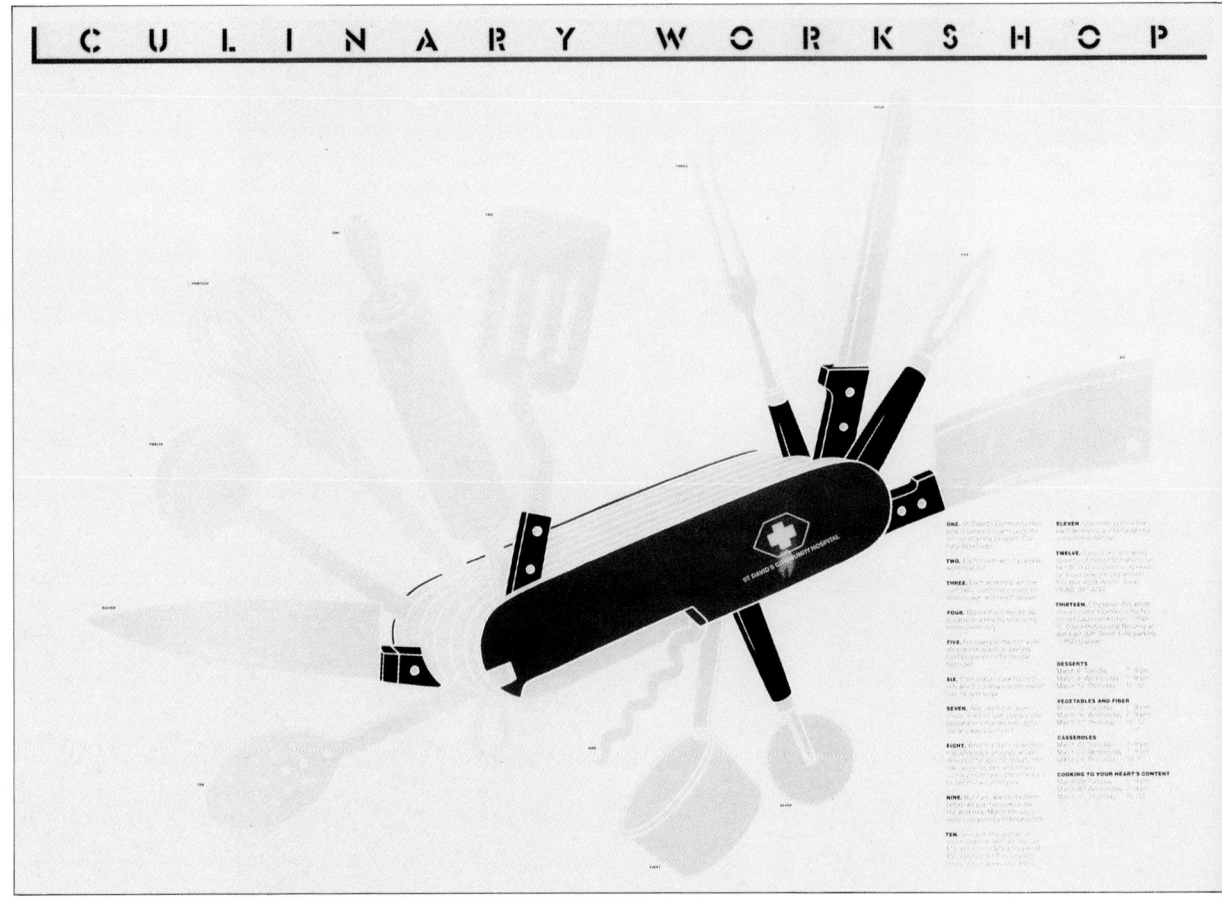

Pirtle Design Logo Book
1981
Woody Pirtle
Art Director, Copywriter
Woody Pirtle, Frank Nichols
Designers
Pirtle Design
Design Firm, Client

Austin Jackson Reilly
1984
Bill Stipp
Art Director, Designer
Bill Baldwin
Copywriter
Benoit Rutter, Inc.
Design Firm
Philip & Donna Reilly
Client

Mardi Gras
1979
Jay Loucks
Art Director
Jay Loucks, Chris Hill
Designers
Jerry Jeanmard
Illustrator
Loucks Atelier, Inc.
Design Firm
Fairmont Hotel
Client

MARDI GRAS BALL

IMPERIAL BALL ROOM, FAIRMONT HOTEL. MONDAY, FEBRUARY 21, 8 P.M.-12 MIDNIGHT, $35 PER PERSON. INCLUDES: DINNER, DANCING, NOISE MAKERS, MASKS AND HATS. DRINKS $2. RESERVATIONS CALL 529-7111

Mardi Gras Poster
1986
Jay Loucks
Art Director
Jay Loucks, Chris Hill
Designers
Jack Unruh
Illustrator
Loucks Atelier, Inc.
Design Firm
Robertson Advertising
Agency
Fairmont Hotel
Client

1985 Marathon Poster
1985

Chris Rovillo
Art Director, Designer

Jack Unruh
Illustrator

Richards, Brock,
Miller, Mitchell & Associates
Design Firm

The Richards Group
Agency

Dallas White Rock Marathon
Client

In the early 1970s, however, most houses on Swiss Avenue could be purchased for under $40,000. The area was zoned for low- and high-rise apartments and there was every reason to believe it would go the way of Gaston Avenue and Live Oak Street, where once-grand houses had been sliced up into cheap apartments managed by absentee landlords.

Homeowners realized that the only way to save Swiss Avenue was to backzone it, about as easy in Dallas as moving the Cowboys football team to Fort Worth. Since few of them knew the National Trust for Historic Preservation from the United Way, they hired an expert on preservation law, Jacob Morrison, to act as their advisor. He recommended that they form a Historic Preservation League to broadcast their objectives to the general public. He also advised the league to publish a series of brochures on the cultural and architectural resources of the proposed district, along with a periodic newsletter that kept residents and potential supporters informed about historic designation procedures.

In the meantime neighborhood leaders beat the bushes generating support for designation. There were many heated community meetings at which realtors fought with planners and residents sometimes fought with both. There were also buffets and cocktail parties in elegant Swiss Avenue mansions at which influential businessmen and public officials were courted and prepped on the benefits of historic preservation.

Upper: Residence, Swiss Avenue, 1916
Lower: Residence, Swiss Avenue, 1917

The Lakewood Bank, in conjunction with the Federal National Mortgage Association, agreed to make $2 million available for mortgage and home improvement loans in the area. Other banks soon followed Lakewood's lead.

The city's new Urban Design staff, led by director Weiming Lu, drew up guidelines for the district that would protect its architectural integrity and insure that new construction was compatible with existing houses. Compatibility rather than rigid conformity was the guiding principle. The final criteria, among the most explicit in the country, have been widely copied by other cities.

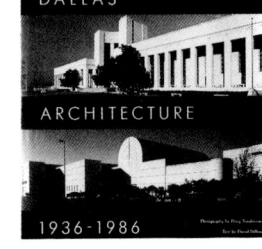

Dallas Architecture 1936–1986
1985

Sibley/Peteet Design
Art Director, Designer, Design Firm

Doug Tomlinson
Photographer

Texas Monthly Press
Client

Some 150 years ago, a small group of businessmen saw in the marshlands of South Boston the opportunity to extend the city's teeming waterfront. In sluggish inlets, they foresaw tall sailing ships; and on tufted grasslands, sturdy wharves laden with silks, sugar and exotic spices for a prosperous New England. Within a few short years, their vision became reality. Tidal flatlands were filled and a stone wharf built in what would turn out to be the Boston Wharf Company's first real estate development venture. At that time, however, the Company's main business was wharfage and storage—a business that grew steadily as Boston became the import capital for the mercantile trade. Graceful clipper ships and schooners lined the wharf, and the sweet aroma of sugar and molasses filled the air. But with the Industrial Revolution, the picture began to change. The emphasis shifted to manufacturing as America's own fledgling industries matured. New enterprises required new facilities for their expanding operations, and many of those facilities were built on Boston Wharf.

The year 1882 marked the beginning of an ambitious construction program that would see some 90 now-historic buildings erected. Streets, too, were developed and miles of spur track laid to meet the needs of an area which soon became the focus of America's wool trade. Now, once again, the area is changing, as Boston strengthens its position as a center of business, finance, technology—and history. In a unique synthesis of past and present, high fashion clothes are sold in old-fashioned marketplaces; computer showrooms rise on renovated piers; artisans practice their crafts where cargoes once were stored. And all along Boston Wharf, the charm of the old blends with the spirit of the new in a continuing process of renewal—a process that has enabled the City of Boston to build its future on the very best of its past.

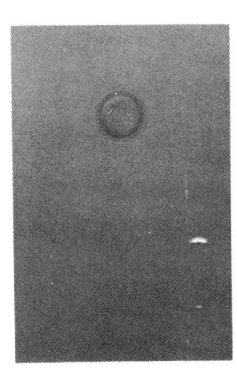

Boston Wharf Brochure
1983

Lowell Williams
Art Director

Lowell Williams, Bill Carson
Designers

Ron Scott, Bob Harr
Photographers

Tom McNeff
Illustrator

Lee Herrick
Copywriter

Lowell Williams Design, Inc.
Design Firm, Agency

Rose Associates
Client

Big Texas Book
1983
Rex Peteet, Marianne Tombaugh
Art Directors
Rex Peteet
Designer, Copywriter
Jerry Jeanmard, Rex Peteet
Illustrators
Sibley/Peteet Design, Inc.
Design Firm
The Hay Agency
Agency
Lomas & Nettleton
Client

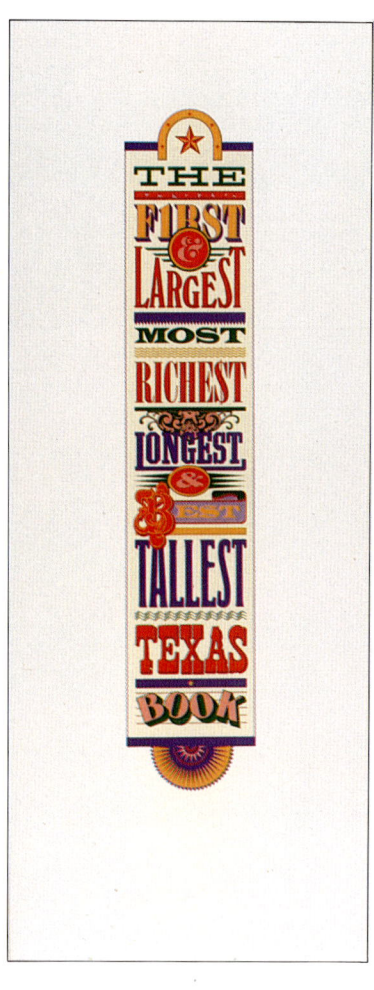

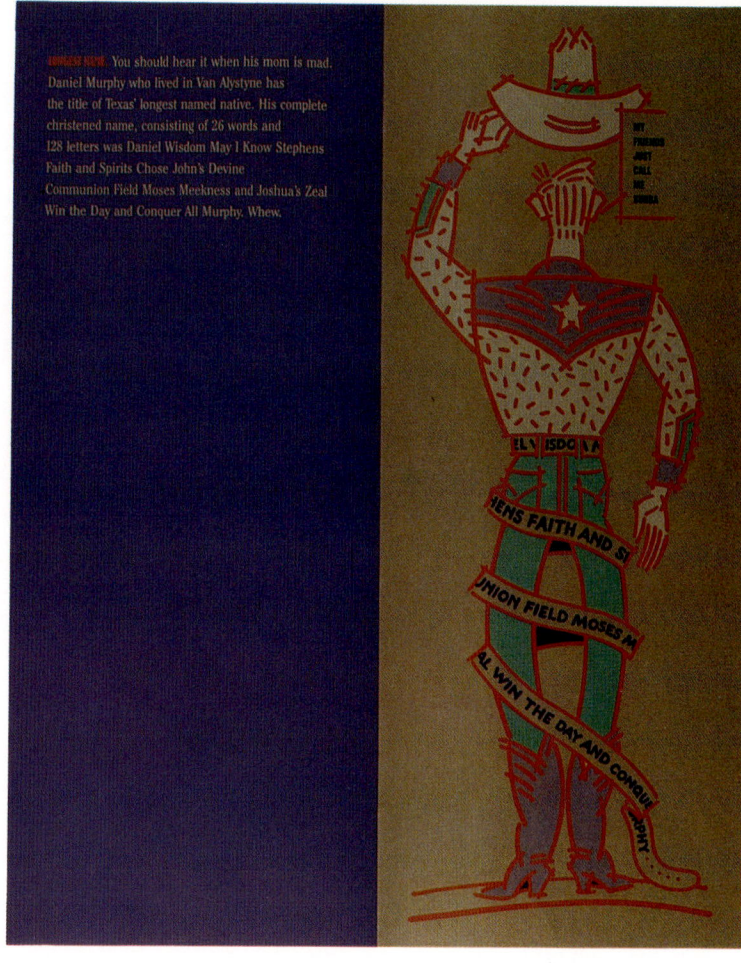

Leggs Poster
1984
Bob Dennard, Glyn Powell
Art Directors
Glyn Powell
Designer, Illustrator, Copywriter
Dennard Creative, Inc.
Design Firm
Susan G. Komen Foundation
Client

200

New York Art Directors Club
63rd Annual Show
1984
Chris Hill
Art Director
Chris Hill, Joe Rattan
Designers
HILL/A Marketing Design Group
Design Firm
New York Art Directors Club
Client

Republic Bank Center Posters
1983, 1984

Lowell Williams
Art Director, Designer

Tom McNeff
Illustrator

Lowell Williams Design, Inc.
Design Firm, Agency

Gerald D. Hines Interests
Client

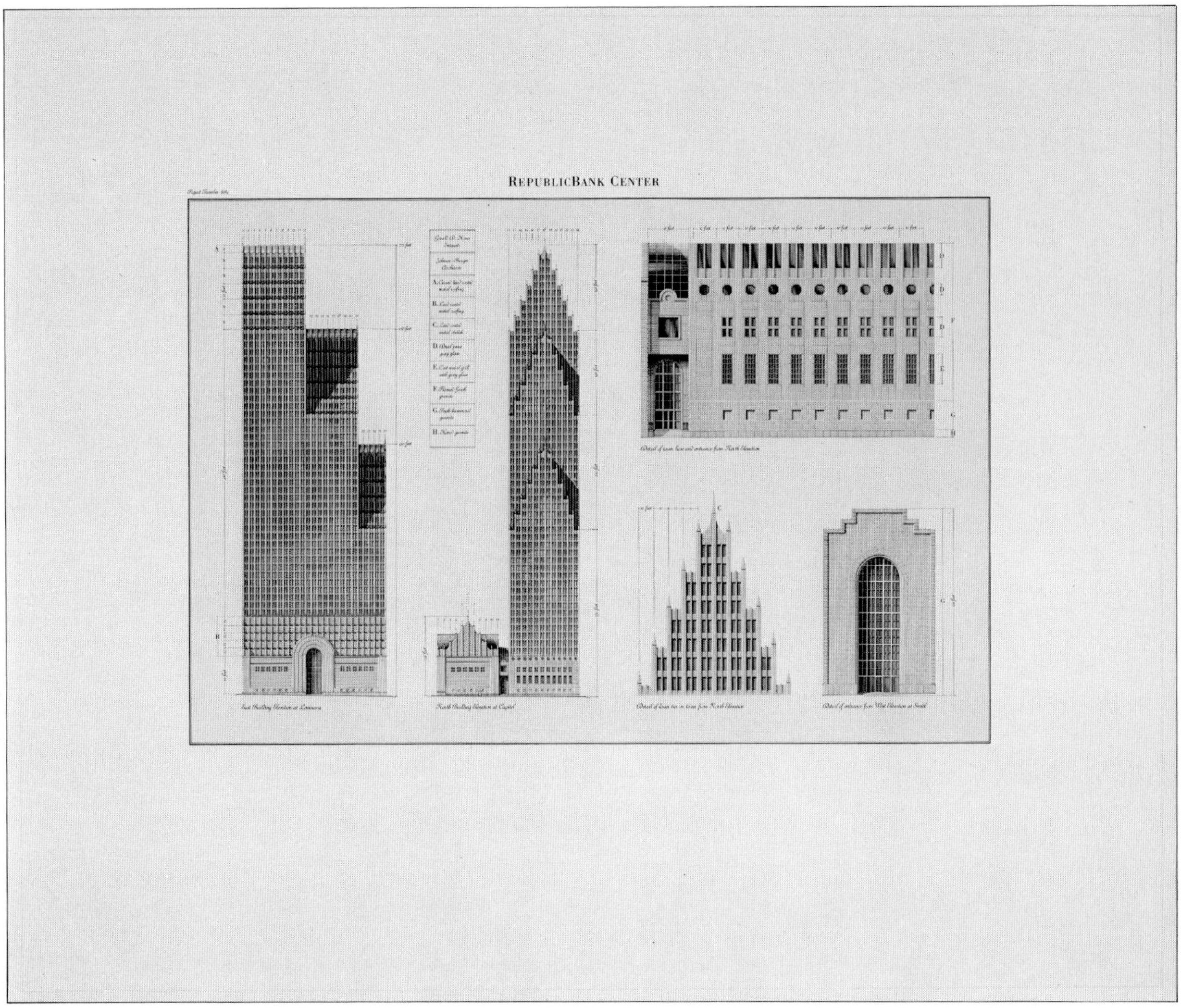

Herring Design Quarterly
(Series)
1979–1985

Jerry Herring
Art Director, Designer, Copywriter

Herring Design
Design Firm, Client

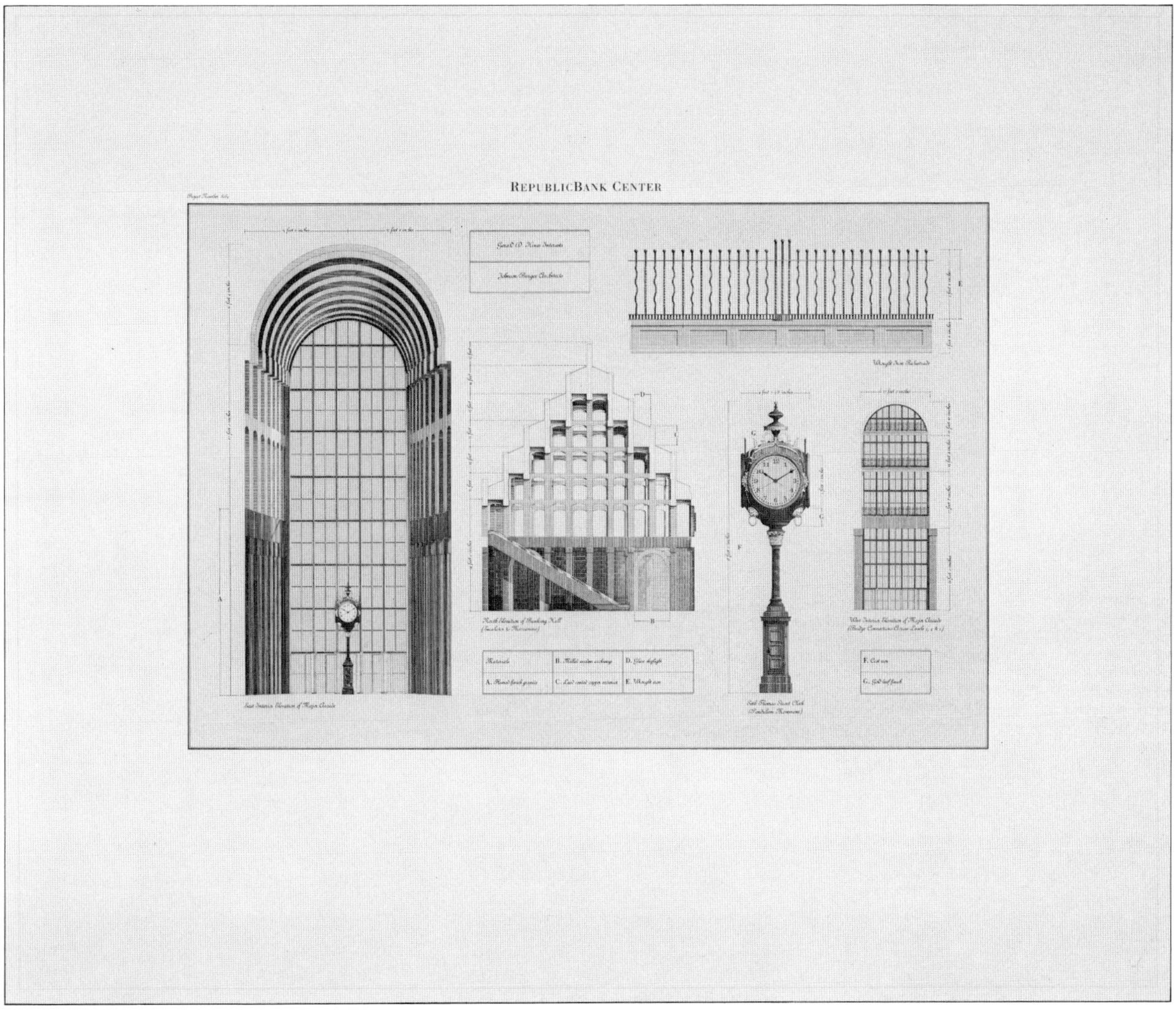

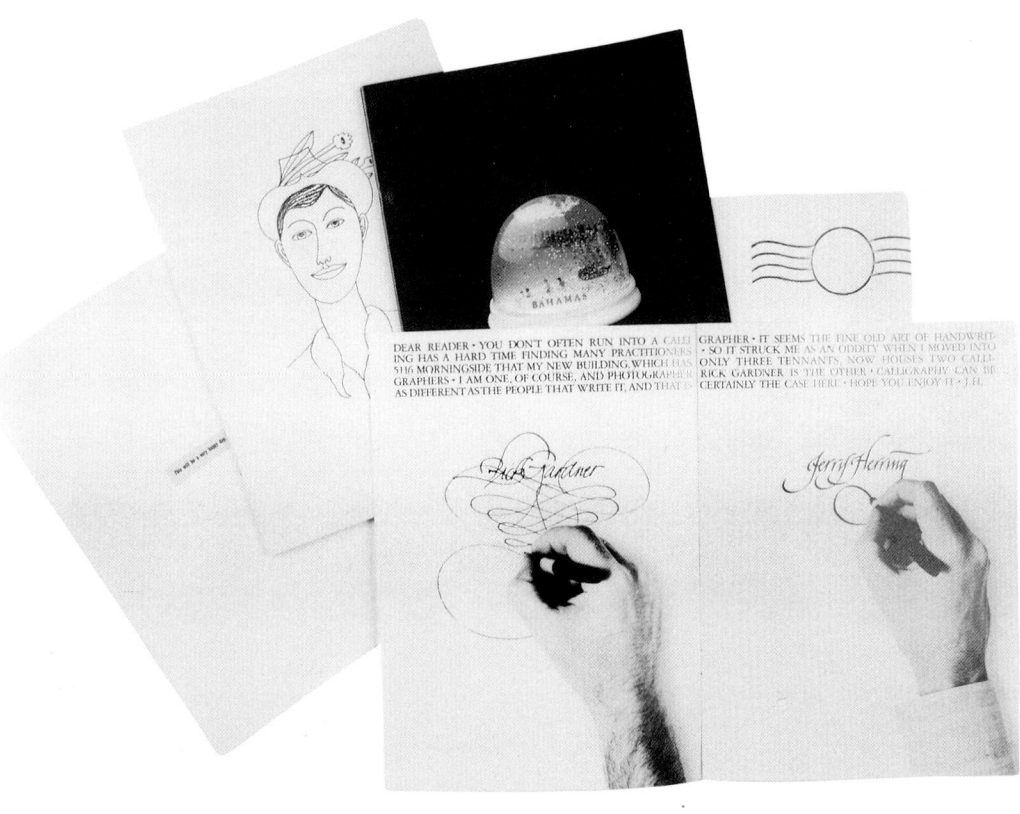

Software Packaging
1985
Cap Pannell
Art Director, Designer, Illustrator
Carol St. George
Copywriter
Pannell/St. George
Design Firm
Alan Weinkrantz & Company
Agency
Learning Technologies, Inc.
Client

Software Packaging
1983

Cap Pannell
Art Director, Designer, Illustrator

Carol St. George
Copywriter

Pannell/St. George
Design Firm

DLM, Inc.
Client

Kuhlen Glacen Yogurt Packaging
1984

David Hopson, Don Sibley, Rex Peteet
Art Directors

Don Sibley, Rex Peteet
Designers

Greg King
Illustrators

Sibley/Peteet Design, Inc.
Design Firm

Saunders, Lubinski & White, Inc.
Agency

Kuhlen Glacen
Client

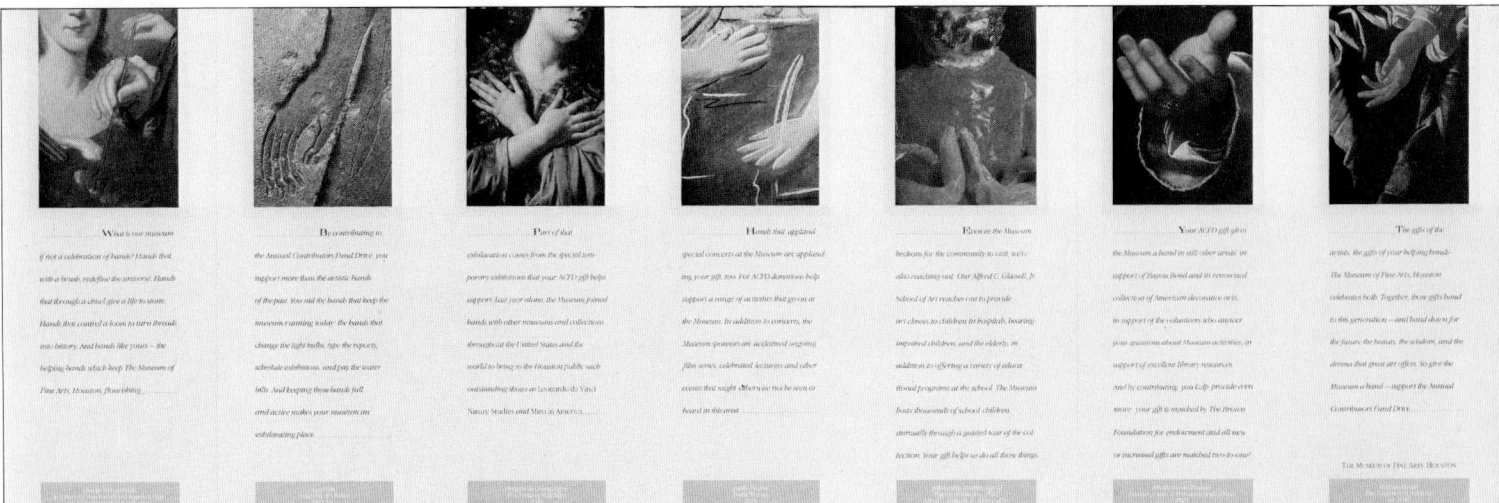

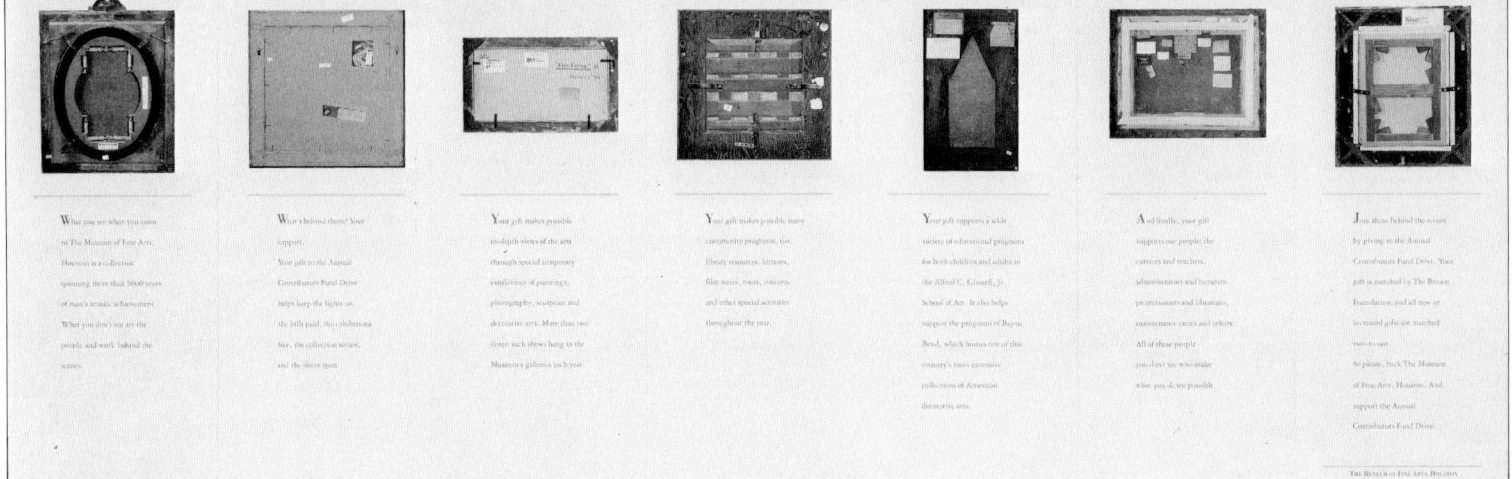

Contributor Fund Drive
1980, 1981

Lowell Williams
Art Director

Lowell Williams,
Bill Carson, Lance Brown
Designers

Jim Sims
Photographer

Lowell Williams Design, Inc.
Design Firm, Agency

Museum of Fine Arts,
Houston
Client

Footprints
1982

Sharon Tooley
Art Director, Designer

Frank White
Photographer

JoAnn Stone,
Paule Sheya Hewlett
Copywriters

Sharon Tooley Design
Design Firm

HRA Associates Architects
Client

Head West With Broadhead
1980

Don Sibley
Art Director, Designer

Jack Unruh
Illustrator

Bob Dennard
Copywriter

Dennard Creative
Design Firm

Paul Broadhead & Associates
Client

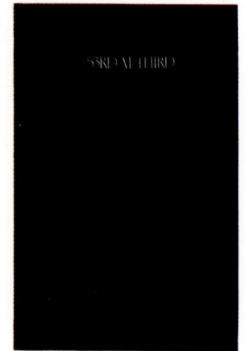

53rd At Third
1984

Jerry Herring
Art Director, Designer

Bob Harr, Steve Brady, Ron Scott
Photographers

Lee Herrick
Copywriter

Herring Design
Design Firm

Gerald D. Hines Interests
Client

When We Dug Into
Dallas Real Estate
1979

Larry McEntire
Art Director

Mike Hicks
Designer

Kirsten Soderlind
Illustrator

Guy Bommarito
Copywriter

Hixo, Inc.
Design Firm

Texas Monthly
Client

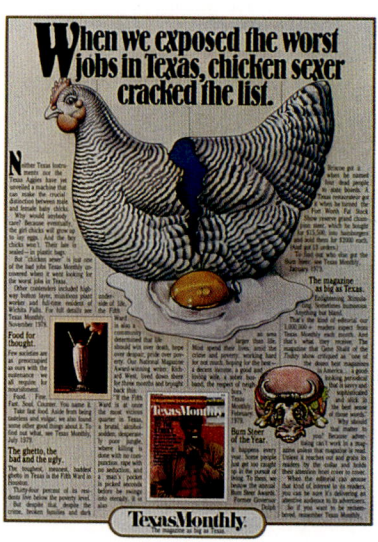
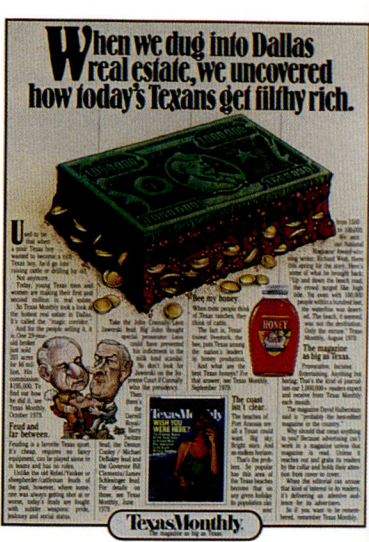

Old City Park Poster
1985
Dale Rushing
Art Director, Designer, Illustrator, Copywriter

The Oakley Company, Inc.
Agency

Williamson Printing Corporation
Client

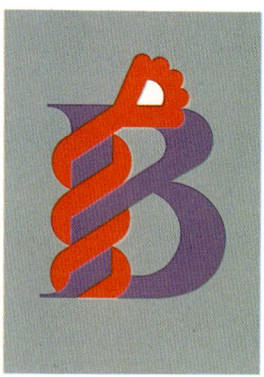

Butler Logo
1980
Woody Pirtle
Art Director, Designer, Illustrator

Pirtle Design
Design Firm

Butler Florist
Client

Heritage Datebook
1981
Jack Summerford
Art Director, Designer
Summerford Design, Inc.
Design Firm
Heritage Press
Client

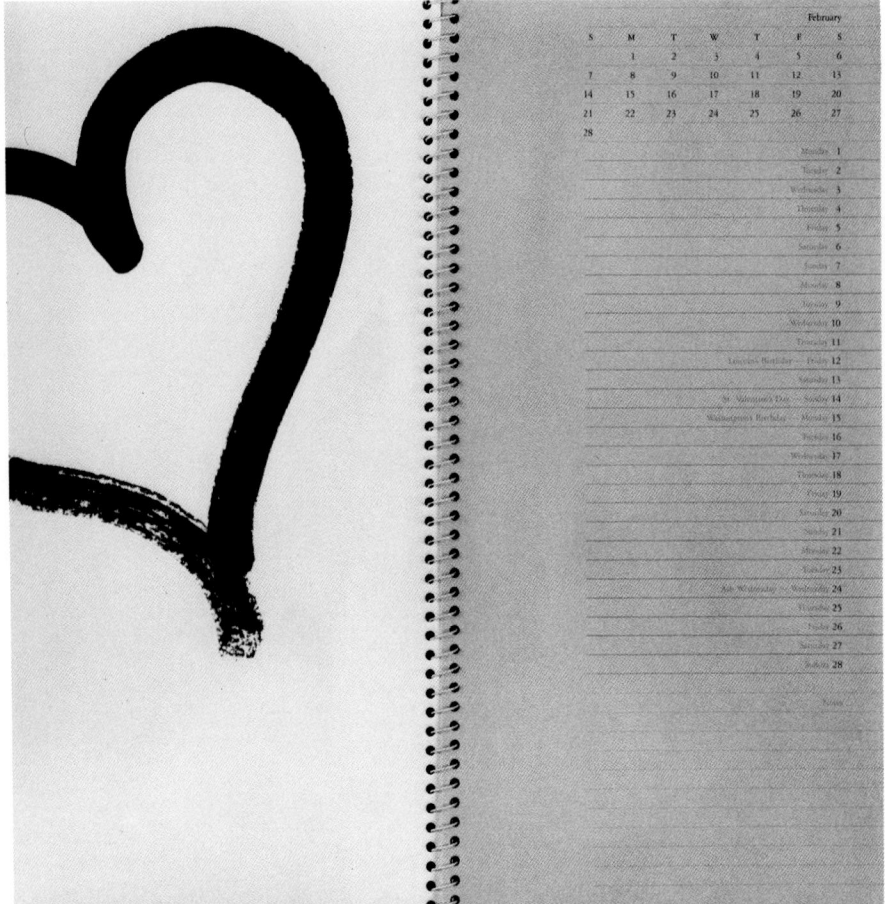

Stop
1978
Carol St. George
*Art Director, Designer,
Illustrator, Copywriter*
Eisenberg & Pannell
Design Firm
City National Bank
Client

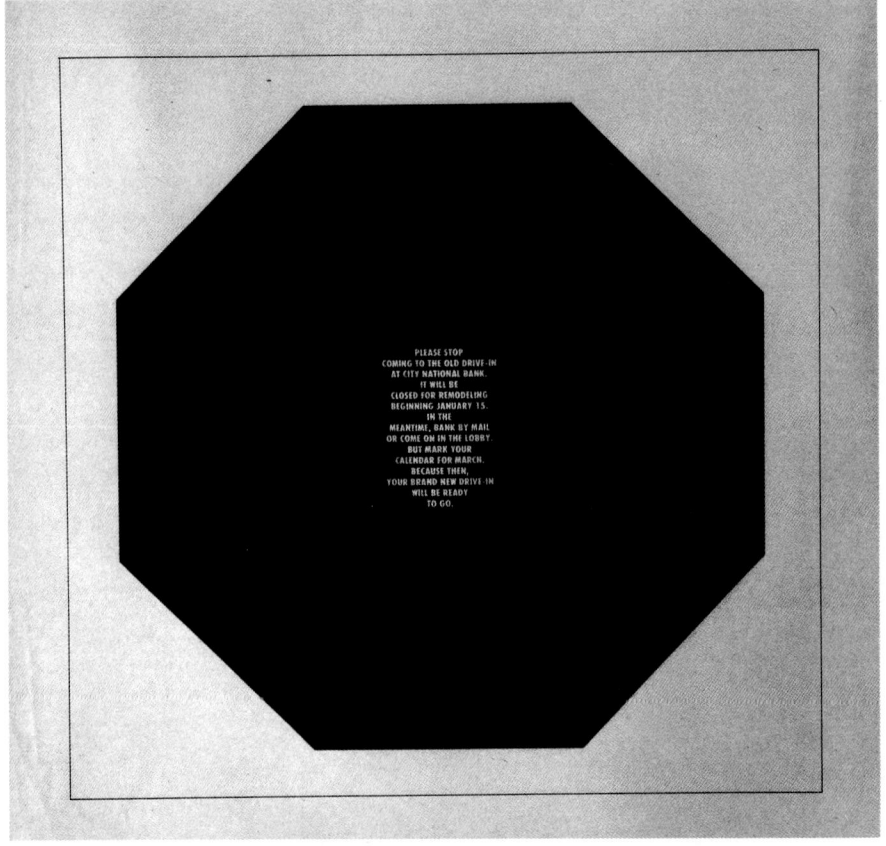

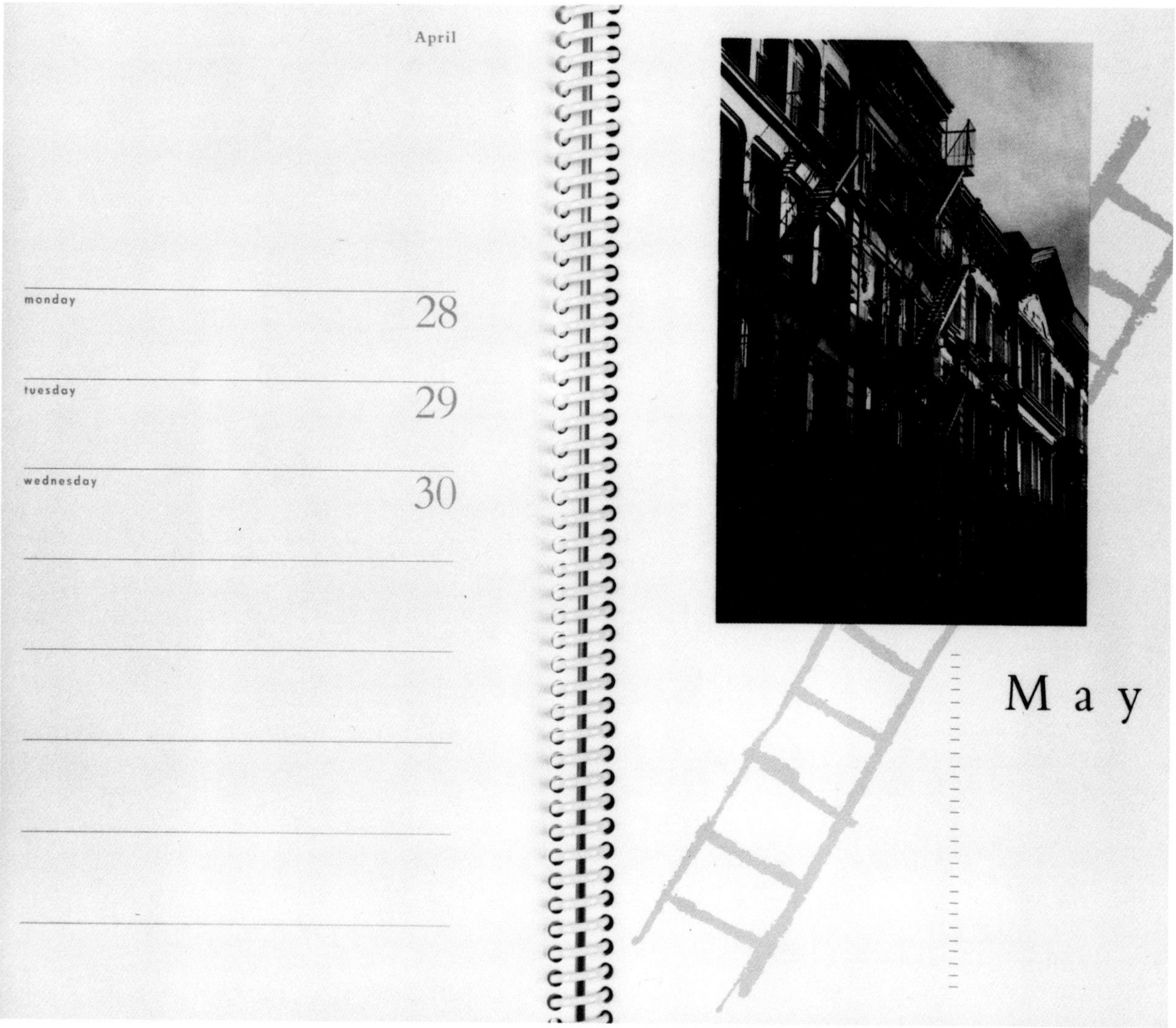

1986 CMI Calendar
1985
Craig Minor
Art Director, Designer
Mark Turkel
Photographer
Creel Morrell, Inc.
Design Firm
CMI
Client

Dallas Symphony Book
1983
D.C. Stipp, Brent Croxton
Art Directors, Designers
Mark Perkins
Copywriter
Richards, Sullivan, Brock & Associates
Design Firm
The Richards Group
Agency
Dallas Symphony
Client

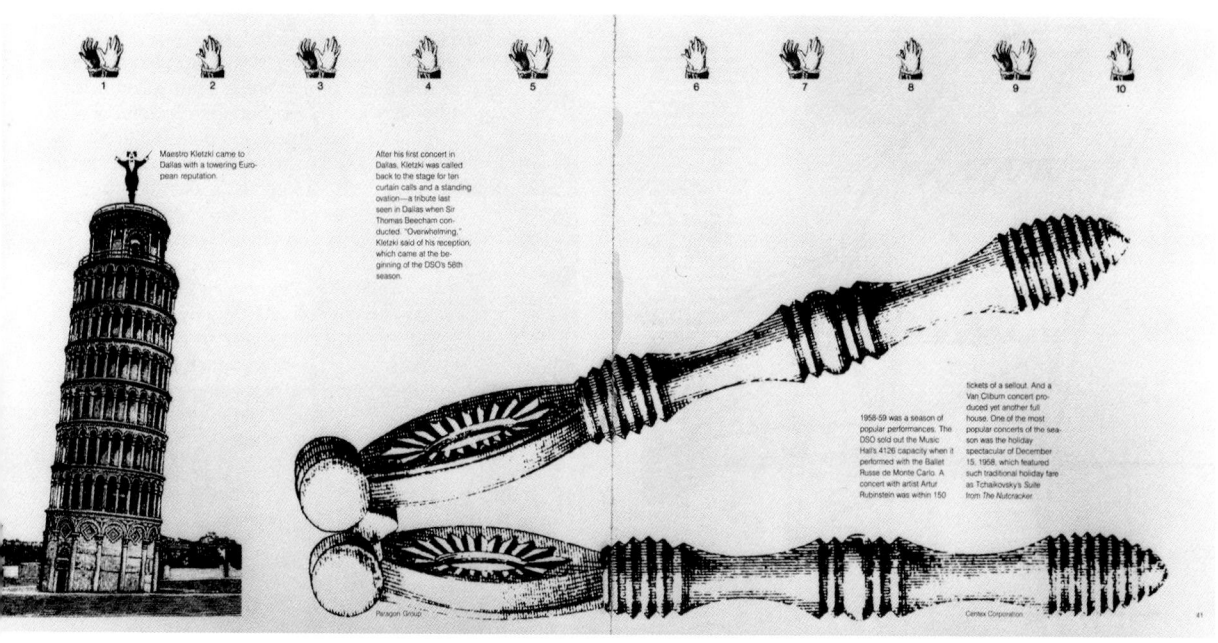

211

Heritage Press
Christmas Greeting
1980
Don Sibley, Bob Dennard
Art Directors

Don Sibley
Designer

Jerry Jeanmard,
Tom Curry, Greg King,
Sue Llewellyn, Bob Dennard,
Rex Peteet, Don Sibley
Illustrators

Bob Dennard,
Don Sibley, Cody Calhoun
Copywriters

Dennard Creative
Design Firm

Heritage Press
Client

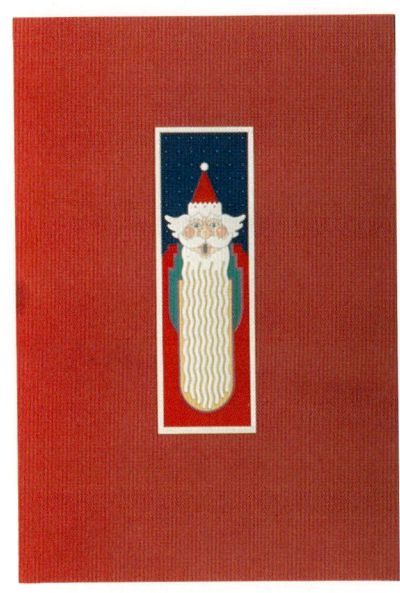

212

Dallas Theatre Center
1983
Don Sibley
Art Director, Designer
Don Sibley, Rex Peteet
Illustrators
Sibley/Peteet Design, Inc.
Design Firm
Dallas Theatre Center
Client

Killeen Mall Campaign
1981
Bob Dennard, Don Sibley
Art Directors

Don Sibley
Designer

Don Sibley, Rex Peteet
Illustrators

Bob Dennard
Copywriter

Dennard Creative, Inc.
Design Firm

Paul Broadhead & Associates
Client

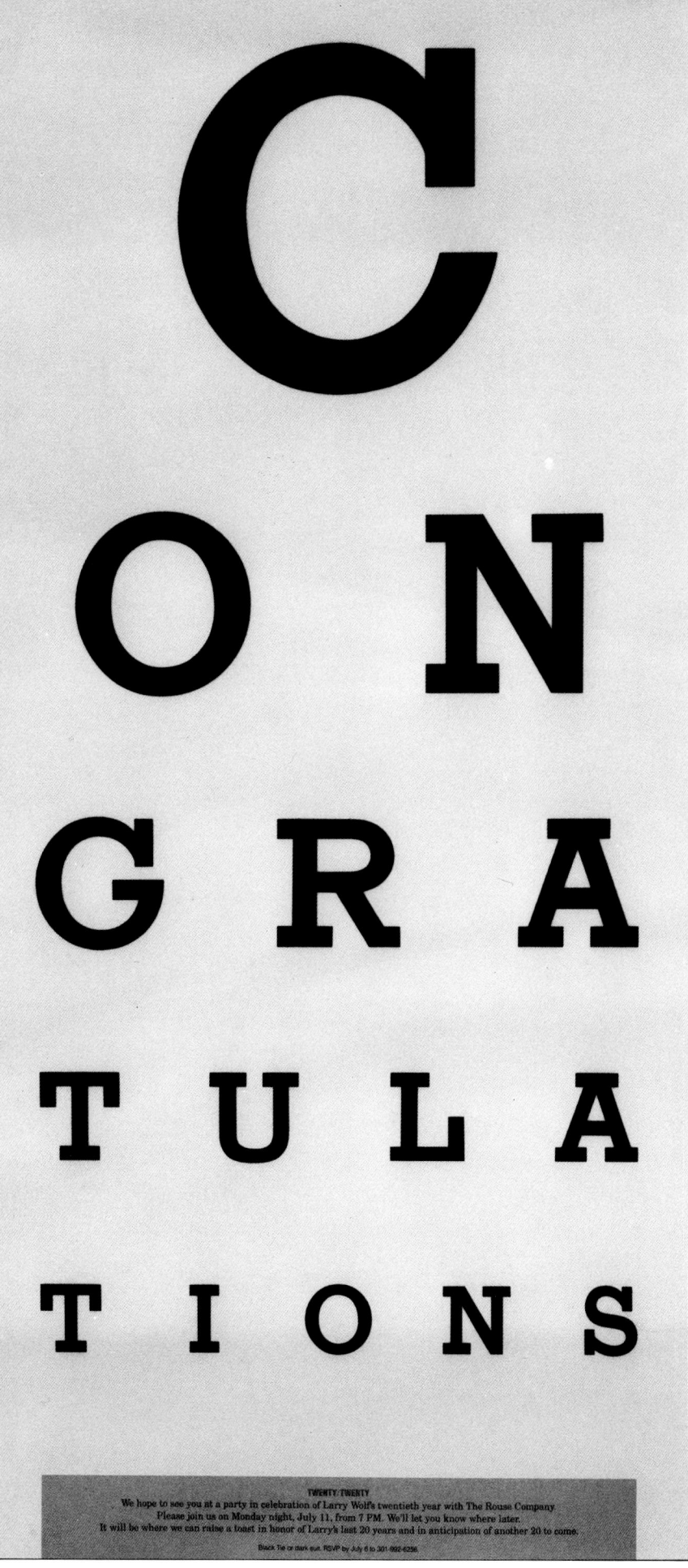

Congratulations Poster
1983

Chris Rovillo
Art Director

Brent Croxton, Chris Rovillo
Designers

Mark Perkins
Copywriter

Richards, Sullivan,
Brock & Associates
Design Firm

The Richards Group
Agency

The Rouse Company
Client

HRA Associates Architects
(Series)
1985
Sharon Tooley
Art Director, Designer

Frank White
Photographer

Paule Sheya Hewlett
Copywriter

Sharon Tooley Design
Design Firm

HRA Associates Architects
Client

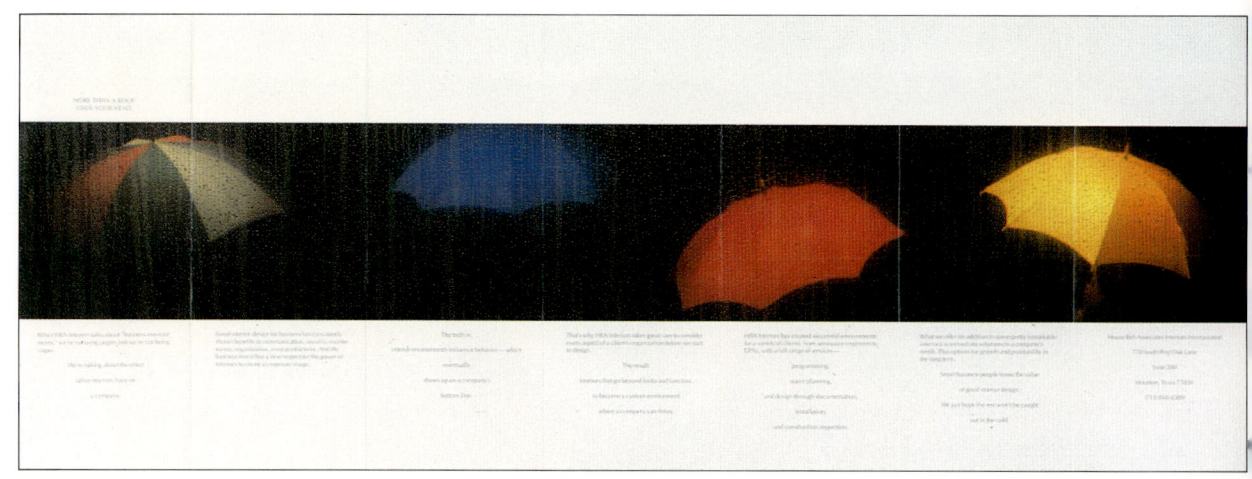

1001 Pennsylvania Ave.
1985
Lowell Williams
Art Director
Lowell Williams,
Bill Carson, Lana Rigsby
Designers
Lana Rigsby
Illustrator
Lee Herrick
Copywriter
Lowell Williams Design, Inc.
Design Firm, Agency
Cadillac Fairview
Client

A Ballad of the West
1983
Larry Smitherman
Art Director, Designer
Barbara Whitehead
Illustrator
Bobby Bridger
Copywriter
The Smitherman Corporation
Design Firm, Agency
Wyaika Press
Client

D Magazine
Moving Announcement
1979
Woody Pirtle
Art Director, Designer, Illustrator
Mary Keck
Copywriter
Pirtle Design
Design Firm
D Magazine
Client

Famous Couples
1985
Glenn Dady
Creative Director
Jim Baldwin, Gena Rogers
Art Directors
Gena Rogers, Paul Von Heeder
Designers
Dennis Murphy
Illustrator/Photographer
David Longfield
Copywriter
The Richards Group
Design Firm
Paige Hutchens, Dan Hutchens
Clients

Skyline High School
Reunion Invitation
1983
Brian Boyd
Art Director, Designer
Mark Perkins
Copywriter
Richard, Brock, Miller, Mitchell & Associates
Design Firm
The Richards Group
Agency
Skyline High School
Client

OPQRSTUVWXYZ

and another couple makes history.

Mr. & Mrs. Robert J. Fleshner, Jr.
and
Barbara Pacífico
request the honor of your presence
at the marriage of their daughter
Paige Fleshner
to
Dan M. Hutcheson
Saturday, the first of June
nineteen hundred and eighty five
at two o'clock in the afternoon
Perkins Chapel
Southern Methodist University
Dallas, Texas

What's happened to the friends and classmates you used to see nearly every day but see no longer? Find out and celebrate on Saturday night, June 11, at the 10-Year Reunion of the Skyline High School Class of 1973. Please join us from 7 PM to midnight at the Lakewood Country Club in Dallas, as we raise a toast to 1973, and renew the memories that may have faded.

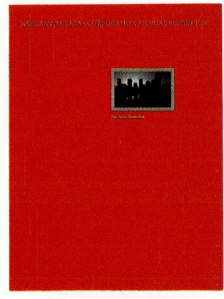

Mercantile Texas Corp.
1981
Dick Mitchell
Designer

Greg Booth
Photographer

Richards, Brock,
Miller, Mitchell & Associates
Design Firm

Mercantile Bank
Client

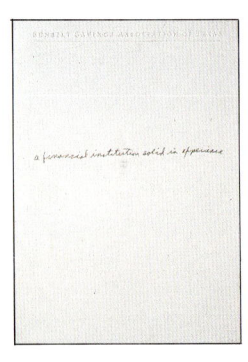

Sunbelt Savings Association
of Texas
1985
Steve Gibbs
Designer

Pharr Cox
Design Firm

Sunbelt Savings
Client

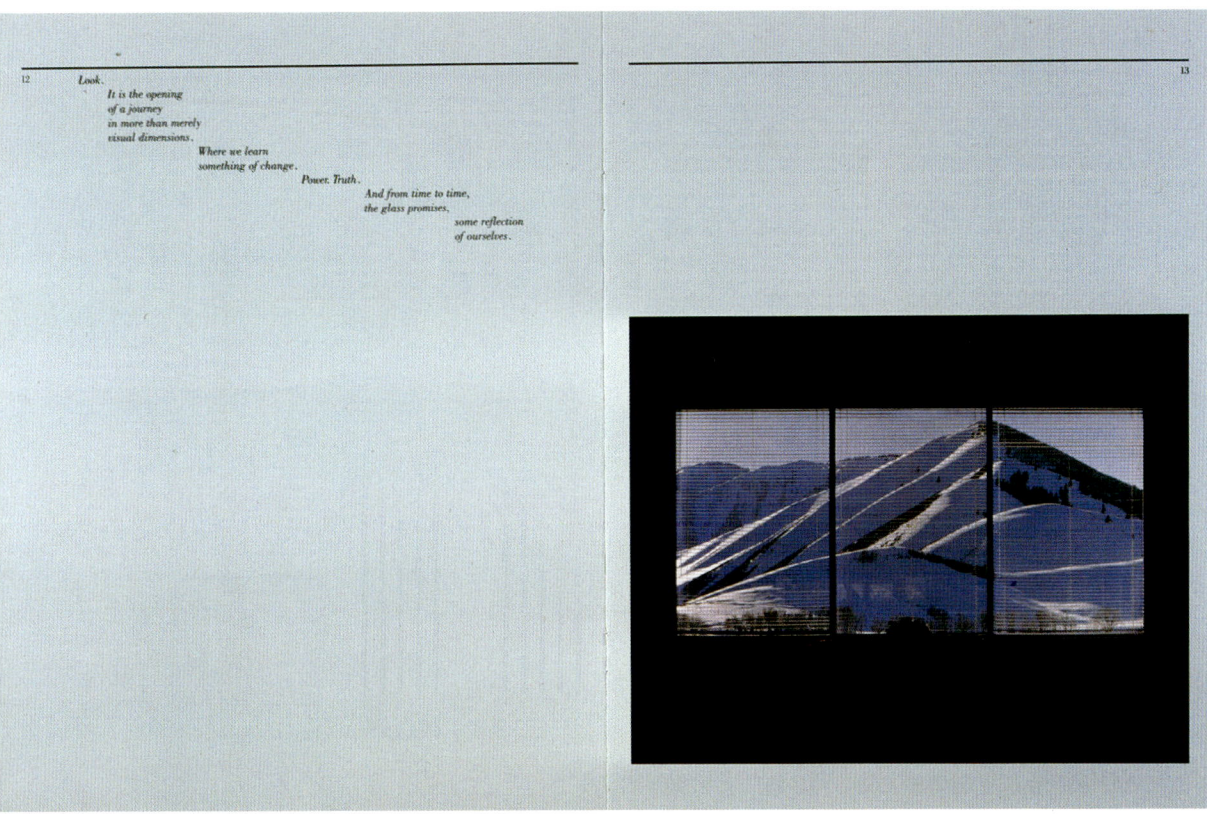

Omega Optical
Annual Report
1981

Woody Pirtle
Art Director, Designer

John Phal
Illustrator/Photographer

Mary Keck
Copywriter

Pirtle Design
Design Firm

Omega Optical
Client

Texas Humanist Covers
(Series)
1985

Richard Whittington
Art Director, Designer

Reagan Bradshaw
Photographer

Marise McDermott
Copywriter

Texas Humanist
Design Firm

Texas Committee For
The Humanities
Client

Perkins/
Image of Happiness
1978

Cap Pannell
Art Director, Designer

Cody Newman
Illustrator/Photographer

Carol St. George
Copywriter

Eisenberg & Pannell
Design Firm

Perkins
Client

A Place for Everything
Black/White
1982

Jim Jacobs
Art Director, Copywriter

Frank Nichols, Jim Jacobs
Designers

Kent Kirkley
Photographer

Jim Jacobs' Studio
Design Firm

A Place for Everything
Client

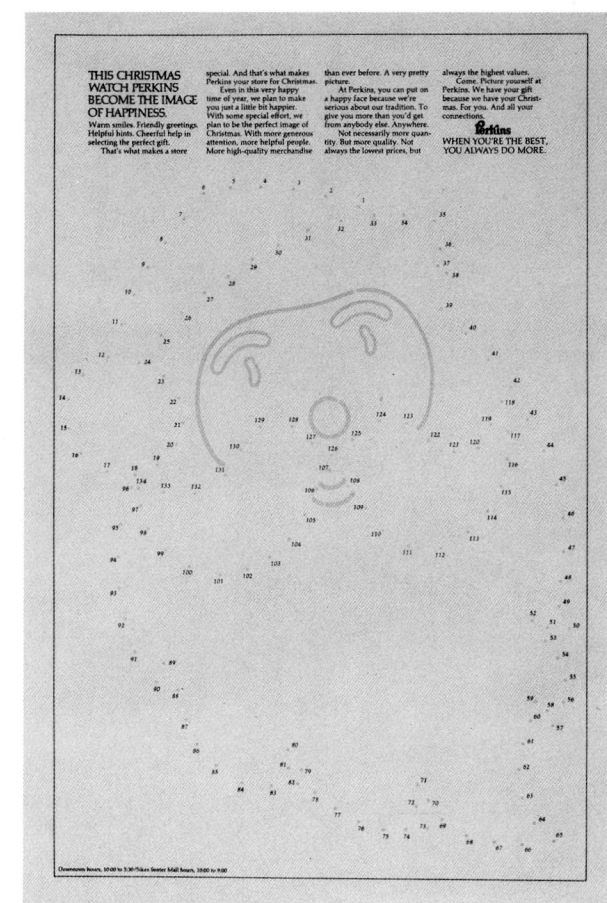
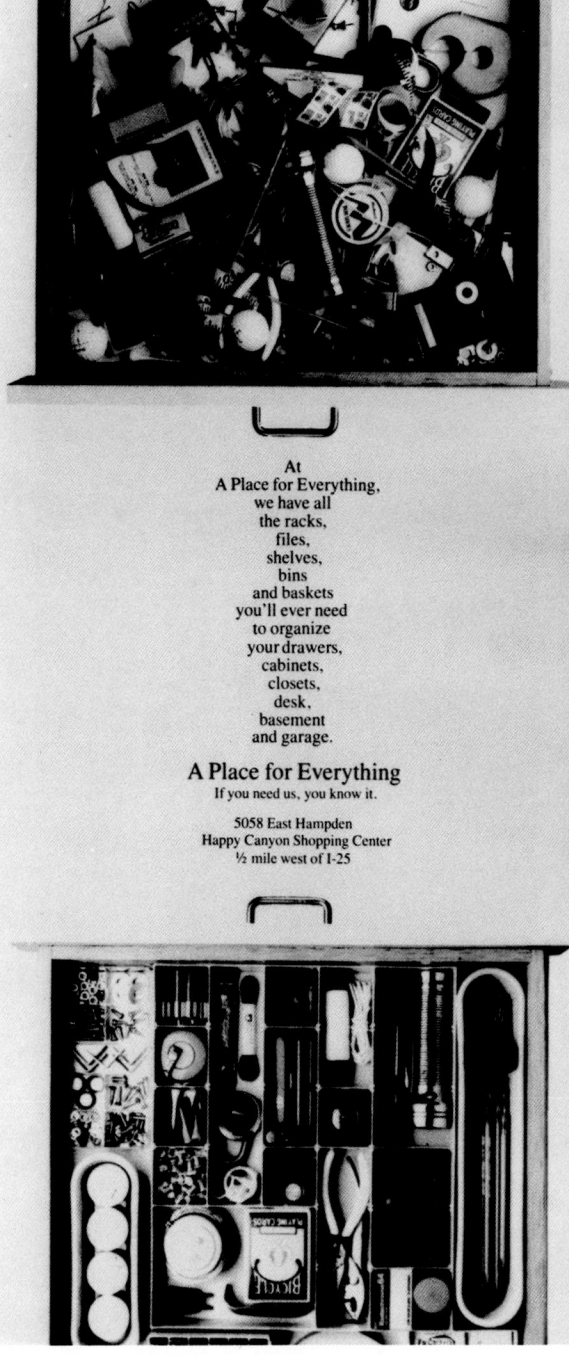

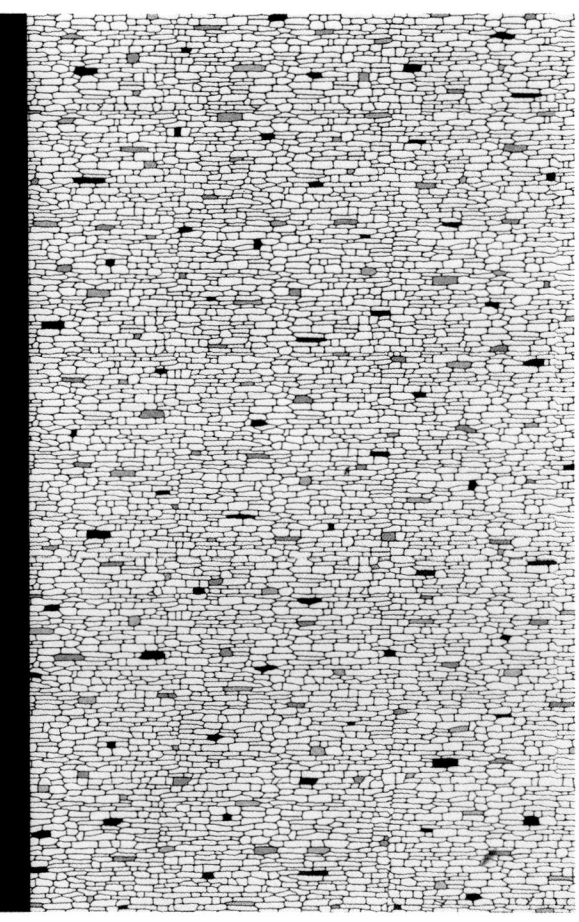

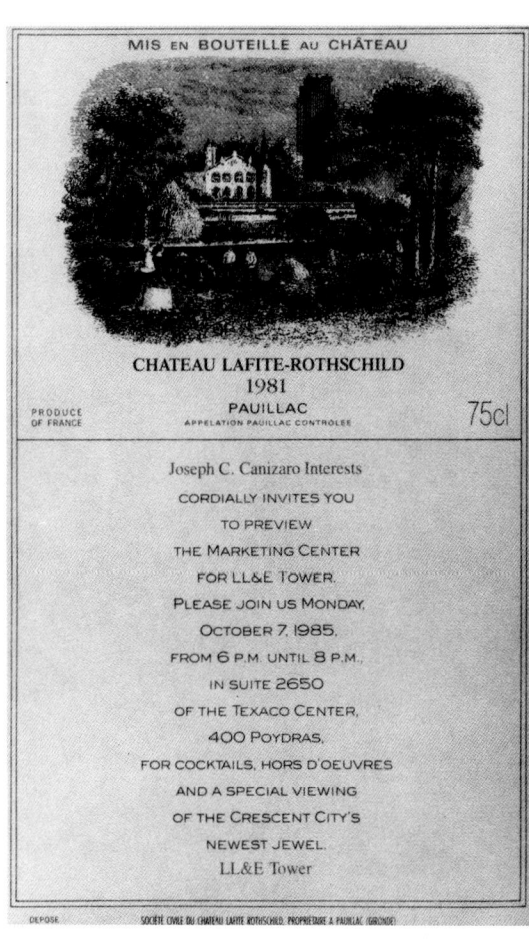

Troubles in Texas
1983
David Holman
Designer
Wind River Press
Design Firm
Southern Methodist University/
Degolyer Library
Client

LL&E Tower Invitation
Wine Label
1985
Blake Miller
Art Director, Designer
Jack Slattery, Blake Miller
Illustrators
Joseph Canizaro Interests
Copywriter
Miller, Judson & Ford, Inc.
Design Firm
Arias, Inc.
Agency
Joseph Canizaro Interests
Client

Dr. Pat Bell
1976
Don Grimes
Art Director, Designer
Don Grimes Design, Inc.
Design Firm
The Richards Group
Agency
Dr. Patrick Bell
Client

Schroder Portfolio
1983
Rex Peteet
Art Director, Designer
Rex Peteet, Don Sibley
Illustrators
Sherry Anderson Koetting
Copywriter
Sibley/Peteet Design, Inc.
Design Firm
Schroder Real Estate
Client

A Rare Site
1982
Paul Black
Art Director, Designer
Robert Latorre
Photographer
Julie Gardner
Copywriter
Levinson, Levinson & Hill
Design Firm, Agency
Los Lomas
Client

Tango Poster
1984
Woody Pirtle
Art Director, Designer
David Kampa
Illustrator
Pirtle Design
Design Firm
Tango
Client

Fresh Films
1983
Cap Pannell
Art Director, Designer, Illustrator
Carol St. George
Copywriter
Pannell/St. George
Design Firm

McGilvray Animals Mailer
1981

Mike Campbell
Art Director, Designer

Jim Jacobs
Illustrator, Copywriter

Jim Jacobs' Studio
Design Firm

Anne McGilvray & Company
Client

Corgan Brochure
1980

Woody Pirtle
Art Director, Designer

Mike Haynes
Photographer

Mary Keck
Copywriter

Pirtle Design
Design Firm

Corgan Associates
Client

Dallas Zoo Endangered Animals
Poster
1985

Brian Boyd
Art Director, Designer

Brian Boyd, Dick Mitchell,
Dianna McKnight, Robin Ayres
Illustrators

Melinda Marcus, Owen Page
Copywriters

Richards, Brock,
Miller, Mitchell & Associates
Design Firm

The Richards Group
Agency

Dallas Zoo
Client

A.I.A.-Dallas
Poster
1981
Woody Pirtle
Art Director, Designer, Illustrator
A.I.A.
Copywriter
Pirtle Design
Design Firm
A.I.A.
Client

Reflect & Remember
Peace Poster
1985

Rex Peteet
Art Director, Designer, Illustrator, Copywriter

Sibley/Peteet Design, Inc.
Design Firm

The Shoshin Society
Client

A Delicate Balance
Peace Poster
1985

Don Sibley
Art Director, Designer, Illustrator, Copywriter

Sibley/Peteet Design, Inc.
Design Firm

The Shoshin Society
Client

T.G.I. Friday's
Annual Report
1984

Woody Pirtle, Alan Colvin
Art Directors

Alan Colvin
Designer

Melissa Grimes
Illustrator

Nathan James
Copywriter

Pirtle Design
Design Firm

Tracy-Locke, Inc.
Agency

T.G.I. Friday's Inc.
Client

Friday's Fan Menu
1979

Woody Pirtle
Art Director, Designer

Gary Templin
Illustrator

T.G.I. Friday's
Copywriter

Pirtle Design
Design Firm

T.G.I. Friday's Inc.
Client

232

Friday's Umbrella Poster
1983
Woody Pirtle
Art Director, Designer

David Kampa
Illustrator

Pirtle Design
Design Firm

T.G.I. Friday's Inc.
Client

Friday's Umbrella Menu
1983
Woody Pirtle
Art Director

Woody Pirtle, David Kampa
Designers

David Kampa
Illustrator

T.G.I. Friday's
Copywriter

Pirtle Design
Design Firm

T.G.I. Friday's Inc.
Client

Friday's Notebook Menu
1973
Woody Pirtle
Art Director, Designer
Don Grimes, Bob Dennard
Illustrator
T.G.I. Friday's
Copywriter
The Richards Group
Design Firm
T.G.I. Friday's Inc.
Client

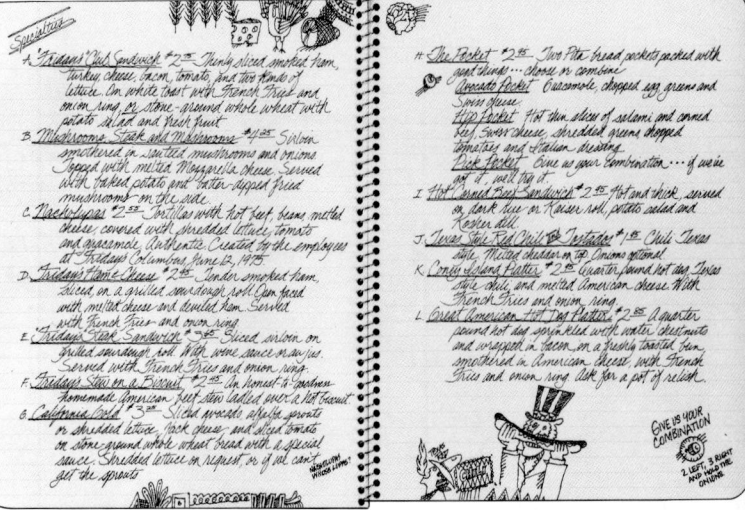

Friday's Egg Book
1979
Woody Pirtle
Art Director, Designer, Illustrator
Mary Keck
Copywriter
Pirtle Design
Design Firm
T.G.I. Friday's Inc.
Client

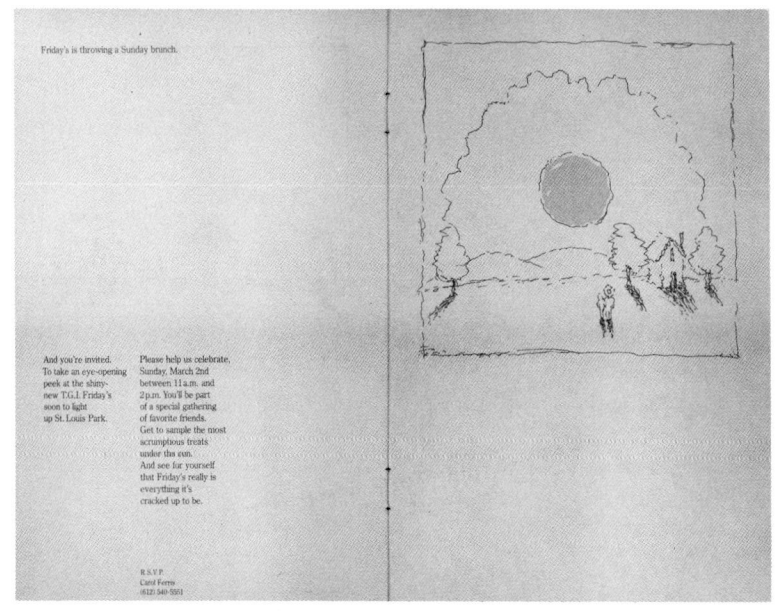

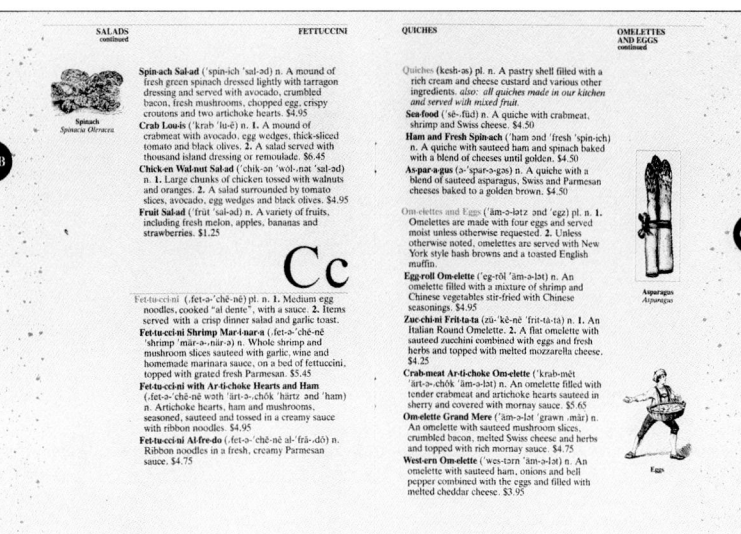

Friday's Dictionary Menu
1981

Woody Pirtle, Luis Acevedo
Art Directors

Luis Acevedo
Designer, Illustrator

T.G.I. Friday's
Copywriter

Pirtle Design
Design Firm

T.G.I. Friday's Inc.
Client

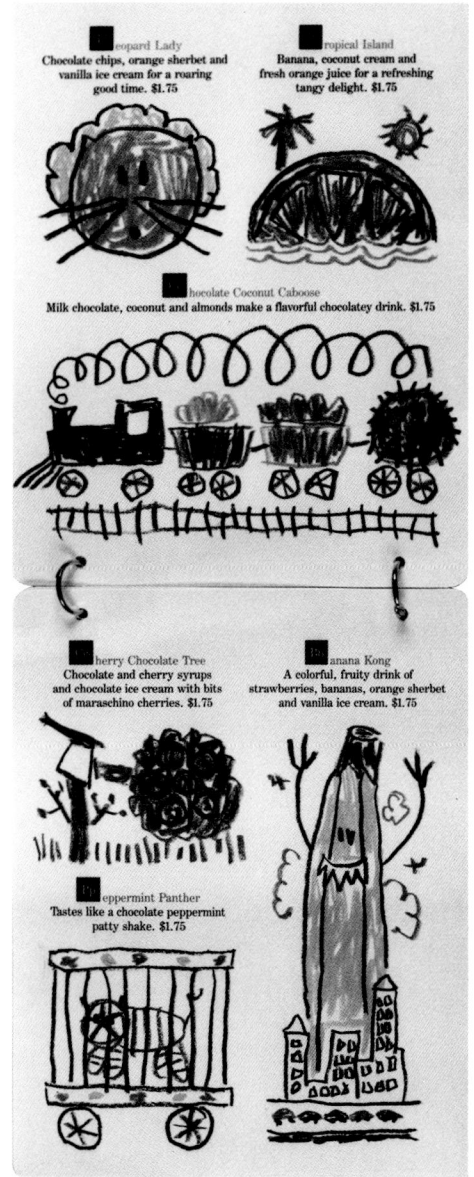

T.G.I. Friday's Kiddie Menu
1985

Mike Schroeder, Woody Pirtle
Art Directors

Mike Schroeder
Designer, Illustrator

T.G.I. Friday's
Copywriter

Pirtle Design
Design Firm

T.G.I. Friday's Inc.
Client

Friday's Sun Reflector
Menu
1982

Mike Schroeder, Woody Pirtle
Art Directors

Mike Schroeder
Designer, Illustrator

T.G.I. Friday's
Copywriter

Pirtle Design
Design Firm

T.G.I. Friday's Inc.
Client

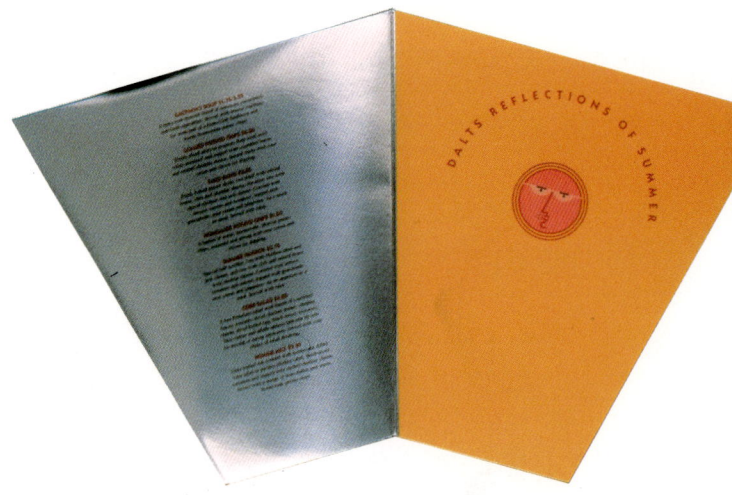

T.G.I. Friday's
Summer Menu
1985

Woody Pirtle
Art Director, Designer

Joe Rattan
Illustrator

T.G.I. Friday's
Copywriter

Pirtle Design
Design Firm

T.G.I. Friday's Inc.
Client

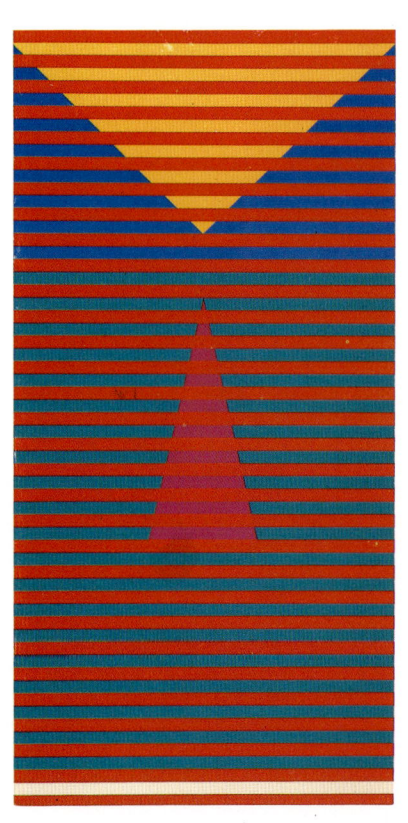

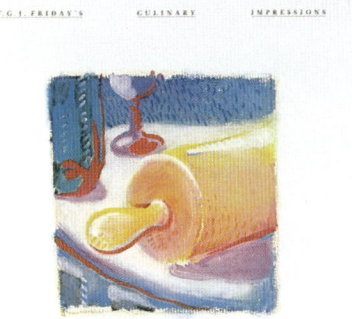

T.G.I. Friday's
Culinary Impressions
1983
Woody Pirtle
Art Director, Designer, Illustrator
T.G.I. Friday's
Copywriter
Pirtle Design
Design Firm
T.G.I. Friday's Inc.
Client

T.G.I. Friday's
Expresso Menu
1982
Woody Pirtle
Art Director
Luis Acevedo, Woody Pirtle
Designers
Luis Acevedo
Illustrator
T.G.I. Friday's
Copywriter
Pirtle Design
Design Firm
T.G.I. Friday's Inc.
Client

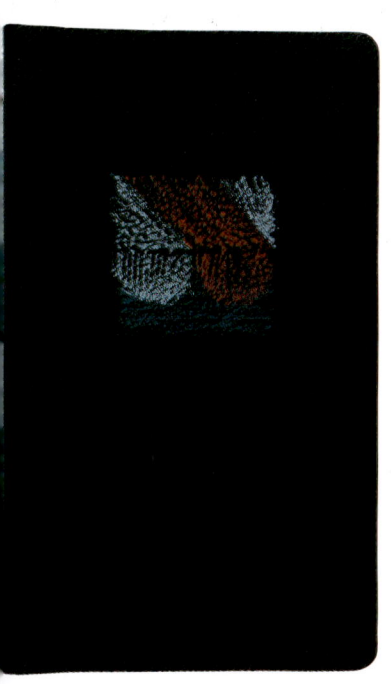
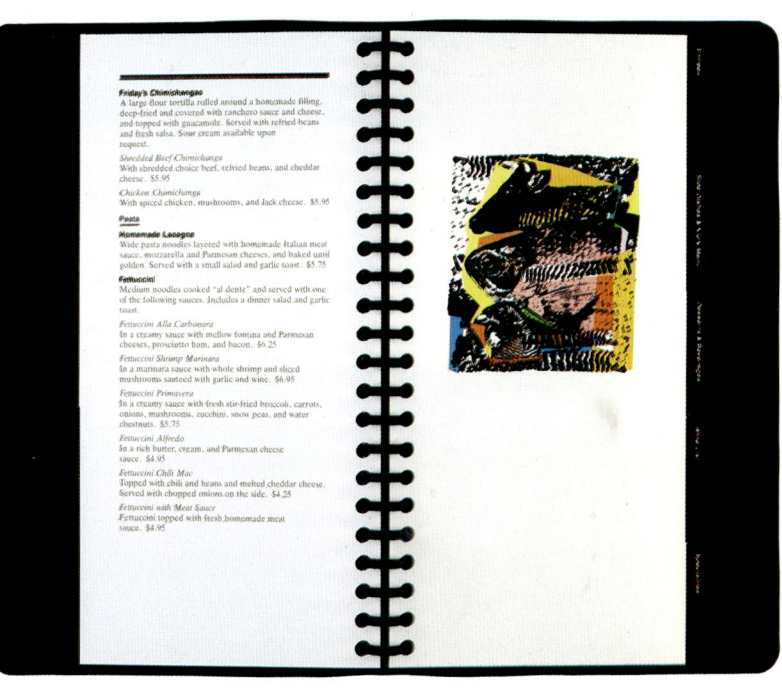

Friday's Main Menu
1982
Woody Pirtle
Art Director, Designer, Illustrator
Pirtle Design
Design Firm
T.G.I. Friday's Inc.
Client

237

LaRue Crow Letterhead
1975
Woody Pirtle, Jerry Herring
Art Director, Designers
Woody Pirtle
Illustrator
Herring & Pirtle, Inc.
Design Firm
LaRue Crow
Client

Radio Ranch
1980
Mike Schroeder
Art Director
Mike Schroeder, Woody Pirtle
Designers
Woody Pirtle
Illustrator
Pirtle Design
Design Firm
Zimmersmith Productions
Client

Jerry Riddle
1981
Don Grimes
Art Director, Designer, Illustrator
Don Grimes Design, Inc.
Design Firm
Jerry Riddle
Client

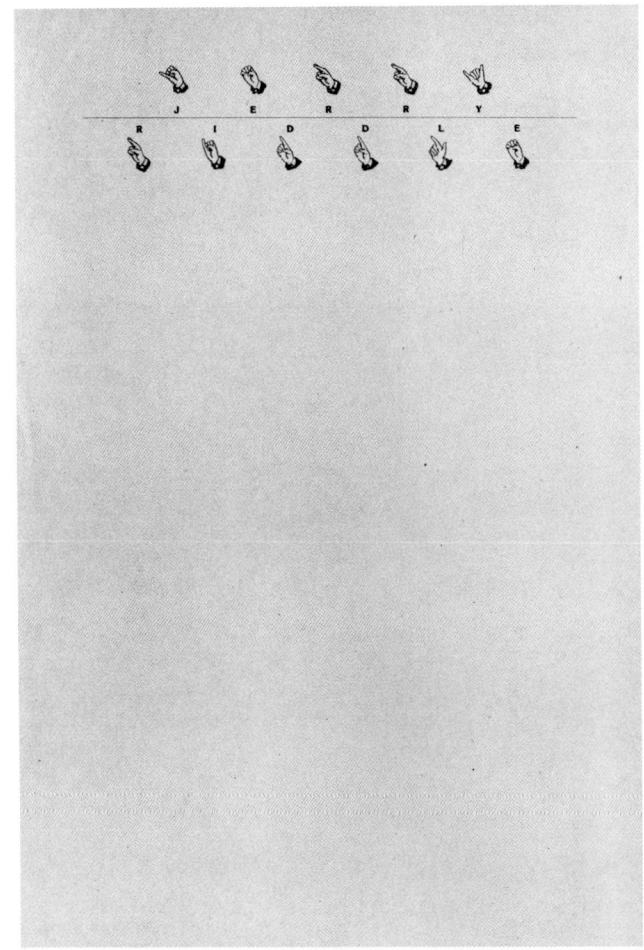

"A Baby Shower"
You are invited to attend a baby shower for Judy and Wayne Marchand on Friday, January 25, 7:30 p.m. at 3902 Marquette in West University.
The shower is compliments of Joyce and Ken Waggoner, Paula and John Heck, Kathy and Rand Kelcely, and the City of Houston. Dress is casual; black towel is optional.

Baby Shower
1979
John Heck
Art Director, Designer, Illustrator
Kerry Oliver
Copywriter
Wayne & Judy Marchand
Client

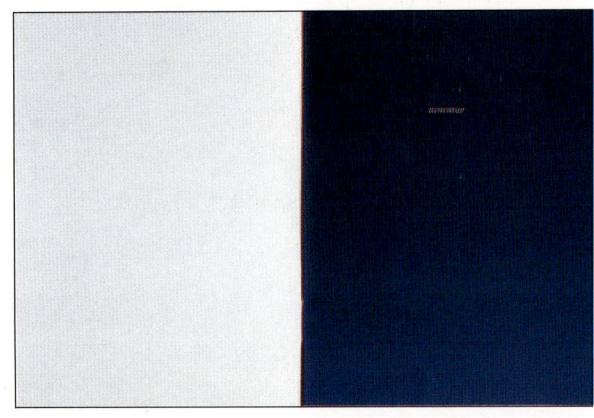

Jackson Myres
Birth Announcement
1983

Danny Kammerath
Designer

Danny Kammerath, Jim Jacobs
Copywriters

Jim Jacobs' Studio
Design Firm

Sherry, Fred and Jackson Myres
Client

Colin In Texas Poster
1984

Chris Rovillo
Art Director, Designer

Gary Gibson
Copywriter

Richards, Sullivan,
Brock & Associates
Design Firm

The Richards Group
Agency

Dallas Society of
Visual Communications
Client

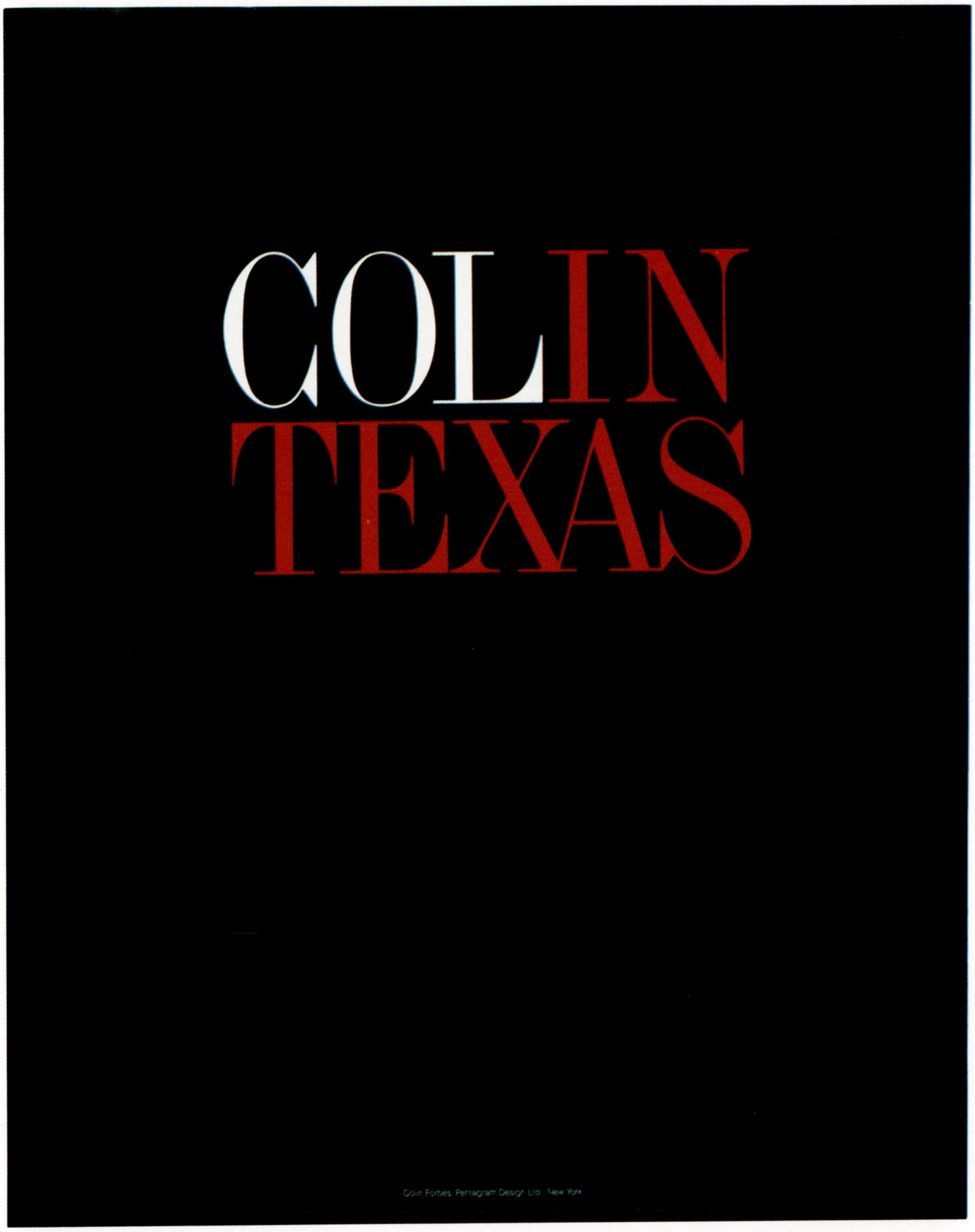

**Goodwill Opens Doors
1981**

Alan Lidji
Art Director, Designer

Alan Lidji, Laynie Lidji
Illustrators

Alan Lidji Design
Design Firm

Goodwill Industries/Dallas
Client

American Tower Campaign
1984

Rex Peteet
Art Director, Designer, Copywriter

Jerry Jeanmard
Illustrators

Sibley/Peteet Design, Inc.
Design Firm

The Harris Group
Agency

Independent American Tower
Client

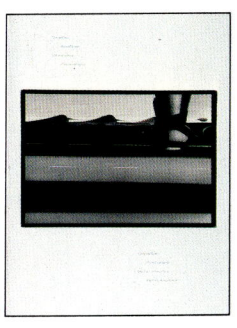

**Printing Resources
1985**

Steven Sessions
Art Director, Designer

Jim Sims
Photographer

Greg Bolton
Copywriter

Steven Sessions Design
Design Firm

Printing Resources
Client

Dr. F. B. Geary Letterhead
1978

Mike Schroeder
Art Director, Designer, Illustrator

Eisenberg, Pannell
Design Firm

Dr. F. B. Geary
Client

Pops in the Park Poster
1984
Nancy Lee-Turner
Art Director, Designer
James E. Tennison
Illustrator
Nancy Lee-Turner Design
Design Firm
Fort Worth Symphony Orchestra Association
Client

Prickley Pear Press Logo
1971
Jim Jacobs
Art Director, Designer, Illustrator
Jim Jacobs' Studio
Design Firm
Prickley Pear Press
Client

Cadillac Poster
1985
Ray Redding
Art Director, Designer
Terry Heffernan
Photographer
David Fowler
Copywriter
The Richards Group
Agency
Omron Financial Systems, Inc.
Client

Out
1985
Cap Pannell, Carol St. George
Art Directors
Cap Pannell
Designer, Illustrator
Pannell/St. George
Design Firm
NCH Corporation
Client

Designers Chili Cookoff Poster
1983
Don Sibley
Art Director, Designer, Illustrator, Copywriter
Sibley/Peteet Design, Inc.
Design Firm
Dallas Designers' Chili Cookoff
Client

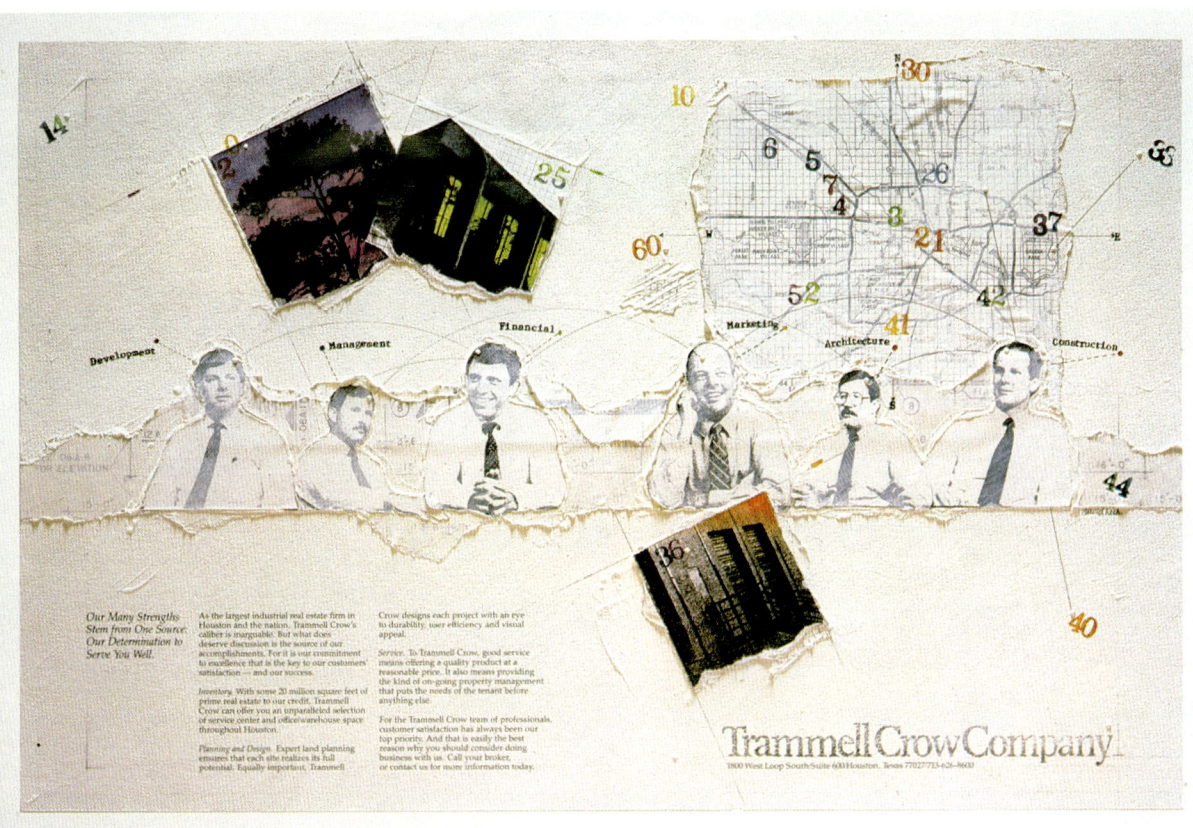

Trammell Crow Company
1983

Diane Butler, Karen Abney
Art Directors

Karen Abney
Designer

David Lesh
Photographer

Mary Langridge
Copywriter

Diane Butler & Associates
Design Firm

Trammell Crow Company
Client

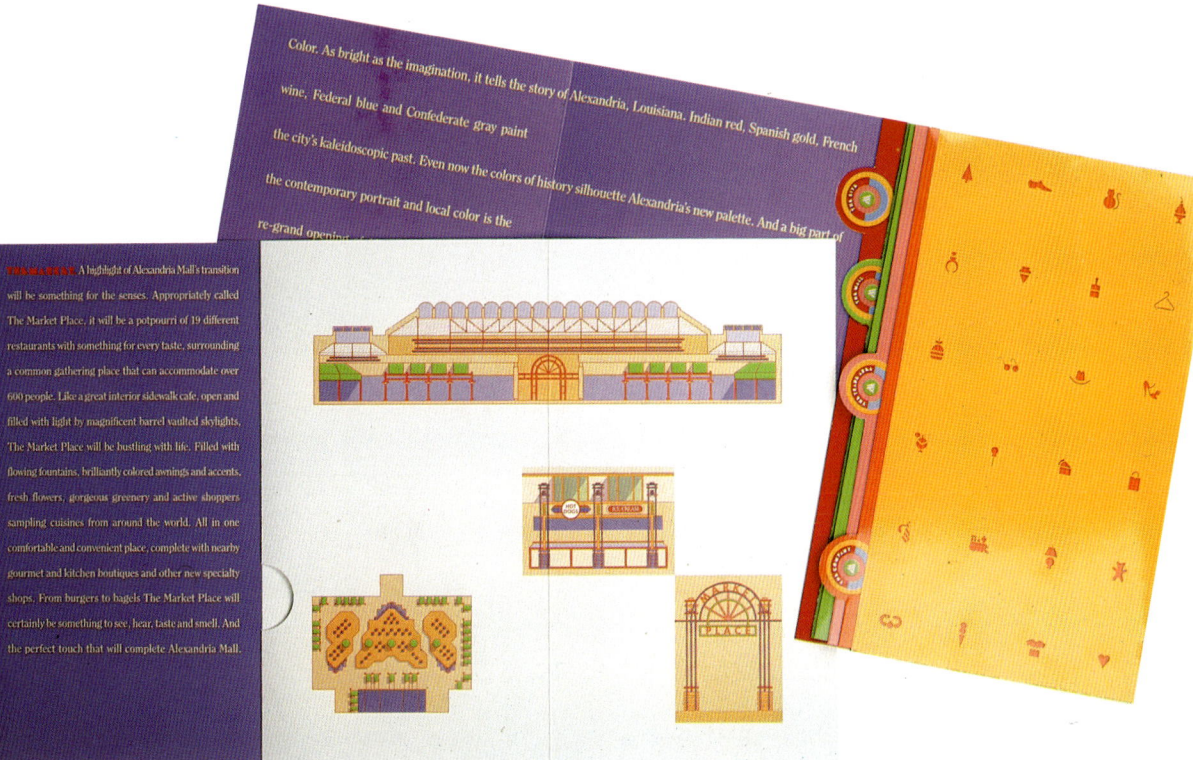

Alexandria Mall Leasing Kit
1985

Rex Peteet
Art Director, Designer

Rex Peteet, Walter Horton
Illustrators

Rex Peteet, Ann Eklund Phillips
Copywriters

Sibley/Peteet Design, Inc.
Design Firm

The Herring Group/
Alexandria Mall
Client

247

Handweaver's Guild Poster
1982

Woody Pirtle
Art Director, Designer, Illustrator

Pirtle Design
Design Firm

Handweaver's Guild
Client

248

Dallas Museum of Art
Sculpture Garden Poster
1984

Rex Peteet
Art Director, Designer

Joan McClendon, Rex Peteet
Illustrators

Sibley/Peteet
Design Firm

Dallas Museum of Fine Art
Client

1983 Christmas Card
1983

Rex Peteet
*Art Director, Designer,
Copywriter*

Sibley/Peteet Design, Inc.
*Design Firm
Client*

A.I.G.A.
Boston Conference Poster
1985

Woody Pirtle
Art Director

Woody Pirtle, Jeff Weithman
Designers

Woody Pirtle
Illustrator

Jim Olvera
Photographer

A.I.G.A.
Copywriter

Pirtle Design
Design Firm

A.I.G.A.
Client

Valley View
Direct Mail Catalogue
1984
Don Sibley, Steve Gibbs
Art Directors
Steve Gibbs
Designer
John Wong
Photographer
Don Sibley
Copywriter
Sibley/Peteet Design, Inc.
Design Firm
Underline, Inc.
Agency
LaSalle Partners/
Valley View Mall
Client

Presence, The Transco Tower
1986
Jerry Herring
Art Director, Designer
Steve Brady
Photographer
Ann Holmes,
Philip Johnson, John Burgee
Copywriters
Herring Design
Design Firm
Herring Press, Inc.
Client

Chow Catering
Packaging
(Series)
1984

Arthur Eisenberg, Linda Eissler
Art Directors

Linda Eissler
Designer, Illustrator

Eisenberg Inc.
Design Firm

The Oakley Company
Agency

Chow Catering
Client

A.M. Cassandre
L'Atlantique
1931

Michael Doret
Poster for Bloomingdale's
1979

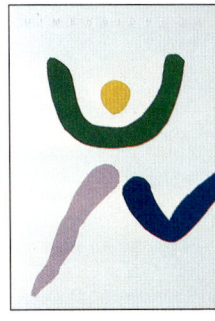

Dimensions Brochure
1984
Woody Pirtle
Art Director
Woody Pirtle, Ken Shafer
Designers
Bud Arnold
Copywriter
Pirtle Design
Design Firm
Simpson Paper Company
Client

Our Lady of Perpetual Motion
1984
Ginny Pitre
Art Director
Tom Zielinski
Designer
Andy Vracin
Photographer
George Toomer
Copywriter
Dallas Life Magazine
Design Firm
The Dallas Morning News
Agency, Client

253

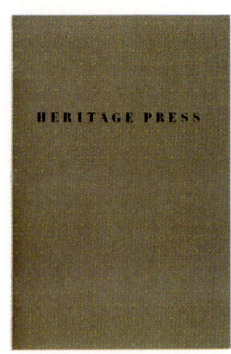

Heritage Press Brochure
1985
Lowell Williams
Art Director
Lowell Williams, Bill Carson
Designers
Arthur Meyerson
Photographer, Copywriter
Lee Herrick
Copywriter
Lowell Williams Design, Inc.
Design Firm, Agency
Heritage Press
Client

McClendon/Schmidt Birth Announcement
1984
Walter Horton
Art Director, Designer, Illustrator, Copywriter
Sibley/Peteet Design, Inc.
Design Firm
Joan McClendon, Donnie Schmidt
Clients

Dr. Bishop Letterhead
1985
Woody Pirtle, Jeff Weithman
Art Directors
Jeff Weithman
Designer, Illustrator
Pirtle Design
Design Firm
Dr. Alton Bishop, DDS
Client

254

Sakowitz Book
1981
Jay Loucks
Art Director, Designer
Ron Scott
Photographer
Loucks Atelier Inc.
Design Firm
Sakowitz
Client

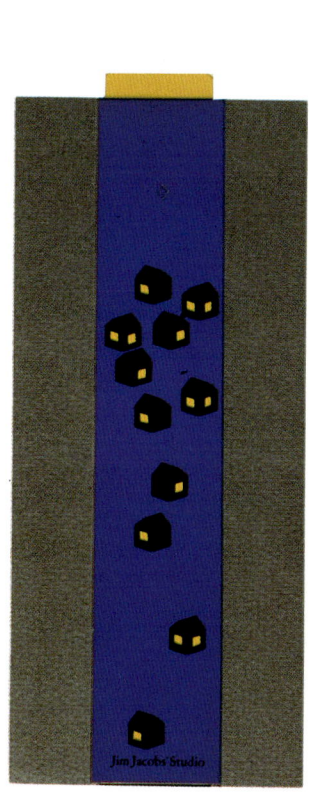

Jacobs/Pirtle
Christmas Card
1979
Jim Jacobs, Woody Pirtle
Art Directors, Designers
Jim Jacobs' Studio, Pirtle Design
Design Firms, Clients

International Paper
Magic Book
1984

Rex Peteet
Art Director, Designer

John Wong, The Bettman Archive
Photographers

Michael Schwab, Rex Peteet,
Luis Escobedo
Illustrators

Mark Perkins, Rex Peteet
Copywriters

Sibley/Peteet Design, Inc.
Design Firm

International Paper Co.
Client

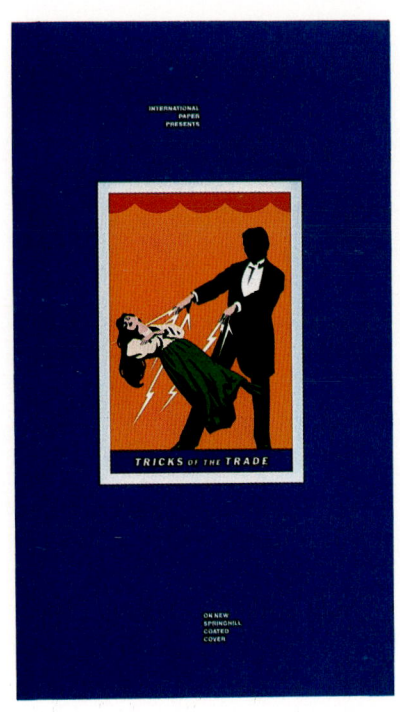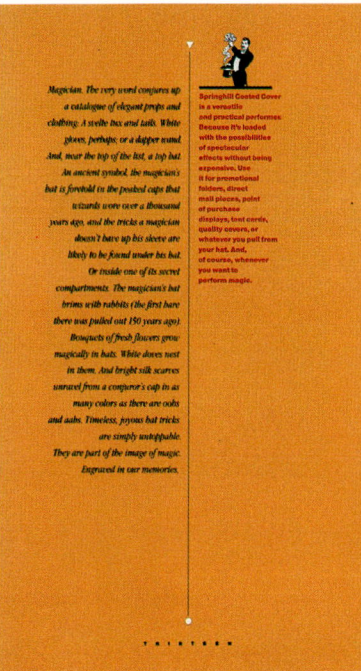

Robert Pirtle, DDS.
1972

Woody Pirtle
*Art Director, Designer,
Illustrator*

Pirtle Design
Design Firm

Robert Pirtle, DDS.
Client

Cow Moo
1985

Steve Connatser
Art Director, Designer

Brian Morrison
Illustrator/Photographer

Connatser & Co.
Design Firm

Texas Homes Magazine
Client

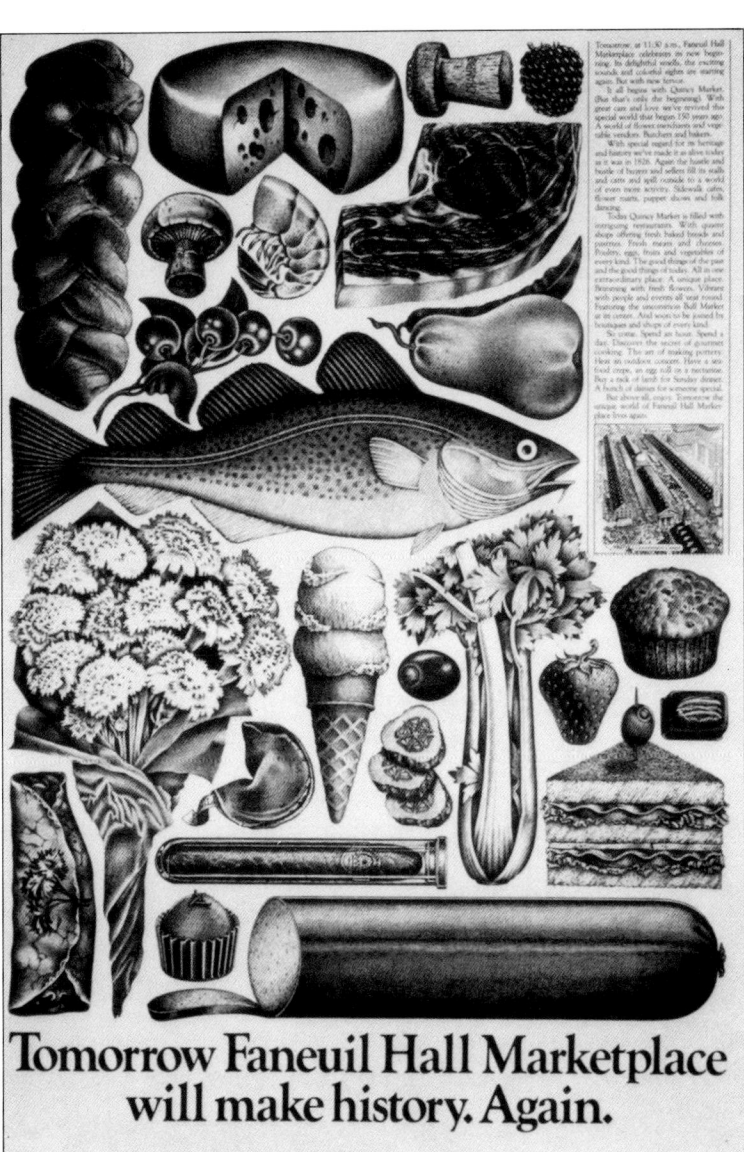

Faneuil Hall Ad
1977

Bob Dennard
Art Director, Designer, Copywriter

Ron Sullivan,
Woody Pirtle, Jim Hradecky,
Steve Miller, Don Grimes
Illustrators

The Richards Group
Design Firm, Agency

The Rouse Company
Client

¼

DSVC Pinball Quarterly
1968

Jim Jacobs
Art Director, Designer

Tom Cansler
Photographer

Spence Michlin
Copywriter

Stan Richards & Associates
Design Firm

Dallas Ft. Worth
Society of Visual
Communications
Client

¼

DSVC
African Drawing Quarterly
1968

Jim Jacobs
Designer

Jim Jacobs, Jack Reed's Mother
Copywriters

Stan Richards & Associates
Design Firm

Dallas Ft. Worth
Society of Visual
Communications
Client

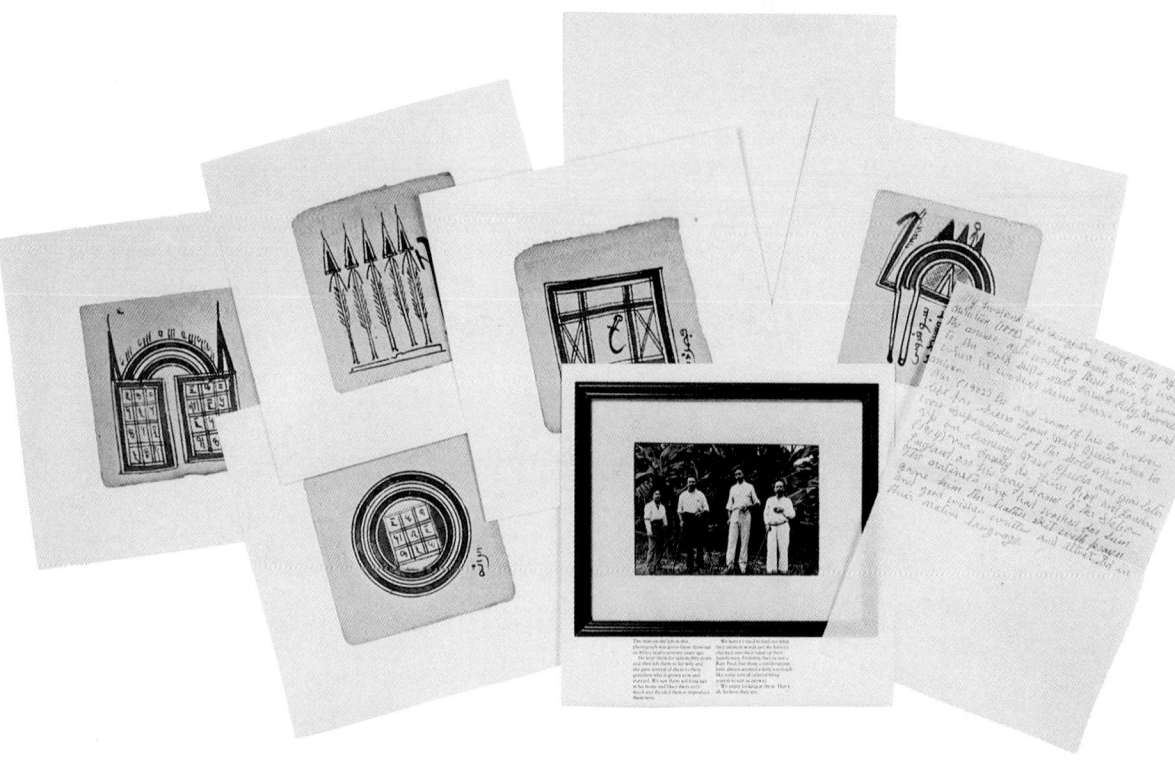

258

Sibley Wedding Announcement
1980
Don Sibley
Art Director, Designer, Copywriter
Dennard Creative
Design Firm
Don & Marilyn Sibley
Client

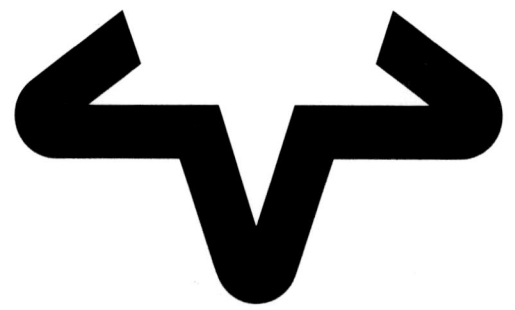

Publisher's Mark
1978
George Lenox
Designer
George Lenox Design
Design Firm
University of Texas Press
Client

259

Mona Lisa/Art Director
1974
Jerry MacPhail
Art Director, Designer
Jim Jacobs
Illustrator
Dallas Ft. Worth Society of Visual Communications
Client

Jo Ann Stone Stationery
1978, 1985

Lowell Williams
Art Director

Bill Carson
Designer

Jo Ann Stone
Copywriter

Lowell Williams Design, Inc.
Design Firm

Jo Ann Stone
Client

Heart With Band-Aid
Logo
1978
Woody Pirtle
Art Director, Designer
Pirtle Design
Design Firm
Heart Center/
Clinic for Cardiological Disorders
Client

Asel Art Logo
1975
Woody Pirtle
Art Director, Designer, Illustrator
Stan Richards & Associates
Design Firm
Asel Art Supply
Client

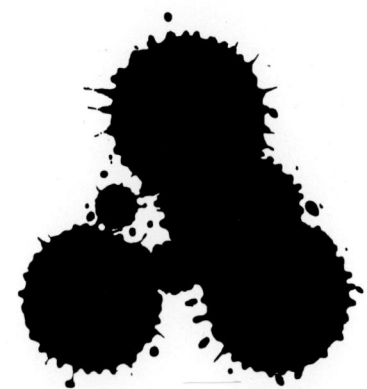

Dallas Opera Logo
1977
Woody Pirtle
Art Director, Designer, Illustrator
Stan Richards & Associates
Design Firm
Dallas Opera
Client

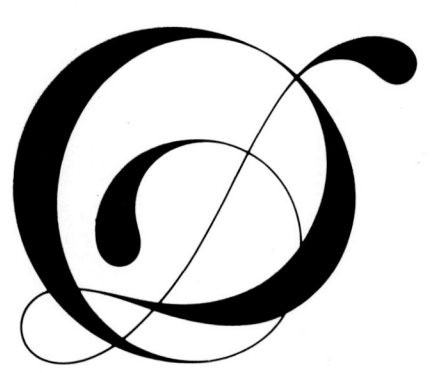

Travis Construction Logo
1982
Woody Pirtle
Art Director, Designer
Pirtle Design
Design Firm
Travis Construction
Client

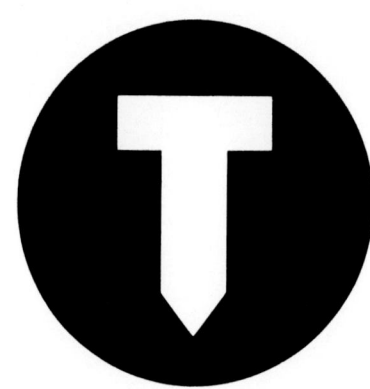

Aubrey Hair
1976
Woody Pirtle
Art Director, Designer
The Richards Group
Design Firm, Agency
Aubrey Hair
Client

Sea Wings Logo
1981
Woody Pirtle
Art Director, Designer, Illustrator
Pirtle Design
Design Firm
Sea Wing Charter Service
Client

Cobb & Friend Logo
1985
Luis Acevedo, Woody Pirtle
Art Directors
Luis Acevedo
Designer, Illustrator
Pirtle Design
Design Firm
Cobb & Friend
Client

Gary Gray Logo
1982
Woody Pirtle
Art Director, Designer
Kenny Garrison
Illustrator
Pirtle Design
Design Firm
Gary Gray, Writer
Client

Landa Pharmaceutical Logo
1979
Woody Pirtle
Art Director, Designer
Pirtle Design
Design Firm
Landa Pharmaceutical
Client

Hyatt Pop Up Cards
1977

Rex Peteet
Art Director, Designer, Illustrator

Mary Keck
Copywriter

The Richards Group
Design Firm

Hyatt Hotels
Client

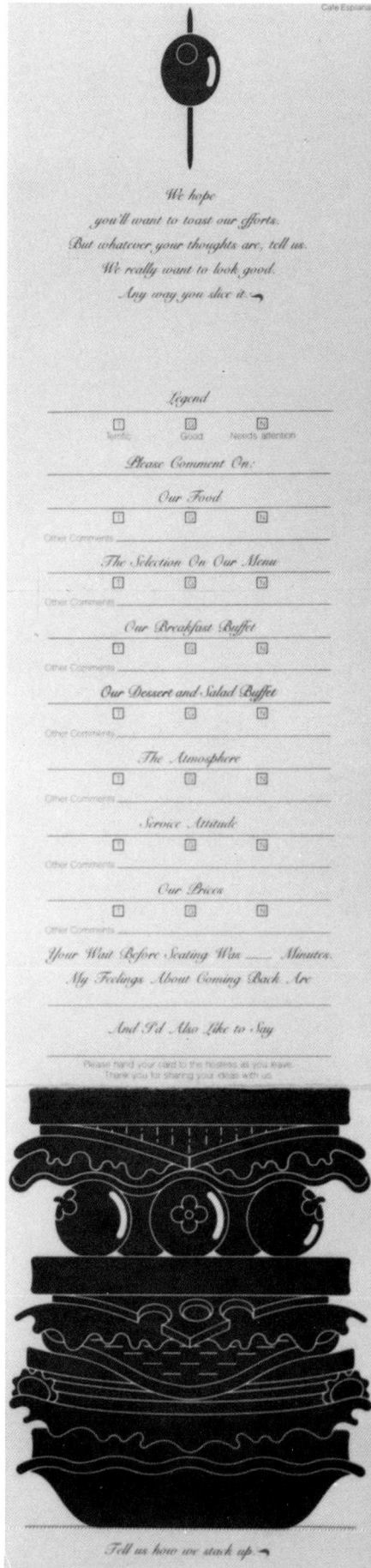

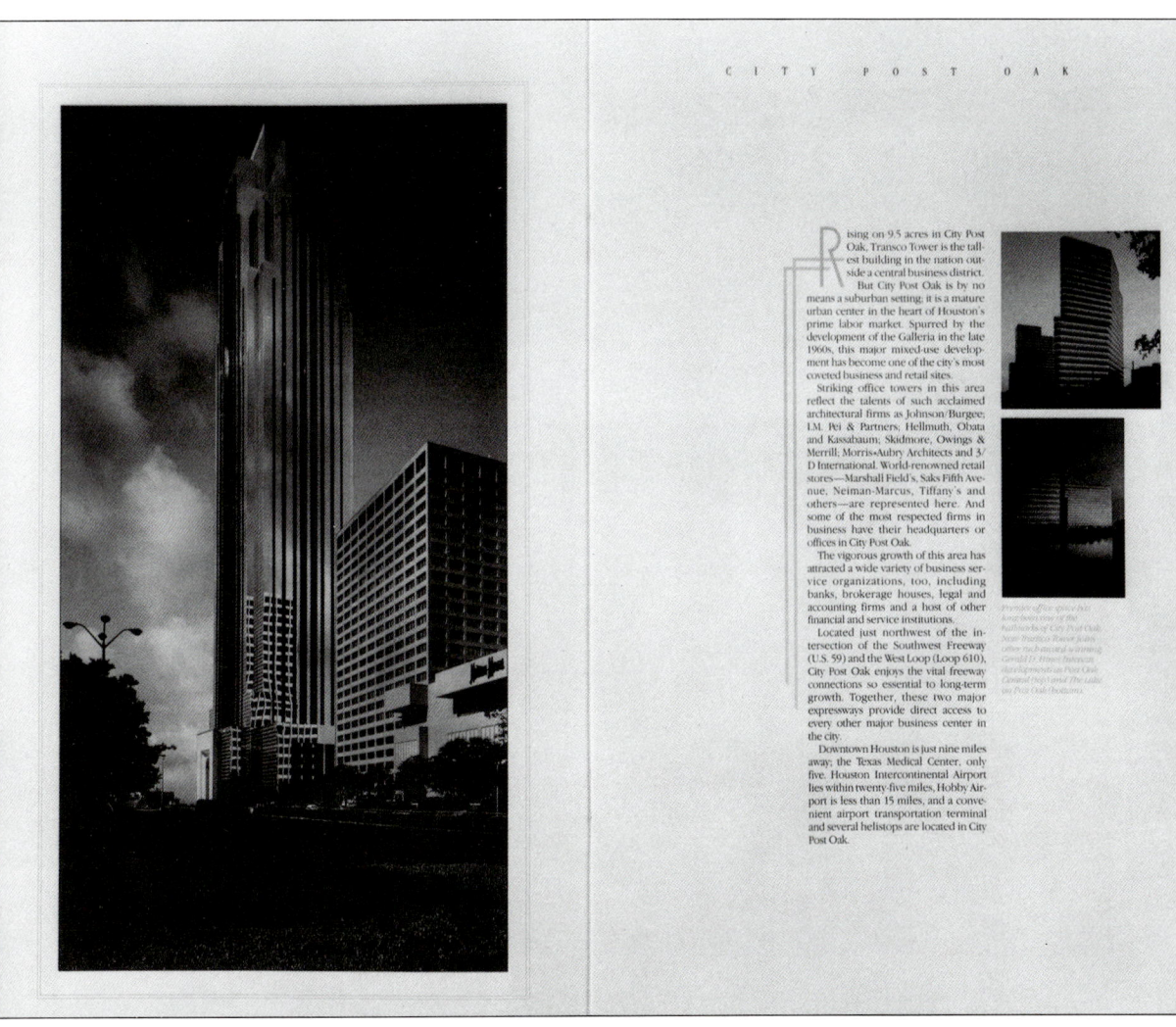

Transco Tower Brochure
1981
Jerry Herring
Art Director, Designer

Bob Harr, Joe Baraban, Ron Scott
Photographers

Lee Herrick
Copywriter

Herring Design
Design Firm

Gerald D. Hines Interests
Client

Dallas Zoo Logo
1983
Dick Mitchell
Art Director, Designer, Illustrator

Richards, Sullivan, Brock & Associates
Design Firm

The Richards Group
Agency

Dallas Zoo
Client

Easter Egg Ad
1978
Rex Peteet
Art Director, Designer
Rex Peteet, Nancy Hoefig
Illustrators
Gary Gibson
Copywriter
The Richards Group
Design Firm
Paul Broadhead & Associates
Client

WATER STREET OYSTER BAR

Casebier Letterhead
1980
Rex Peteet
Art Director, Designer, Illustrator
Pirtle Design
Design Firm
Ed Casebier
Client

Waterstreet Oyster Bar
1984
Janis Koy Beveridge
Art Director, Designer
Koy Design, Inc.
Design Firm
Waterstreet Oyster Bar
Client

A
A.I.A.-Houston 145, 229
A.I.G.A. 40, 250
A.I.G.A.-Texas 127, 167
Abney, Karen 247
Abramowitz, Jerry 105
Acadiana Symphony Orchestra 150
Acevedo, Luis 96, 97, 98, 156, 169, 235, 237, 263
Adams, Laurie Foreman 68
Ad Works 183
Aker, Joe 117
Akers, Terrall 148
Alexandria Mall 247
Allen, Charlie 118
Allen, Gerald 105
Amon Carter Museum 51
Anderson, Sherry 95, 224
A Place for Everything 222
Arday, Don 155
Arias, Inc.
Arnold, Bud 253
Arnold, Harwell, McClain Assoc. 129
Artworks 30
Art Directors Club of Houston 130, 166, 182, 189
Art Directors Club of New York 92, 201
Art Investors Gallery 182
Asel Art Supply 262
Asheland Design, Inc. 26
A.S.M.P. 157
Aubrey Hair 262
Autohaus 33
Ayres, Robin 228

B
Baker, Beth 90
Baker, Dot 70
Baker, Kipp 62
Baldwin, Bill 195
Baldwin, Jim 218
Baraban, Joe 28, 35, 43, 54, 96, 97, 131, 145, 265
Barney, William 170
Barnhill, Steve 68, 81, 126, 131, 134
Steve Barnhill & Company 90
Barrington, Ann 143
Baronet, Willie 150
Bayou City Oyster Company 186
Bell, Patrick MD 223
Bennigan's 112, 113
Benoit, Dennis 68, 179
Benoit Rutter, Inc. 68, 179, 195
The Bettman Archive 51, 187, 256
Beveridge, Janis Koy 36, 68, 73, 267
Bishop, Alton MD 254
Bishop, Patti 110
Black, Paul 38, 66, 99, 121, 224
Paul Black Design 66
Bolton, Greg 243

Bommarito, Guy 53, 194, 208
Greg Booth And Associates 143
Booth, Greg 26, 45, 46, 47, 48, 49, 50, 51, 52, 53, 87, 146, 166, 220
Bordelon, Melinda 192
Boswell Byers & Stone 54
Boy Scouts of America 85
Boy Scouts, Circle 10 Council 85, 146
Boyd, Brian 91, 128, 146, 151, 168, 218, 228
Bramalea Texas, Inc. 180
Braasch, Gary 140, 186
Bradford, Linda 27, 126
Bradshaw's Prime Beef 68
Bradshaw, Reagan 221
Brady, Steve 68, 76, 102, 181, 208, 251
Braniff International 146
Branner, Phil 64
Brazeal, Lee Lee 192
Bridger, Bobby 217
Paul Broadhead & Assoc. 57, 84, 101, 137, 139, 183, 207, 214, 266
Brown, Cathy 148
Brown, Lance 206
Burget, Russell 140
Burgee, John 251
Burke, Carol 104, 182, 184, 185
Busby, Jim 180
Butler Florist 209
Butler, Diane 247
Diane Butler & Associates 247
Butyl Rubber Producers 41

C
Cadillac Fairview 132, 217
Calhoun, Cody 57, 112, 212
Campbell, Mike 227
Canizaro, Joseph 223
Cannedy, Carl 194
Cansler, Tom 258
Canterbury Press 171
Carson, Bill 35, 54, 65, 87, 104, 108, 126, 129, 132, 199, 206, 217, 254, 261
Ben Carter & Associates 140
Casebier, Ed 267
Celusniak, Chris 30
Cenergy Corporation 131
Cenikor Foundation 131
Chambers, Bart 189
Chambers, Steve 165
Chapman, Greg 76
Chapman, Ron 151
Chasey, Diane 143
Chaucer Group, The 150
Chavigny, Neil L., Jr. 148
Chimayo 127
Chow Catering 252
City National Bank 210
Clicks Billiards, Inc. 64
Clinic for Cardiological Disorders 262
Clock, Argus 148

CMI 211
Cobb & Friend 169, 263
Cober, Alan 189
Colling, Dana 153
Collins, Bryan 165
Collage Systems 79
Colvin, Alan 85, 132, 145, 232
Compendium 140
Connatser & Crum 122
Connatser & Company 34, 115, 121, 257
Connatser, Judy 121
Connatser, Steve 34, 115, 121, 257
Copp, Jeff 123
Corgan Associates 227
Cotton Club 148
Craig, John 131
Crawley, John 147
Creel Morrell, Inc. 211
Crittenden, Susan 64
Crow, LaRue 238
Cross, James 134
Cross Associates 134
Croxton, Brent 56, 211, 215
Crum, Don 57, 114, 122, 123
Don Crum & Company 57, 114
Curry, Tom 184, 212

D
Dady, Glen 218
Dallas Advertising League 63, 115, 122
Dallas Designers' Chili Cookoff 116, 246
Dallas Life Magazine 90, 253
Dallas Market Center/Infoworks 152, 153
The Dallas Morning News 90, 158, 253
Dallas Museum of Fine Art 121, 175, 249
Dallas Opera 262
Dallas Public Library 86
Dallas Symphony Orchestra 128, 211
Dallas Society Visual Comm 33, 35, 56, 57, 89, 96, 98, 114, 160, 165, 172, 174, 194, 240, 258, 260
Dallas Theatre Center 213
Dallas White Rock Marathon 198
Dallas Zoo 228, 265
Daues, Dan 43
Davis, Bruce Henry 150
Dearwater, Andy 27, 132
Degolyer Library 223
Dennard Creative 84, 96, 101, 112, 113, 116, 137, 139, 147, 148, 165, 192, 200, 207, 212, 214, 259
Dennard, Bob 45, 57, 84, 96, 101, 105, 112, 113, 137, 139, 147, 148, 165, 180, 192, 200, 207, 212, 214, 234, 257
DiBaggio, Brad 36

Dimperio, Mr. & Mrs. 94
Ditch, Scott 75
DLM, Inc. 205
D Magazine 184, 185, 218
Dolim, Judy 95, 165
Dunnick, Regan 59, 61, 65, 82, 92
Dunnick/Hill Productions 65

E
Eastfield College 66
Eggers, Scott 75, 118
Eickmeyer, John 178
Eisenberg, Arthur 35, 155, 252
Eisenberg, Inc. 35, 155, 252
Eisenberg & Pannell 108, 210, 222, 243
Eissler, Linda 252
Engle, Cathy
Episcopal School of Dallas 147
Escobedo, Luis 256
Evans, John 155

F
Fairmount Hotel 196, 197
Fallon McElligott Rice 132
Federated Stores Realty, Inc. 156
The 500 Inc. 56
Flaming, Jon 164
Ford, Wayne 28, 54
Forsbach, Robert 91
Fort Worth Symphony Orchestra 244
Fowler, David 245
Freeman, Charlie 119
Frost, Robert 186
Ft. Worth Linotyping, Inc. 62

G
Gardner, Rick 102, 175
Gardner, Julie 224
Garrison, Kenny 81, 93, 141, 263
Gary, Wayne 122
Geary, F.B. MD 243
Geer, Mark 27, 29, 90, 140, 166
Gibbs, Steve 39, 135, 136, 154, 220, 251
Gibson, Gary 125, 240, 266
Gill, Duana 167
The Glassell School of Art 38
Good Earth Restaurant 162, 163
Goodwill Industries 241
Goodwin Dannenbaum Littman Wingfield 162
Goodwin, Gary 82, 178
The Grape 94
Grace School 27
Grahnquist, Mr. & Mrs. 67
Graphic Design Press 141
Gray, Gary 263
Gray, Jon & Toni 32
Green, A.C. 166
Greenville Avenue Merchants Guild 55
Don Grimes Design, Inc. 32, 83, 223, 238, 257

268

Grimes, Don 32, 83, 160, 194, 223, 234, 238, 257
Grimes, Melissa 43, 53, 232

H

Hammer, Stanley 63
Handweavers Assoc. 83, 248
Harr, Bob 108, 129, 132, 199, 208, 265
Harris, Pat 61
The Harris Group 242
Hart, Chuck 31
Harwell, Barbara 187
Hawkins, Jill 111
Jill Hawkins Design 111
The Hay Agency 69, 76, 200
Hay, Jess 46, 47, 48, 49, 50, 52, 53
Haynes, Mike 41, 62, 81, 227
Heart Center 262
Heck, John 39, 41, 83, 162, 175, 239
George Hederhorst Company 54
Heffernan, Terry 245
Helton, Linda 164
Hendel, Richard 110
Heritage Press 161, 210, 212, 254
Herrick, Lee 35, 76, 87, 102, 108, 126, 129, 199, 208, 217, 254, 265
Herring Design 39, 55, 70, 76, 99, 102, 126, 131, 134, 141, 171, 175, 187, 202, 208, 251, 265
Herring Group 158, 192, 247
Herring & Pirtle, Inc. 83, 130, 238
Herring Press, Inc. 251
Herring, Jerry 39, 55, 70, 76, 83, 99, 102, 126, 130, 131, 134, 141, 151, 171, 175, 187, 202, 208, 238, 251, 265
Hershorn, Shel 127
Hewlett, Paule Sheya 28, 207, 216
Hicks, Mike 43, 53, 110, 167, 190, 191, 192, 208
Hightower, Jim 43, 147
Hill, Chris 37, 43, 59, 61, 65, 73, 82, 92, 97, 101, 123, 140, 145, 181, 182, 186, 189, 196, 197, 201
HILL/A Marketing Design Group 37, 43, 59, 61, 65, 82, 92, 97, 101, 181, 182, 186, 189, 201
Gerald D. Hines Interests 61, 76, 102, 103, 108, 202, 208, 265
Hixo, Inc. 43, 53, 110, 167, 190, 191, 192, 194, 208
Hoefig, Nancy 50, 136, 154, 266
Hollenbeck, Phil 57
Holman, David 223
Holmes, Ann 251
Hopson, David 205

Horton, Walter 60, 84, 118, 247, 254
Horton, Sharon 62
Houston Metropolitan Ministries 126, 134
Houston Zoological Society 27
Howard/Gossett Co. 29
HRA Associate Architects 207, 216
Hradecky, Jim 33, 56, 164, 257
Hubler, Olivette 143
Hubler, Roseburg, & Associates 143
Hussey, Katherine Sheehy 88
Hutchens, Paige 218
Hutchens, Dan 218
Hyatt Regency Dallas 31
Hyatt Hotels 264

I

Independent American Tower 242
Interfirst Bldg. 180
International Paper Co. 256
International Assoc. of Business Communicators 109

J

Jackson, Thom 74, 136
Jacobs, Jim 64, 77, 79, 82, 86, 88, 118, 127, 143, 157, 159, 163, 170, 171, 175, 183, 222, 227, 240, 244, 255, 258, 260
Jim Jacob's Studio 64, 77, 79, 82, 86, 88, 143, 157, 159, 163, 170, 175, 183, 222, 227, 240, 244, 255
James, Nathan 232
Jeanmard, Jerry 112, 137, 162, 163, 196, 200, 212, 242
JMB Federated 138, 189
Joseph Canizaro Interests 223
Johnson, Chuck 96, 165, 192
Johnson, Philip 251
Jones, Dick 64, 175
Judson, Mark 28

K

Kagan, Brian 141
Kammerath, Danny 26, 240
Kampa, David 88, 225, 233
John Katz Photography 33, 120
Katz, John 33, 78, 120
KCBN Advertising 187
Keck, Mary 89, 94, 117, 144, 154, 156, 158, 160, 218, 221, 227, 234, 264
Kerm, Judy 31
Kilmer, Brenda 38
Kilmer Design 38
Kilmer-Geer Design 27, 29, 90, 166
Kilmer, Richard 27, 29, 90, 140, 166
Kim, Margaret 59
King, Greg 165, 205, 212
Kirkley, Kent 26, 34, 64, 111, 222

Knoll International 42
Koester, Ken 147, 165, 192
Koetting, Sherry Anderson 95, 224
Koetting, Richard 95
Susan G. Komen Foundation 200
Kondos, Theo 189
Kotarski-McCue, Cheryl 192
Koy Design, Inc. 36, 68, 267
Krause & Young 31
Kuhlen Glacen 205
KVIL Radio 151

L

Lakewood Theatre 85
Lakewood Yacht Club 87
Landa Pharmaceutical 263
Langridge, Mary 43, 82, 101, 182, 247
Larkin, Sharon 109
LaSalle Partners 74, 251
La Salle, Patti 107
Latorre, Robert 184, 224
Learning Technologies, Inc. 178, 204
Legal Assistant Today 88
Lehndorff Group, The 173
Lenox, George 107, 122, 154, 259
George Lenox Design 259
Leon, Paul 108
Lesh, David 247
Leslie & Company 55
Levinson, Levinson & Hill 224
Liddell, Thom 124
Alan Lidji Design 119, 158, 178, 241
Lidji, Alan 119, 158, 178, 241
Lidji, Laynie 241
Lincoln Property Company 106
Lindlof, Ed 110, 122, 154
Lindstrom, Eric 194
Llewellyn, Sue 212
Lomas & Nettleton 69, 200
Lomas & Nettleton Financial Corp. 46, 47, 48, 49, 51, 52
Lomas & Nettleton Housing Corp. 50
Lomas & Nettleton Mortgage Co. 45
Lomas & Nettleton Mortgage Investors 45, 46, 47, 48, 49, 50, 51, 52, 53
Lone Star Donuts 155
Longfield, David 218
Los Lomas 224
Loucks, Jay 140, 176, 196, 197, 255
Loucks Atelier, Inc. 123, 140, 145, 176, 196, 197, 255
Lovell, Rick 73
Luby's Cafeterias 68
Al Lum Properties 175

M

MacPhail, Jerry 260
Madrulli, Pete 173

Magleby, McRay 53
Manhattan Laundry & Dry Cleaning 155
Marchand, Wayne & Judy 239
Marcus, Melinda 104, 168, 228
Marschall, Dorothy 32
Martin, David 96, 165, 192
Martin, Mo 57
Mary Kay Cosmetics 105
May, Doug 147
MBank 58
McBride, Dealey & Day 106
McCoy, Gary 121
McClendon, Joan 249, 254
McDermott, Marise 221
McElgunn, Jim 175
McEntire, Larry 194, 208
McGrath, Michael 31
Anne McGilvray & Company 143, 227
Michael McGrath Design 31
McKay, Jeffrey 59, 65, 82, 182
McKnight, Diana 40, 79, 91, 164, 228
McNeff, Tom 108, 199, 202
Mead Paper Company 72
Media Communications 101
Mental Health Assoc. of Texas 154
Mercantile Bank 87, 220
Mercantile Texas Corporation 26, 166
Arthur Meyerson Photography 44
Meyerson, Arthur 44, 65, 80, 81, 101, 145, 254
Michlin, Spence 258
Miller Outdoor Theatre 78
Miller, Blake 28, 223
Miller, Madelyn 63
Miller, Judson & Ford Inc. 28, 54, 223
Miller, Steve 46, 47, 48, 49, 73, 257
Minor, Craig 211
Mitchell, Dick 46, 47, 56, 70, 87, 114, 136, 166, 220, 228, 265
Moore, Ann
Moonlight Beach Development 84
Morrison Design 58
Morrison, Brian 257
Morrison, Penny 58
Muhlherr, Michael 38
Murphy, Dennis 218
Museum of Fine Arts, Houston 206
Myers, Jim 40
Myres, Sherry, Fred & Jackson 240

N

Narahara, Dean 150
The Nasher Company 160, 180

National Gypsum Company 80, 81
NCAA 181
NCH Corporation 245
NCR Corporation 97
Neiman Marcus 136, 143
Newman, Cody 222
Nichols, Frank 129, 195, 222
North Hills Mall 189
Northern Telecom 168
North Star Mall 79
North Park 160

O
The Oakley Company 209, 252
Odom, Roby 69
Ogilvy & Mather 78
Oiltools International, Ltd. 35
Oliver, Kerry 39, 239
The Olivet Group 43
Olmos, Moses Photographer 151
Olmsted-Kirk Paper 170
Olson, Peggy 106
Olvera, Jim 250
Omega Optical 221
Omron Financial Systems, Inc. 245
One Realty Corporation 99
Orchard, Liza 148

P
Page, Owen 73, 147, 228
Palmer Paper Company 176
Pannell, Beverly 41
Pannell, Cap 34, 41, 127, 133, 138, 142, 149, 178, 182, 204, 205, 222, 226, 245
Pannell Creative 34
Pannell/St. George 41, 133, 138, 142, 178, 182, 204, 205, 226, 245
Park Central 173
Parrish, John 74, 136
Payne, Richard 76, 102
Perkins, Mark 46, 47, 49, 50, 56, 69, 77, 79, 114, 118, 128, 136, 164, 174, 211, 215, 218, 256
Perkins 222
Peteet, Rex 33, 38, 39, 60, 63, 74, 84, 89, 94, 98, 101, 109, 112, 113, 116, 117, 118, 121, 134, 155, 156, 160, 162, 163, 183, 184, 194, 200, 205, 212, 213, 214, 224, 230, 242, 247, 249, 256, 264, 266, 267
Peterson & Company 107, 193
Peterson, Bryan L. 107, 193
Phal, John 221
Pharr Cox 220
Pharr, Tom & Cynthia 118
Phillips, Ann Eklund 84, 247
Pierce, Donald L., Jr. 55, 141, 145, 176

Pirtle Design 33, 42, 44, 55, 62, 71, 72, 80, 81, 85, 89, 93, 94, 97, 98, 100, 103, 117, 120, 129, 131, 132, 141, 144, 145, 152, 153, 156, 161, 169, 170, 172, 177, 184, 185, 188, 195, 209, 218, 221, 225, 227, 229, 232, 233, 234, 235, 236, 237, 238, 248, 250, 253, 254, 255, 256, 262, 263, 267
Pirtle, Robert 256
Pirtle, Woody 33, 42, 44, 55, 62, 67, 71, 72, 80, 81, 83, 85, 89, 93, 94, 97, 100, 103, 117, 120, 124, 129, 130, 131, 132, 141, 144, 145, 146, 152, 153, 156, 160, 161, 164, 169, 172, 177, 180, 184, 185, 188, 194, 195, 209, 218, 221, 225, 227, 229, 232, 233, 234, 235, 236, 237, 238, 248, 250, 253, 254, 255, 256, 257, 262, 263
The Pitluk Group 73
Pitre, Ginny 253
Pitts, Ann 78
Pizza Inn 148
Pollack, Denise 87
Post, Andy 49, 73, 75, 105, 151
Poth, Tom 110, 190, 191, 192, 194
Powell, Glyn 35, 113, 165, 192, 200
Prickly Pear Press 159, 170, 244
Printing Resources 243
Priore BMW Autocare 163
Professional Typographers 36, 39

R
Rattan, Joe 37, 43, 61, 92, 97, 101, 131, 132, 141, 181, 186, 201, 236
Ravseh, Trisha 36
Redbird Mall 144
Redding, Ray 245
Jack Reed's Mother 258
Reilly, Philip & Donna 195
Renfro, Mike 58
Stan Richards & Associates 36, 83, 124, 146, 151, 160, 171, 258, 262
Richards, Brock, Miller, Mitchell & Assoc. 36, 46, 47, 73, 87, 91, 146, 147, 151, 168, 198, 218, 220, 228, 265
Richards, Grant 26
The Richards Group 26, 33, 36, 45, 46, 47, 48, 49, 50, 51, 52, 53, 56, 58, 67, 70, 73, 75, 77, 83, 91, 105, 114, 116, 118, 125, 128, 136, 138, 146, 147, 149, 151, 154, 160, 164, 166, 168, 174, 180, 183, 194, 198, 211, 215, 218, 223, 228, 234, 240, 245, 257, 262, 264, 265, 266
Richards, Stan 83, 116, 151, 171

Richards, Sullivan, Brock & Assoc. 26, 36, 48, 49, 50, 53, 56, 70, 75, 77, 114, 116, 118, 125, 128, 136, 154, 166, 174, 211, 215, 240, 265
Riddle, Jerry 238
Rigsby, Lana 27, 54, 65, 217
Rivers, Laura 136
Riverside Square 138
RMI
Robertson Advertising 197
Rogers, Gena 58, 218
Rose Associates 129, 199
Rosemarin, Mickey
Rosler, Peter 77
The Rouse Company 40, 75, 79, 136, 164, 183, 215, 257
Rovillo, Chris 77, 125, 147, 174, 198, 215, 240
Roy, Don 40
RTKL Associates, Inc. 173, 180, 189
Rucker, Doug 36
Rushing, Dale 209
Russel, David 105
Rust, Ann 79

S
Sailor, Jim 180
Sakowitz 255
Sallis, James 90
Sanders, Jim 38, 41, 83
Sands, Suzi 88
Saunders, Lubinski & White, Inc. 155, 205
Savage Design Group, Inc. 142
Savage, Paula 142
Schorre, Charles 171
Schmidt, Donnie 254
Schroeder, Acevedo 37
Schroeder, Mike 37, 55, 85, 89, 94, 100, 103, 108, 153, 161, 170, 177, 235, 236, 238, 243, 293
Schroeder Real Estate 224
Schwab, Michael 256
Schwartz, Daniel 52
Schwartz, Rona 27
Scoggin, Dan 71
Scott, Ron 35, 39, 76, 81, 87, 104, 108, 132, 199, 208, 255, 265
Scott Towel 170
Seashore Press 171
Sea Wing Charter Service 263
Secker, Beth 173, 180, 189
Serve-Rigs 126
Sessions, Steven 243
Steven Sessions Design 243
Shafer, Ken 39, 163, 253
Shakespeare Festival of Dallas 177, 188
Sheers, Melissa Lane 34
Sherman, C. Randall 176
Shimkus Design 63
Shimkus, Barbara 63

The Shoshin Society 59, 119, 230, 231
Sibley, Don 39, 57, 101, 112, 135, 136, 137, 139, 158, 163, 187, 205, 207, 212, 213, 214, 224, 231, 246, 251, 259
Sibley/Peteet Design, Inc. 38, 39, 60, 63, 74, 84, 95, 99, 109, 117, 118, 121, 134, 135, 136, 155, 158, 162, 163, 199, 200, 205, 213, 224, 230, 231, 242, 246, 247, 249, 251, 254, 256
Sibley, Marilyn 259
Silverman, Jay 157
Simpson Paper Company 93, 134, 253
Sims, Jim 27, 29, 35, 37, 55, 90, 126, 134, 146, 168, 185, 186, 206, 243
Skyline High School 218
Slattery, Jack 223
Pat Sloan Design 62
Sloan, Pat 62
Smith, Cerita 34, 138, 142
The Smitherman Corporation 217
Smitherman, Larry 217
Sneath, Lee 80
Soderlind, Kirsten 208
Sons, Larry 155, 180, 183
Southern Methodist University 107, 193, 223
Southwestern Bell 133
Southwest Conference 73
Southwestern Typographics 102
Stanley, Steve 41
State Dept. of Agriculture 43
State Fair Texas 179
St. Clair, Dean 32
St. David's Hospital 194
Steak, Pat 143
Steed, Marguerite 38
Stevens Interiors 101
St. George, Carol 127, 142, 170, 178, 204, 205, 210, 222, 226, 245
St. Gill, Marc 87
Stinson, Mark 63
Stipp, Bill 195
Stipp, D.C. 116, 211
St. Louis Union Station 164
Stone, Jo Ann 132, 207, 261
Stone, John 26, 45, 48, 49, 50, 51, 52, 53
Stribling, Kelly 136
Studio Ten Productions 83
Sullivan Perkins 40, 79, 164
Sullivan, Ron 40, 48, 49, 50, 51, 52, 53, 56, 75, 79, 136, 149, 160, 164, 180, 257
Summerford, Jack 26, 33, 40, 45, 51, 52, 67, 102, 105, 124, 155, 210

Summerford Design, Inc. 33, 40, 102, 105, 124, 155, 210
Sunbelt Savings 220
Sunwest Communications 182
Superb Litho 186
Superior Land & Cattle Company 28

T
Tango 225
Taylor, Inc. 145
Tele-Image 142
Temple Mall 183
Templin, Gary 232
Tennison, James E. 244
Texas Committee for Humanities 221
Texas Department of Agriculture 147
Texas Homes Magazine 34, 121, 257
Texas Humanist 221
Texas International Company 140
Texas Junk Company 58
Texas Monthly 88, 118, 190
Texas Monthly Press 190, 191, 199, 208
Texas Special Olympics 90
Texas Toffey, Inc. 38
T.G.I. Friday's Inc. 100, 232, 233, 234, 235, 236, 237
Thrasher, Dennis & Lisa 82
Thumb-Page, Tom 187
Tidwell, Bieber 32
Todd, Doris 73
Tombaugh, Marianne 200
Tomlinson, Doug 199
Tooley, Sharon 28, 207, 216
Sharon Tooley Design 28, 207, 216
Toomer, George 112, 253
Tootsies 142
Total Picture 142
Tracy-Locke, Inc. 232
Trammell Crow Company 38, 60, 117, 135, 247
Travis Construction 262
Turkel, Mark 211
Nancy Lee Turner Design 244
Turner, Nancy Lee 244
Turtle Creek Center For The Arts 26
Typographers International Asso. 155

U
Underline, Inc. 251
Universal Signs
University of Texas Press 107, 110, 122, 154, 259
Unruh, Jack 33, 47, 50, 107, 139, 170, 179, 197, 198, 207
USA Film Festival 67, 111, 138, 149
U.S. West 132
UPI 51

V
Valley View Mall 74, 251
Vansyckle, Martha 104
Vecta 73
Villa Linda Mall 158
Von Heeder, Paul 218
Vracin, Andy 253

W
Water Street Oyster Bar 267
The Watson-Casey Companies 110
Webb & Sons 31, 178
Weekley & Penny 41, 83
Alan Weinkrantz & Company 204
Weithman, Jeff 72, 141, 152, 153, 172, 250, 254
Werfel, Amy 114
Wesko, David 106
White, Frank 28, 207, 216
Whitehead, Barbara 217
Whitmore Manufacturing Company 76
Whittington, Richard 221
Whole Foods Company 53
Widener, Terry 90, 154, 192
Miss Williams 37
Lowell Williams Design, Inc. 27, 35, 54, 65, 87, 104, 108, 126, 129, 132, 186, 199, 202, 206, 217, 254, 261
The Williams Group 84
Williams, Lowell 27, 35, 54, 65, 87, 104, 108, 126, 129, 132, 186, 199, 202, 206, 217, 254, 261
Williams, Melinda 167
Williamson Printing 91, 117, 209
Wilson, Jan 148, 192
Wind River Press 223
Wingfield, Anna Jane 162
Wong, John 47, 58, 251, 256
Woodward, Fred 88
Wood, Keith 50
Wyaika Press 217

Y
Young Presidents Organization 77

Z
Zapf, Herman 176
Ziebell, Robert 38
Zielinski, Tom 90, 253
Zimmersmith Productions 238

AIGA-Texas Members

ARLINGTON
Jim Nelson Black
Susan Murphy

AUSTIN
Linda Adkins
James Ammenheuser
Richard Bartholomew
Vernon Berger
Richard Brinkman
Jim Cinq-Mars
Thomas A. Darnell
Cinda Debbink
Herman Dyal
Claire A. Fisher
Mike Flahive
Stephen Freeman
Ransom B. Green, Jr.
David Grosvenor
Sue Heatly
Ray Helmers
Mike Hicks
Susan Hicks-Sands
Chris Jagmin
Mary Jarowitz
Terry Johnston
Larry Jolly
Diana Kipfer
Alison Klassen
William Korbus
Claire Maeder
Helen McCarty
Marcellina McNally
Mark S. Mitchell
Eric Morrell
Tom Poth
Gerald F. Tucker
John A. Wilson
Jane Wu

BEAUMONT
Michael Lee

BELLAIRE
Elizabeth Krueger
Gee Lindblom

BRYAN
Luis D. Gonzalez

CORPUS CHRISTI
David Bridges
Debbie Wingfield

DALLAS
Luis Acevedo
Willie Baronet
Betsy Berger
Robert A. Bernardini
Dan Blackburn
Greg Booth
Brian K. Boyd
Ron Bryan
David Carter
Gaylene Cochran
Alan Colvin
Steve Connatser
Dean Corbitt
Don Crum
Christi Daniel
Virginia S. Dismukes
Stephanie Donon
Marsha Drebelbis
Mark Drury
Linda Eissler
Kathleen A. Ferguson
Lynne Ferguson
Bill Ford
Jay Franklin
Sandra Freeman
Kenny Garrison
Rick Gavos
David Gillespie
James Good
Don Grimes
Chuck Hart
Linda Helton
Jack Hermsen
Duncan Hopkins
Olivette Hubler
Ron Hudson
Jim Jacobs
Brian Kagan
Clare Adams Kittle
Alan Lidji
Tommy J. Lout
Douglas May
Terrence Meacher
Genevieve Meek
Madelyn Miller
Stephen Miller
Sherry Myres
Jim Olvera
Randy Padorr-Black
Cap Pannell
Rex Peteet
Woody Pirtle
Ginny Pitre
Glyn Powell
Ken Pugh
Joe Rattan
Rick Reeves
Shannon Reeves
Sue Reynolds
Pamela Roseburg
Chris Rovillo
Mike Schroeder
Virgil Scott
Beth Secker
Don Sibley
Arthur Simmons
Cerita Smith
Linda C. Smith
Douglas J. Sprague
Carol St. George
Mark Steele
D.C. Stipp
Ron Sullivan
Jack Summerford
Alan Taylor
Larry E. Taylor
Jeri Taylor
Becky Wade
Jeff Weithman
Alice Word
Edward Zahra

EL PASO
Scott Goodwin

GARLAND
Judy Kriehn

HOUSTON
Anthony C. Adduci
Chris Alexander
Abraham Amuny
Paula S. Andell
Jo Bertone
George Buckow
William M. Burwell
Chuck Carlberg
Scott Carothers
Bill Carson
James Cauthorn
Tonnie Chamblee
Phil Chrzanowski
F. Clendaniel
Tom Ewasko
Jeffry A. Flasik
Hope Fonte
Wayne Ford
Mark Geer
Mark Gelotte
Hunter George
Robert T. Gibson
Don Goodell
Jan M. Green
Kathleen Groble Kelly
Stephen Harding
Michael Hart
John Heck
Bob Heliton
Jerry Herring
Richard High
Chris Hill
Peat Jariya
Monica Keogh
Brenda Kilmer
Richard Kilmer
Johann Kohl
Rosario Laudicina
Paula Leone
Jay Loucks
Christopher Mayes
Jeff McKay
Ferdinand Meyer V
Blake Miller
Gerald Motley
Marilyn Muller
Ward G. Pennebaker
Todd Pomeroy
Rosalie Ramsden
Julie Ray
Donette Reil
Lana Rigsby
Jana Ross
Pat Schrader
Leon Simeon
Jim Sims
Marilyn Van Cleave
Kathryn Van Dyke
Ellis Vener
Phil Watkins III
Teddy Weingarten
Lowell Williams

IRVING
Dale Henry
Ken Koester
Robert Mynster

LANCASTER
Cody Calhoun

LUBBOCK
Texas Tech University

MISSION
Katherine Kelley

MISSOURI CITY
Susan Waggoner

PORT ISABEL
Linnitt Duflon
Charles Fincher

RICHARDSON
Linda Kingsbury
Michael McGrath
John Swieter

ROANOKE
Bev Shumate

SAN ANTONIO
William Bellamy
Stephen Bisch
Roger Christian
John Crain
Jeannette Cuevas
Swain Edens
Michelle Friesenhahr
Jill Giles-Cardellino
Dawn S. Gwin
Jeff Jackson
Cornelia A. Kosfeld Ki
Janis Koy
Liz Martinez
June Robinson
San Antonio College
Barbara Shimkus
Peter Szarmach
M.E. Twomey

SAN MARCOS
SW Texas State Univers

SPRING
Carrie Reeves Davis

TYLER
Matthew Watson

WACO
Charlotte Potts
Terry M. Roller

FORT WORTH
Margie Adkins
John R. Anglim
Ray Gulick
Carolyn Hoefelmeyer
Sandra Sawyer
Pat Sloan